D1266734

DIPLOMACY AND DOGMATISM

Bernardino de Mendoza
and the French Catholic League

DIPLOMACY AND DOGMATISM

Bernardino de Mendoza
and the French Catholic League

✤ ✤ ✤ ✤

De Lamar Jensen

HARVARD UNIVERSITY PRESS

Cambridge, Massachusetts

1964

Distributed in Great Britain by Oxford University Press, London

Publication of this book has been aided by a grant from
the Ford Foundation

Library of Congress Catalog Card Number 63-20769

Printed in the United States of America

TO MY FATHER
JACOB A. JENSEN
(1883–1961)

PREFACE

In the last two decades of the sixteenth century, France, and Europe, passed through a period of turbulent crisis, the outcome of which has had both immediate and lasting effects. This epoch, the final stage of the French religious wars, saw institutions, ideologies, and men pitted against each other in a bitter and desperate struggle for survival. The repercussions and implications of the French wars were international, and their lessons still have significance today.

The following study is an attempt to show, through the activities of the Spanish ambassador in France, Don Bernardino de Mendoza, the nature and extent of the connection between Spain and the French Catholic League (known also as the Holy League, *Sainte Ligue*, or *Sainte Union*) and to indicate the broader role played in the Counter Reformation and in the diplomatic affairs of all Europe by both the League and Mendoza. I have no illusions that this will be a definitive account. It is intended rather as a preliminary study which may serve as an aid to further investigations into this fascinating phase of European history.

In many respects the restless world of Bernardino de Mendoza was very much like our own, and thus its study can shed valuable light on many current problems and attitudes. It also has similarities with the chaotic decades of the French Revolution. In all three times great importance has been attached to dogmatic ideological loyalties and to an impassioned war of ideas. In the half-century following the Protestant Reformation, European society was dominated by ideological absolutes. To Catholic and Protestant alike religious creeds and affiliations were not just matters of personal faith and worship; they formed part of the basic structure of society and added intensity to the general intolerance of that day. In a very real sense the vital issue in all three of these periods has been the underlying disagreement over the nature of man and his relation to the institutions which govern him, and toward which he feels an allegiance.

After the middle of the sixteenth century, the multitude of problems and passions unleashed by the Reformation tended to become polarized into two violently antagonistic groups — Catholic and Calvinist. The lines of conflict were being sharply drawn and the opposing parties were closing ranks for the inevitable encounter. The growing strength of Calvinism in Catholic France soon plunged that kingdom into this whirlpool of doctrinal fervor. From the turmoil came one of the most active politico-religious institutions of the sixteenth century, the French Catholic League, created to suppress heresy in France, maintain the Catholic tradition of the crown, and help restore the religious unity of western Europe. During its short but turbulent existence the League channeled Catholic political and religious thought in France, while developing a quasi-democratic organization unique in its time, and took the lead in the bitter Counter Reformation fight against Protestantism.

The role of the League in the vanguard of reactivated Catholicism soon brought it into close contact with Spanish diplomacy and foreign policy. The intimacy of this relationship has not been fully recognized by historians of the period, and has never been investigated in more than restricted areas. I hope here to show the exact affiliation between the Spanish ambassador in Paris and the Holy League, the part he played in shaping League policy and directing its activities, what he saw and how he commented on French and League affairs, and how he contributed to the methods and purposes of Spanish diplomacy in France. Mendoza, a capable scholar as well as an experienced soldier and diplomat, served as resident ambassador to France from 1584 until 1591, during the culmination of the religious struggles. In this key position he led the Spanish diplomatic offensive in France, and, through his agents and friends in England, Scotland, and the Netherlands, exercised a great influence on the entire European scene. Yet, surprisingly enough, very little has ever been written about Mendoza and his important ministry.

The principal source material for this study has been Mendoza's own dispatches, letters, and papers, which fill sixteen large bundles in the Sección de Estado of the Simancas Archives. These manuscripts, which are indispensable to any study of Philip's relations with France, have only recently been returned to Spain after they were removed by Napoleon Bonaparte during the Peninsular War. Few of his documents dealing with affairs in France have been used before, and those still in diplomatic cipher have been passed over completely. My own months of discouraging struggle to decode these ciphered dispatches finally resulted in success, and I have been able to make use of the letters in this research. In addition to the Simancas papers, I found a number of valuable sources at the Bibliothèque Nationale and at the Archives Nationales in Paris, and some helpful material on Mendoza's earlier life at the Biblioteca Nacional in Madrid.

My sincere appreciation goes to Dr. Ricardo Magdaleno Redondo, director of the Simancas Archives, for his friendship and generosity during my stay there, and to many others whose help was freely given. They cannot all be acknowledged by name, but I owe particular gratitude to Don Angel de la Plaza, vice-director of the Archives; Doña Concepción Alvarez Terán, archivist; Don Amando Represa Rodríguez, archivist, and Manuel Garrido Valentín of the microfilming facilities; and to the patient and helpful archival assistants. The willing cooperation of the staff at the Bibliothèque Nationale in Paris is also appreciated.

I am thankful to the Institute of International Education for a generous Fellowship which enabled me to pursue the archival research for this study in Europe, and to the Brigham Young University for providing me with a series of research grants for its completion. I am especially indebted to Professor Garrett Mattingly of Columbia University, whose kindly encouragement and valued criticism during much of the research have been the real inspiration behind this work. It was he who, eleven years ago, first introduced me to Mendoza and provided the continuing interest and stimulus which enabled me to complete this book. His recent death is a great loss to all who admire and respect meticulous scholarship, sympathetic and inspirational teaching, and artistic writing.

Parts of the manuscript have been read and constructively criticized by the late Professor Walter L. Dorn, and by Shepard B. Clough, René Albrecht-Carrié, and John H. Mundy. Professor Helmut G. Koenigsberger, of the University of Nottingham, has followed the evolution of this study from an early stage and has offered many perceptive suggestions for its improvement. I am grateful also to Professor E. Harris Harbison of Princeton University for reading the completed manuscript and for his recommendations, and to Miss Nancy Lyman Roelker, of Cambridge, Massachusetts, who carefully went over the entire manuscript contributing valuable comments and observations, particularly in regard to the *Politiques*. Mr. John R. Cousins and others of my graduate students have helped in many ways. Although her numerous tasks have permitted only an indirect involvement in the project, my wife has contributed immeasurably to its successful completion.

Brigham Young University   De Lamar Jensen
June 1963

CONTENTS

ILLUSTRATIONS

[Holograph letter in 16th-century Spanish secretary hand]

Muy illustres señores

por entender que el señor Don Alonso mi hermano
es uno de la congregación eclesiástica
y conocer quan activas es su condición
para inflamar demás en los buenos ofi-
cios que me ymagino que para ello y a
todos los demás le escrivo respondi-
endo a las suyas porque no parezca artifi-
cio el capítulo que Vuestra Merced verá en la obli-
gada que va a ver se y que Juzgue Vuestra Merced
que no se que me ha de ayudar a errar y en o dar
lla a mi señora Doña Clara mi hermana por cu-
yos manos velas mías para que la de que el
deseo de acertar en todo me ha hecho es-
crivírselo con su ruego por el término que en ti-
endo que puede ser mas conveniente y fruc-
tuoso. nuestro señor &c. de París a 24 de octubre
1586.

B. las manos a Vuestra Merced
Juan

don Bernardino
de Mendoza

Holograph letter from Mendoza to Juan de Idiáquez

Chapter I

THE WARS OF RELIGION IN FRANCE

✤ ✤ ✤ ✤

Bʏ the middle of the sixteenth century the fluid period of the religious reformation was drawing to a close. Until the last sessions of the Council of Trent (1562–63) it might still have been possible to stem the spread of religious revolt and perhaps even win back the majority of dissenters to the Catholic fold. This, at least, was the opinion of some European statesmen at the time; and, had the Reformation consisted only in the revolt of Martin Luther and his immediate followers, it is conceivable. A more conciliatory policy by the Catholics at the first two sessions of the Council of Trent — for example, such as was advocated by the Emperor Charles V — could have placated many of the German Lutherans. Furthermore, the relatively successful compromise effected in Germany between Catholics and Lutherans by the Religious Peace of Augsburg (1555) suggests the likelihood of a workable coexistence for a considerable period of time.

But there were other and more dynamic forces pressing for radical changes in sixteenth-century Europe. During the time of the Catholic-Lutheran struggles in Germany, an active and militant Calvinism had gained momentum in the Swiss city of Geneva. Between 1541 and 1559 the reorganization of religion and government along the lines of Calvin's conception of the "City of God" was carried out, and after 1555 this movement spread rapidly into France, the Netherlands, western Germany, and Scotland. It was 1559 before Calvin actually became a citizen of Geneva; but after his execution of Servetus in 1553, there was no longer any doubt that he was the ruler of both church and state and that he meant to accept no compromise with "papists or sinners" in his crusade to gather the "elected" and build the kingdom of God. Politically as well as religiously, Europe was approaching a mid-century watershed, but in 1559 it would still have been difficult to predict whether this turning point meant the beginning of an era of peace and relatively harmonious development or the acceleration and more violent continuation of the religious conflict begun in the first half of the century.

END OF THE HAPSBURG-VALOIS WARS

The last major battle of the chronic Hapsburg-Valois wars was fought at St. Quentin in August 1557. The commander of the Spanish Flanders army, Emanuele Filiberto, duke of Savoy, won a decisive victory over the French forces of the constable Anne de Montmorency. The defeat was an ignominious one for France, and for the illustrious constable, but was partially equalized by the French seizure of Calais from the English a few months later; a stroke which, planned and executed by Francis of Lorraine, duke of Guise, ended two centuries of English control of the channel coast.

It was apparent to many, and particularly to the rulers of the two main opponents, Spain and France, that the struggle could not be continued. Both states were on the verge of bankruptcy and each had growing domestic troubles which demanded both attention and money. There were many voices among France's allies in Germany and Italy clamoring for a continuation of the war, but the French king, Henry II, was only too aware of the impossibility of pursuing it further. Beginning in September 1557, his credit fell so rapidly on the Lyon market that it became virtually impossible for him to borrow more money. What Henry was not fully aware of was the equally untenable economic position of the Spanish monarch. Philip II tried desperately to maintain his declining credit but, as the leading Hapsburg creditors (the Welsers, Tuchers, and even the Fuggers) closed their windows to the Spanish monarch, he was forced into bankruptcy. On 10 February 1558, Philip sent the following plea to his regent in Spain, disclosing the acuteness of his financial troubles:

We realize that now that Calais and Guines have fallen, and the King of France is powerfully armed and we the opposite, there is little to be done. The only remedy is to take the field as quickly as possible, and this will cost much money. What with the arrears owed to the German cavalry which has been disbanded and the German infantry which is being kept up, we owe more than one million by the end of this month of February, besides the pay for afterwards and what we owe the merchants with whom we negotiated on (the security of) what Don Luis de Carvajal brought and has not been paid to them. This amounts to another 600,000 ducats. We will try to manage to settle these claims without destroying our credit altogether, making part payment in cash and putting off the rest, on condition that our factor, Hernan López de Campo, can manage to send us something here, and we succeed in borrowing the balance. . . . The 600,000 remaining from the 900,000 to be brought by Pero Menéndez in cash will serve to meet the most urgent payments; we have used some of this money already. Thus everything you will be sending us, including what is being held in Seville, is already spent or ear-marked. Over and above this, we shall need another large sum, which we hope we shall get from the Estates here, to raise and pay an army of over 18,000 foot and 8,000 horse, with which we trust we can defend ourselves from the King of France and even attack him. . . . I therefore charge you to lose not one minute in taking this matter up with the Council of Finance, so that they may raise the largest possible sum in the shortest time, . . . You may use the powers I have sent you by two different routes to sell jurisdictions and other posts, at moderate prices, in order that many buyers may be attracted; and you will send me the money raised thereby as a matter of greatest urgency.[1]

In the autumn of 1558, Philip dispatched a peace commission to France to begin negotiations for ending the war. The talks dragged on through October and November after striking an impasse over the French refusal to return Calais to the English. Late in November, Philip's wife, the queen of England, died, and with the uncertainty of the English position he was even harder pressed to reach an agreement with France. In February 1559, he wrote to his peace commission at Cateau-Cambrésis:

I find myself under an absolute impossibility of continuing the war. I have already spent 1,200,000 ducats which I raised from Spain two or three months ago, and I have need of another million in the coming month of March. From Spain they have sent me Doctor de Lasco to assure me that they cannot do anything more for me. The situation seems to me so very grave that, under pain of losing everything, I must come to some sort of an arrangement. I am waiting with a very active impatience for news, but on no account whatever must these negotiations be broken off.[2]

On the question of Calais, Philip conceded to the French — much to the humiliation of his English allies — and on 3 April 1559 the Treaty of Cateau-Cambrésis was formally signed. By the terms of this important agreement the long Hapsburg-Valois struggle for Italy was finally ended, with political hegemony over the peninsula going to Spain. The few territorial successes of France against the duchy of Savoy in the southeast were likewise forfeited. But in the north and the northeast France made significant gains, which suggest the new direction of French territorial ambitions in the next two centuries. The recent acquisitions of Metz, Toul, Verdun, and Boulogne were guaranteed by the treaty, as well as the retention of the important port of Calais.[3]

As was customary at the conclusion of an important peace settlement, the principal parties to the treaty gave evidence of their good will by a marriage contract between them. In the case of Cateau-Cambrésis, a double ceremony took place between Philip II (who was now widowed as a result of the death of Mary in November 1558) and Elizabeth of Valois, eldest daughter of King Henry II and Catherine de' Medici; and between the duke of Savoy and Marguerite, younger sister of Henry II. The banquets and celebrations accompanying the royal marriages and the ratification of peace were among the most festive of the century, but they ended suddenly in personal and national tragedy. In 1559 no celebration of any importance would have been complete without a day or more of gala tournaments and jousts. In the final clash of lances on 30 June, Henry II was accidentally but mortally wounded by young Gabriel de Lorges, count of Montgomery, captain of the king's Scottish Guard. The death of the king marked the beginning of almost half a century of civil and religious turmoil in France, and brought the recently powerful and splendid monarchy to the verge of complete political and social disintegration.

EUROPE ON THE EVE OF THE RELIGIOUS WARS

The position of France vis-à-vis her neighboring states was crucial and volatile during the last half of the sixteenth century. Without the firm leadership which had been provided in the early part of the century by Francis I and Henry II, French policy was buffeted by the monthly and even daily shifts in domestic and international events. The peace of Cateau-Cambrésis was supposed to begin a new era in friendly relations with Spain, but in fact the greatest change to take place in their relationship was the shift in their relative power. Mutual distrust continued to prevail, and the peace which was precariously maintained was due more to the inability of France to strike a bold policy against her southern rival (France had usually been the aggressor in the Hapsburg-Valois wars), than to any newly found cordiality. After 1559 Spain occupied the role of European arbiter, and as long as Spanish policy was motivated by a dogged determination to maintain the *status quo* (which meant a continuation of the Spanish hegemony), Philip II's interests were best served by conservatism and universal peace.

There were cracks in the structure, however, and powerful forces were at work pulling it apart. The unleashing of more violent religious forces in France and the Netherlands converted these areas into seed beds of unrest and agitation which were certain to arouse the armed intervention of Spain — for Philip was as dedicated to preserving the religious *status quo* as he was the political. Whenever the government of France took a virorous stand against the threatening forces of Protestantism, Philip's attitude was peaceable and cooperative, but when the Huguenots appeared to be increasing their strength Spanish policy toward France became obdurate and aggressive.

There were many points of contact between the two countries, and these soon became areas of tension and rivalry. The border separating France and Spain was one of these lines of friction. The entire saddleback kingdom of Navarre was claimed by Philip, but the northern third of it (that part lying to the north of the crest of the Pyrenees) was also claimed — and effectively occupied — by the Bourbon king of Navarre, who paid his only allegiances to the crown of France. Philip stubbornly refused to recognize the separate existence of a crown of Navarre, and when it became apparent after June 1584 that Henry of Navarre (who was also the leader of the Huguenots) might, as first prince of the blood, ascend to the throne of France, Philip's alarm moved him to diplomatic and military intervention. The northern frontier between France and the Spanish provinces of Artois and Luxembourg was another perennial trouble-spot in Franco-Spanish relations. The French seizure of Cambrai, and the disagreement over control of Rocroi were problems brought up at almost every diplomatic encounter between the two governments in the last two decades of the century. And of course the growing religious unrest in the entire area did nothing to reduce the causes of friction. Calvinist activity in Spanish Flanders — especially in the cities of Valenciennes and Tournai, where French influence was notoriously prominent — accentuated the commercial and political tensions. As organized revolt and open rebellion spread in the Netherlands, French Huguenots became intimately connected with that movement, both in France and in the Low Countries.[4] When the French crown attempted to capitalize on this situation, a clash of arms became almost inevitable.

The central figure of European affairs in the second half of the sixteenth century was Philip II, king of Spain, whose territorial possessions and religious commitments involved him in almost every European problem and affair. By heritage Philip was well qualified to cope with the immense task of governing a disparate empire of Castilians, Aragonese, Catalans, Portuguese, Neapolitans, Milanese, Burgundians, Luxembourgers, Flemings, Walloons, Brabanters, Zeelanders, and Dutch (not to mention Arowaks, Tlaxcalans, Aztecs, Chibchas, and Incas), without the benefit of central institutions of revenue or government; but by training, temperament, and personality he was disastrously inadequate to the role for which he had been capriciously cast by history.

Philip II was aware of his royal prerogatives and unusually conscientious about his duties and responsibilities as a Christian sovereign. He was also devoted to the political and religious causes which he espoused, according to the rules of conduct conceived by his curiously legalistic mind. But he was quite unable to understand the economic and religious upheavals of his time that were helping to convert the Christian commonwealth into divergent and autonomous national states. Gallicanism, that tendency in France to view the church as a uniquely French institution, for example, was incomprehensible to Philip. He was equally unable to adjust to the administrative necessities of his own polyglot empire. Philip recognized the need for greater governmental centralization, and he contributed significantly to its realization; but he failed to see that institutional centralization without an accompanying social integration was bound to bring trouble. Not only that, by insisting upon supervising every detail of administration himself, he also failed to take the required steps toward a rationalized and departmentalized administrative structure on the highest governmental level. The minutiae of diplomatic correspondence and municipal jurisdiction received the same meticulous and torpid personal attention as did the most urgent communication or pressing political decision. The resulting sluggishness of government during the period of the religious wars prompted more than one Spanish diplomat to quip that he wished "death might come by way of Spain, thus we would live to a good old age." [5] The observation of a Venetian ambassador in 1557, that the Spanish king was "phlegmatic and melancholy," [6] was still true in 1598.

In 1559, after the conclusion of the treaty of Cateau-Cambrésis, another Venetian ambassador noted that Philip's foreign policy was likewise a direct reflection of his slow, meticulous, judicious nature, that

> At an age which ordinarily manifested great inclination toward belligerency and insatiable desire for glory and power, all the actions of His Majesty are aimed, not toward the enlarging of his possessions by war, but their conservation by peace. . . . The Emperor [Charles V] took pleasure in matters of war, and he understood them well, but the king [Philip] knows little about war, and cares for it even less. With ardor and zeal the Emperor launched great enterprises; Philip tries to avoid them if he can.[7]

This cautious and prudent attitude toward external affairs appears to have been more consistently followed in the first twenty-five years of Philip's reign than it was after 1580 when the magnitude and urgency of the religious situation moved even this circumspect monarch to decisive and aggressive — though not always sound — diplomatic and military activity.

The position of Rome in the international affairs of the late sixteenth century — particularly papal relations with Spain and France — was ambiguous. The complexity of papal policy stems from the fact that the pope, in addition to being the spiritual head of Catholic Christendom, was also the secular ruler of a large and significant Italian state with frontiers bordering those of Spanish possessions in Italy. The irritations caused by this territorial proximity and by the even more serious clashes over high level ecclesiastical matters were deep and vital. The result was an inevitable rivalry between Philip, as he gradually accepted the role of political champion of the Counter Reformation, and the pope, who continued to assert his claim to universal pre-eminence.

When Philip II arrived in Spain in September 1559 to take personal control of the government which three years before he had inherited from his father, he had already been engaged in one major conflict with the pope (an encounter which produced a papal alliance with both France and the Turks and the threat of excommunication), a Spanish invasion of the Papal States, and finally the defeat of the papal army and the occupation of Rome. But, on 18 August 1559, Pope Paul IV died and was succeeded by the mild and peace-loving Pius IV. It looked now as if a new era of cordial relations was about to open with the papacy as well as with France. But the expected tranquillity failed to result. Philip quarreled with the pope over the jurisdiction of the Spanish Inquisition and the financing of the crusade against heretics, disagreed violently with him over the calling of the Council of Trent (January 1562),[8] and then broke off diplomatic relations after the pope granted the French ambassador ceremonial precedence over the Spanish.[9]

In January 1566, Pius IV was succeeded by the austere, zealous, and energetic, ex-inquisitor, Michele Ghislieri, who took the name Pius V. Because of the new pontiff's vigorous commitment to extirpate heresy in Italy, Philip, thinking this pope would be less likely to interfere in international affairs, supported his election, though far from wholeheartedly.[10] Again the competition between the Catholic king and Catholic pope strained relations between them, although they were able to cooperate sufficiently to bring about a concerted naval campaign against the Turks, resulting in the victory at Lepanto in 1571. Yet, as the religious and political crises in France and the Netherlands mounted after 1572, Philip found Pope

Gregory XIII (1572–1585) no more favorable to Spanish policy than his predecessors had been. Whereas Pius V had prodded the king to take more violent measures to stamp out heresy, Gregory XIII was so reluctant to support Philip's attempts to put down the Dutch revolt that the latter accused him of actually desiring the Spanish loss of the Netherlands.[11] Finally, with the election of the impetuous and politically ambitious Pope Sixtus V, in April 1585 (against Philip's loud protests), relations reached still another peak of intense friction and discord. Sixtus V was the most political-minded of all the late-sixteenth-century popes, and in most of the issues involving the two rulers Philip II and Sixtus V were aligned on opposite sides.[12]

Relations between the papacy and France were likewise strained and irregular during the period of religious wars. Pius IV opposed Catherine de' Medici's early conciliatory policy toward the Huguenots, and took great offense at the Gallicanism expressed by the Estates General in 1560–61 [13] and by the French refusal to adopt the decrees of the Council of Trent. Pius V urged the total destruction of Protestantism in France by force, and his successor was delighted by the news of the massacre of St. Bartholomew's Day, but the policies of Sixtus V seem to have been aimed more against Spanish or League domination of France than against the Protestants. He usually supported the king against the Huguenots and Catholic League, and sided with the more moderate Leaguers in opposition to the radical Spanish-led Parisian group.

England's role in the struggles of the late sixteenth century was more political than religious in the early years of Queen Elizabeth, but with the mounting friction between Catholics, Calvinists, and Anglicans at home, and the increased pressures from Jesuit- and Seminary-trained missionaries, following the papal excommunication of Elizabeth in 1570, the foreign policy of England also became Protestant-orientated and eventually resulted in armed conflict with Spain. Nevertheless, in 1559, and for some years thereafter, the diplomatic connections between England and Spain were predominantly cordial. The two powers were so closely allied at the time of Elizabeth's accession that, had it not been for Philip's friendly disposition toward her and his threat to intervene in her behalf, it is quite possible that the Franco-Scottish attempt to place young Mary Queen of Scots on the English throne would have been successful.[14]

It appears to be one of the fascinating paradoxes of the sixteenth century that during the first years of her reign, while Elizabeth was gradually breaking away from the Roman church and laying the foundations of Anglicanism, Philip of Spain was her most conscientious protector against European rivals (particularly against France and Scotland). Yet upon closer scrutiny it is not so strange after all. For more than a half-century England and Spain had maintained friendly relations, and for much of that time they were diplomatic and military allies. From 1554 until 1558 Philip was king consort of England, and there was no immediate indication that England would soon cease to be a protectorate of the Spanish king. Furthermore, a Franco-Scottish defeat of England, resulting in the establishment of Mary Queen of Scots (and queen of France) as ruler of England, would have been disastrous to Philip's position in the Netherlands. A policy of friendship and support, therefore, was the only reasonable one Philip could have pursued under the circumstances. There is little doubt that both Elizabeth and Philip preferred peace, and that for more than twenty-five years they were generally unmoved by the clamorings of their more ardent advisors. But Anglo-Spanish amiability was strained precipitously by repeated English support of the Dutch rebels (as well as by privateering actions against Spanish shipping), and by the harsh Spanish treatment of English seamen. The eventual result was the Armada war.

English relations with France during the first thirty years of Elizabeth's reign were also largely contingent upon the situation in the Netherlands. Elizabeth's vacillating policy across the Channel is not so puzzling when it is remembered that, as far as England was concerned, the only thing worse than a Spanish-dominated Netherlands would be a French-dominated one. Thus Elizabeth assisted the rebels to prevent a Spanish conquest, and reversed that policy whenever it appeared that the French would reap the greater benefits.

Further tensions with France resulted from English determination to regain Calais and any other channel ports which might be advantageous. That is why most of Elizabeth's treaties with the French Huguenots stipulated the return of Le Havre, Dieppe, and Calais to England as a *sine qua non* for the employment of English troops and money in France. After the outbreak of the religious wars, an English force did occupy Le Havre for a short time, but it was driven out again in August 1563. Throughout the period of religious tumult, negotiations were frequently opened by Elizabeth for the return of Calais, but the French insisted that it had now been returned to its original and rightful owner and there it would remain.[15]

CALVINISM AND ITS FOES IN FRANCE

The rapid growth of Calvinism in France during the middle decades of the sixteenth century was one of several unforseeable phenomena of the period which had immediate and far-reaching effects upon the political and international life of that nation. At the beginning of 1562 the Huguenots themselves claimed some 2,150 organized congregations,[16] each varying in size from a few dozen to over a thousand.[17] Estimates of the total Huguenot population in 1562 range from 600,000 to 4,000,000,[18] and some believe that they continued to increase during the course of the religious wars. This amazing growth of Calvinism between 1555 and 1562 can be explained in part by the organized missionary aggressiveness of John Calvin and the Geneva Company of Pastors, by the tight discipline and organization of the French Calvinists, and by the great increase of soldier-nobles in the movement after 1559.

There is little doubt that Calvin intended to win France to the cause of Reformed Christianity and that the Genevan Academy and the organization of missionaries were instruments for achieving that goal. The pastors sent into France, beginning in 1555, were carefully screened and chosen, trained thoroughly in Calvinist doctrines and organization, and dispatched in utmost secrecy to key locations in the cities and provinces.[19] It appears that the provinces of southern and southwestern France, particularly the cities, had the heaviest concentration of Huguenots, with Normandy and some of the central areas following closely behind.[20] Northern and eastern France remained predominantly hostile to the Calvinist reform, as did Paris and some of the other large cities such as Toulouse and Bordeaux.[21]

The organization of Calvinism in France was carried out in great detail and dispatch by the Genevan pastors and by locally appointed officials. The structural network was built up from the foundation of widely scattered and heterogeneous congregations, varying considerably in size and importance, through representative regional colloquies, provincial synods, and finally to the national synod. Calvinism, like Catholicism, was a militant international organization demanding the complete allegiance and discipline of its adherents. Thus the congregations, colloquies, and synods of the Huguenots could be quickly converted into military units under the leadership of their respective captains, colonels, and commander-in-chief.[22]

The growing militancy of the Huguenots between 1559 and 1562 was largely due to the influx of French nobles into their ranks after the peace of Cateau-Cambrésis had deprived the nobility of its principal career and livelihood. The lower nobility in France was particularly affected by the economic and political changes of the sixteenth century. The chronic inflation enveloping Europe after mid-century resulted in a steady drop in the value of fixed rents, which were the nobles' chief sources of income, while the costs of living continued to rise.[23] As their economic status gradually declined, the nobles held desperately to their rank by increasingly luxurious dress, display, and disorder. Some of them turned to brigandage and piracy for a livelihood, others sought the patronage of the wealthier lords, while many more found hope by joining the spirited and active Huguenots, among whom they could maintain their prestige and perhaps even engage in the occupation they knew best.[24] Naturally, the Calvinists of France made no attempt to dissuade these nobles. Calvin saw as clearly as did the Huguenot leaders the advantages to be gained by courting the support of the nobility. So successful were the Calvinists in recruiting the country gentry that, by the outbreak of the civil wars in 1562, an estimated one-half of the French nobility was on the side of the Huguenots.[25]

It would be a mistake to assume that this trend affected only the lower nobility. The upper ranks of French aristocracy, even the princes of the blood, were also attracted to the Protestant cause, and they soon dominated the movement through their influence, leadership, and political following. The ensuing religious wars are seriously misunderstood when it is not recognized that they were also personal and dynastic struggles between rival families and segments of the French high nobility. One of the leading noble houses to be attracted to the Reformed religion was the Châtillon-Coligny of southeastern France. In the middle sixteenth century the fortunes of this family rested on the shoulders of the three sons of Gaspard, seigneur de Châtillon (one-time marshal of France): Odet, cardinal-bishop of Beauvais; Gaspard de Coligny, admiral of France; and Francis, sieur d'Andelot, colonel-general of infantry. Andelot and Coligny were active as Huguenot leaders, particularly Coligny, who was head of the movement until his assassination in 1572. The Châtillons were also closely related to another of the great noble families of France, the Montmorency, lords of the Ile-de-France, and Languedoc. Anne de Montmorency, renowned constable of France, was uncle to the Châtillons and, although Montmorency and his sons remained loyal to the Catholic faith, he promoted the best interests of his nephews at every opportunity.

Of greatest significance to the course of French history was the association of the house of Bourbon-Albret with the reform movement in France. In 1548, Antoine of Bourbon, duke of Vendôme, head of the family which was next in line for the crown, married Jeanne d'Albret, heiress of the tiny kingdom of Navarre and of the adjoining principality of Béarn. Navarre had been a center of Reformed ideas and literature ever since Jeanne d'Albret's mother, Marguerite d'Angoulême (sister of King Francis I), became queen of Navarre in 1527. Antoine of Bourbon, now king of Navarre, became an early friend of the Reformation, but he was far from being a dependable supporter or leader of the Huguenots. When it came to a showdown, he renounced any Protestant affiliation and threw his support to the Catholics. Not his wife, however. Until her death in 1572, Jeanne d'Albret remained an implacable enemy of the Catholics, and especially of Philip II who represented the most serious threat to her possessions and throne.[26] The most devoted Huguenot leader in the early years of the civil wars was Antoine's younger brother, Louis of Bourbon, governor of Picardy and prince of Condé. By temperament and ability, Condé was the natural field general and driving force of the Huguenots.

The relentless rival of these noble families (and of Protestantism in general) was the house of Guise-Lorraine-Joinville. Claude, the son of Duke René of Lorraine, attached himself to the court of France during the reigns of Louis XII and Francis I, and as a reward for his faithful and energetic support of the French king during the Hapsburg-Valois wars he was created duke of Guise and became a peer of the realm. Before reaching his eighteenth birthday, Claude married Antoinette of Bourbon, aunt of Antoine the future king of Navarre. From this marriage came nine children, each of whom played a decisive role in the history of France and Europe in the late sixteenth century. The eldest son was Francis, second duke of Guise, who became one of the leading soldiers of France — having commanded the successful defense of Metz in 1552–53, participated commendably in the French campaign in Italy in 1556–57, and led the capture of Calais from the English in 1558 — before he was killed by a Huguenot assassin in 1563. Next to Francis was Charles, whose profession was the church. He advanced rapidly in the ecclesiastical hierarchy until he became the primate of France as archbishop of Rheims and cardinal of Lorraine. During the middle years of the sixteenth century the cardinal of Lorraine was one of the wealthiest and most powerful men in France. Louis, the third son, became the cardinal of Guise; Claude, the duke of Aumale; René, marquis of Elboeuf; and Francis (it was not uncommon to give two children in the family the same name), duke of Longueville. Mary, the eldest of three sisters, became the wife of King James V of Scotland, and subsequently the mother of Mary Stuart, Queen of Scots.

The family left by Duke Francis of Guise became the leading force in supporting the Counter Reformation in France and the Catholic League, which was its primary instrument of opposition to the Huguenots. These children were: Henry (born in 1550), who became duke of Guise upon the death of his father in 1563, and leader of the League; Catherine, duchess of Montpensier, its strongest supporter in Paris; Charles, duke of Mayenne, who succeeded his brother as head of the League in 1589; and Louis, cardinal of Guise.

Occupying the middle ground between these disruptive forces, and trying to maintain and promote its own dynastic as well as national position, was the declining Valois monarchy. In spite of the gradual development of administrative institutions and machinery in Renaissance France, governmental control still depended primarily upon personalities and private interests. The evolution from private rights to public law, or from feudalism to monarchical consolidation, was far from complete in sixteenth-century France.[27] But the last Valois ruler who could command allegiance, respect, and admiration (even if not love or sympathy) from the French people died in 1559. Henry II's four sons were not only deficient in the administrative skills and patience required to be successful monarchs in the sixteenth century, but they also lacked the strength of character and personality to manage or direct the centrifugal forces that were tearing France apart. As a result, the fortunes of the crown fluctuated violently with the successes and failures of groups and individuals over whom the government had little or no control.

The only consistently stable element in the French government after the treaty of Cateau-Cambrésis was that represented by the widowed queen mother, Catherine de' Medici. Catherine's life spanned the reigns of three of her sons, and provided a degree of continuity and moderation — with one notable exception — without which the dynasty might very well have collapsed completely. Even the terrible massacre of St. Bartholomew's Day was more a result of mounting political pressures and Catherine's own fear than of premeditated treachery on her part.[28] Her policies were dictated by interests of state, in the best Machiavellian tradition of her native Italy, and by a warm and doting affection for her children. These interests, she believed, could be promoted best by domestic peace and international amity. Toward these goals she continually applied her influence. Nevertheless, Catherine was scarcely more successful in governing France or achieving peace than were her sons. She possessed considerable charm and finesse in negotiation, had a perceptive insight into the judgment of character, and was doggedly persistent in pursuing a course of action; but her own personality — as well as her ancestry — promoted suspicion instead of confidence, and her statesmanship lacked a grounding in sound political morality. Not only was she wanting in moral principles (which was characteristic of the times), but she identified too closely the needs of the nation with her personal and dynastic interests. Undoubtedly she thought the crown of France *was* the nation, and that any promotion of royal and family advantage was for the benefit of all; but she never succeeded, as did Elizabeth of England, in convincing the people that her actions were in their best interest.

BEGINNING OF THE RELIGIOUS WARS

Francis, the eldest son of Henry II, was only fifteen years of age when he became king of France in 1559, and was ill-prepared to assume the responsibilities of ruler. In such a situation the first prince of the blood might have stepped in as a personal abutment to the crown, but Antoine of Navarre was not the man to make so decisive a move. Others at court were much less reluctant to seize power. Close behind Francis II and his young wife, Mary Stuart, titular queen of Scotland, stood Mary's ambitious uncles, the duke of Guise, the cardinals of Lorraine and Guise, and the dukes of Aumale, Elboeuf, and Longueville. As long as Francis and Mary were king and queen of France the Guise influence in the government was strongly felt. Yet this was not the only pressure exerted after 1559. Many of the Huguenot nobles, led by the prince of Condé and later by Coligny, became alarmed over the Guise domination, which they knew would mean an increase in persecution of the Protestants. Soon an active party of resistance was taking shape both at court and in the provinces. The Tumult of Amboise, in which a number of Huguenot nobles plotted to seize the young king, assassinate Guise and the cardinal of Lorraine, and elevate Antoine of Navarre to chief advisor of the crown, was only the first in a series of upheavals which soon led to open hostilities.[29]

Caught between Guise domination and Protestant heresy, Catherine de' Medici tried desperately to mark a middle course of compromise and appeasement. In this she was supported by the new chancellor of France, Michel de l'Hôpital, a sympathetic man whose desires for peace and moderation were as strong as the queen mother's. By nature L'Hôpital was a Christian humanist, desiring social harmony through the maintenance of religious unity and the peaceful reform of clerical abuses. He followed Erasmus in his greater concern for morality and reason than for theology,[30] but L'Hôpital's responsibilities as a politician, statesman, and man of affairs forced him into a more active role in the politico-religious struggles than was taken by the great Rotterdam humanist. L'Hôpital saw the political, social, and economic chaos that would result from religious war, and, though he still dreamed of the unity of the Christian commonwealth, he became convinced that its cost was too great. Far better would it be to tolerate several religious beliefs than to force religious conformity if that meant national upheaval.[31] This opinion was very close to the ideological position of the *Politiques*, who later became an active and important third party.

L'Hôpital became chancellor on 27 March 1560, and from that time until his dismissal in September 1568 he worked tirelessly (and hopelessly) to conciliate the disruptive forces through toleration and cooperation and to promote loyalty and devotion to the monarchical government of France. But the trend of the time was toward greater intolerance and fanaticism, not less, and the forces leading France toward disaster were growing daily. In desperation Catherine summoned an assembly of the notables to Fontainebleau to air the questions of religion and control of the government.[32] The session ended in an impasse and it was finally decided to turn to the nation for consultation. Thus, after seventy-six years the Estates General of France was convoked to share in the making of vital decisions of state.

On 5 December 1560, one week before the opening session of the Estates General at Orléans, Francis II died, leaving his ten-year-old brother, Charles IX, as king of France. Confusion and disorder mounted. The deputies at the Estates General were noncommittal about a regency or interim government, but on matters of political and religious administration they were adamant, demanding immediate reforms in both church and state and refusing to accept the taxes requested of them by the government.[33] On 31 January 1561 the assembly was prorogued until August so the deputies could be reinstructed by their constituents on the matters of finances and the regency. The skeleton Estates General which met at Pontoise (August 1st to 27th) was equally outspoken and hostile, but it did agree to recognize the queen mother as regent.[34]

In the meantime, in an attempt to reach some settlement of the religious controversy, Catherine called an assembly of the French clergy to meet with Huguenot leaders at Poissy. She hoped that this Colloquy of Poissy would function as a national council of the French church in working out a much needed program of reform (thus enabling the French to present a stronger front at the forthcoming general council of the church at Trent) and at the same time reconcile the doctrinal differences between Catholics and Protestants in France. But again, although the colloquy had an auspicious beginning, neither side was willing to compromise on what each considered "the basic issues" and the result was stalemate plus increased tensions and aroused feelings.[35]

By the beginning of 1562 it was becoming more and more obvious that the political power in France was shifting to the radical forces outside of the government, and that no matter what steps Catherine took to reconcile these groups they were growing more petulant and belligerent. Many of the clergy were outspoken in their criticism of the government and its failure to extirpate heresy. Echoes of papal dissatisfaction also resounded in Paris with the arrival of the new papal legate, Hippolyte d'Este, cardinal of Ferrara, who accused the queen mother of irresponsibility in her toleration of the Huguenots. And Philip of Spain reacted with unusual precipitancy to warn Catherine of the international risks she was taking by coddling the Calvinists in France. "Make the queen understand," he wrote to his ambassador in France, "that by following such a course her son will lose his kingdom as well as the obedience of his vassals." [36]

On the other side, the Huguenots were becoming more restless as the government vacillated between repression and collaboration. In October they seized several towns in western Languedoc and at the same time strengthened their position at court by a temporary closing of ranks among the Bourbon, Montmorency, and Châtillon factions. In the early weeks of 1562, Catherine took the fateful step of recognizing the Huguenot strength by issuing a statement of tolerance and coexistence, known as the Edict of January. This edict gave legal status to the Protestant religion in France, granted the Huguenots places of worship in the city suburbs, authorized their assemblies of synods and consistories, and forbade the involuntary imposition of additional taxes upon them.

Again the result was an increase of tensions. Catholics were enraged, and Protestants confidently defied their former tormentors at the slightest provocation. The situation was dangerously volatile, and when on 1 March 1562 the duke of Guise and a company of soldiers attacked a congregation of Huguenot worshipers outside of Vassy, France was thrown into civil war. Thousands of Huguenot nobles and foot soldiers immediately responded to Condé's mobilization call. Protestant congregations throughout France supported the appeal to arms with men and money. In Geneva, too, and wherever the Reformed Church had spread, funds were solicited and raised for the campaign.[37] A contingent of Swiss soldiers joined the Huguenots, and in Germany Coligny's brother Andolet busily recruited mercenaries from the rich cities and provinces of the Rhineland.

It is outside the scope of this book to follow the ebb and flow, the campaigns and sorties, and the atrocities and excesses of the French religious wars. They were punctuated by frequent truces and treaties only to flare up again in more ruthless attacks and sieges. Major battles were fought at Dreux in December 1562, at Saint-Denis in November 1567, Jarnac, March 1569, and Moncontour, October 1569, all of them resulting in serious but not decisive victories for the Catholic-royalist forces. Fighting raged all over France, with the strongest Huguenot positions remaining in the south (but with constant harassment from the rugged and ruthless Catholic general, Blaise de Monluc), and with central and northeastern France staunchly loyal to Catholicism and the house of Guise-Lorraine. Antoine of Navarre, who had defected to the Catholics, died in 1562 at Rouen. In February 1563 the duke of Guise was assassinated outside of Orléans; in 1567 Montmorency was killed; and at Jarnac, in March 1569, Condé fell. By 1572 a new generation of leaders was taking command on both sides.

In August 1570 the peace of Saint-Germain was negotiated, and the most violent and excessive of the religious wars was brought to a temporary close. Two years later a more formal recognition of amity was arranged by a marriage alliance between Marguerite of Valois, second daughter of Catherine de' Medici, and Henry, king of Navarre, son of Antoine Bourbon of Navarre. This was the reason for the presence of several thousand Huguenots in Paris on the eve of St. Bartholomew's Day, August 24, 1572. The savage massacre which began that night with the assassination of Coligny and then spread convulsively into the provinces, has been the subject of too many lengthy monographs and scholarly exercises (as well as fanciful melodramas) to take time and space retelling here.[38]

HUGUENOT POLITICAL THOUGHT

The St. Bartholomew massacre marked an important turning point in the spirit and direction of the French domestic wars, and caused serious repercussions throughout Western Europe. Instead of being destroyed by the brutal stroke of the sword, the Huguenot party was actually pulled tighter together by this ruthlessness of the government. Previously the Protestants had been divided on many issues of politics, religion, and war; but now their differences were minimized as their conception of the enemy became more clarified. Even after the outbreak of the wars in 1562 most of the Huguenots viewed the government as basically just, sympathetic, and honorable — a divinely ordained institution for executing the political laws of the land for the temporal benefit of all subjects of the king. The monarchy was the apex of a legitimate and acceptable system of political jurisdiction, according to Calvinist views, and in times past had even been boldly solicitous of Huguenot welfare. For thirteen years most of the Huguenots had been able to distinguish in their own minds between the French government (represented normally by the king and council, but since 1559 by the queen mother), to which they paid homage and loyalty, and the Catholic-Guise conspiracy which threatened to pervert the country into a tyranny. By this view the Huguenots were not at war with the crown, but were supporting and defending it against its real enemies.

Obviously this view was shattered in the St. Bartholomew massacre. The hand which had been extended to steady the tottering throne was suddenly struck off at a single blow; not by the Lord, as in the Biblical case of Uzzah and the Ark, but by the treachery and deceit of the government. Immediately a change took place in the Huguenot attitude toward government in general and toward the French monarchy in particular. Not only was the person of the king (and the queen mother) violently attacked, in a new outburst of polemical writings, but the idea of kingship itself was critically questioned. Most of the Huguenot pamphleteers and political writers now emphasized the limited nature of monarchy, and stressed the authority of the people as expressed through the Estates General and the magisterial role of the nobility. These *monarchomachs* (monarch-eaters), as William Barclay called all of the sixteenth-century proponents of limited monarchy, took a position in political thought which, although not immediately successful in France, helped circulate and popularize ideas about the limited and contractual nature of the state and which subsequently had an immeasurable effect upon the development of political theory, especially in England.[39]

Of the hundreds of Huguenot political pamphlets and books appearing after St. Bartholomew's, the following four are typical and unusually significant for their political perception, clarity of exposition, and influence on the period.

Late in 1573 the eminent Huguenot jurist, and one-time professor of law at the University of Bourges, Francis Hotman, published the remarkable *Franco-Gallia*.[40] In it he examined the medieval history of France and found a significant contrast in the spirit and structure of Germanic and Roman Gaul. In pre-Roman days and among the ancient Franks, said Hotman, the king was bound by law and was responsible to representative bodies of the people for all of his official acts. He was elected to his position and could be deprived of it if he failed to rule justly. Hotman then equated modern France with ancient Gaul and demanded the restoration of this natural state which since the Roman domination had been perverted by Roman law with its promotion of centralized rule. Hotman's appeal, then, was for a monarchy limited and controlled by the Estates General and the aristocratic magistrates.

In 1574 Theodore Beza's influential *Du droit des magistrats sur leurs sujets* appeared in France, opening a new phase of polemic religious literature against the government.[41] Only God possesses absolute power, said Beza, arguing primarily from Biblical precedent, and, since people are created by God, and kings are created by the people (through contract), the authority of the French monarchy is contingent upon the king's observance of his political and religious duties. If he violates God's will he can, through the proper authorized bodies, be resisted and deposed. This idea was pressed much further by the pseudonymous author of *Le Réveil-Matin* (1574), who boldly advocated tyrannicide and even called upon the Guises to strike down the treasonous Valois king.[42]

A much less known book in our time, but one which was widely circulated and read during the religious wars, was Innocent Gentillet's *Contre Machiavel*, published anonymously at Lausanne in 1576.[43] Gentillet was another Huguenot lawyer and jurist, who fled to Geneva after St. Bartholomew's Day, then returned in 1576 to occupy various positions in the *Chambres mi-parties* and parlements at Grenoble, Toulouse and at Die. He also wrote several pamphlets and books against the despotic government and against the Catholic League.[44] Entwined with a somewhat superficial analysis and critique of what he considered were Machiavelli's political maxims, is Gentillet's attack on the French government of Catherine de' Medici which had violated the historical traditions and patterns of benevolent French monarchy by introducing Machiavellian cynicism and despotism into France from Italy. Like Hotman's, Gentillet's approach was primarily historical, with a heavy reliance upon classical mythology, and appealed strongly to those who wanted to believe they were really loyal to the government while fighting against foreign-inspired tyranny. The appeal to patriotism was not entirely new, but in Gentillet's handling of it we find an important doctrinal link between the Huguenots and the later Politiques, who proclaimed this as their cardinal principle.

From the point of view of significant political theory these writings were all surpassed by a short book appearing in 1579 under the title *Vindiciae contra Tyrannos*.[45] Although considerable disagreement over the authorship of *Vindiciae* still exists, there seems to be convincing evidence that young Philippe du Plessis-Mornay, the active Huguenot intellectual leader, and later counselor and secretary to Henry of Navarre, was at least co-author — and probably sole author — of the book.[46] The approach of the *Vindiciae*, similar to that of Beza's *Du droit des magistrats*, is philosophical rather than historical and attempts to set forth the basic premises of a rational (though strongly theistic) contractual monarchy. Its essence is the answering of four basic questions on the constitutional and moral relation of the government and the governed: (1) "Are subjects bound to obey princes if they command that which is contrary to the law of God?" (2) "Is it lawful to resist a prince who infringes the law of God, and ruins the Church, and, if so, who ought to resist him, by what means, and how far should resistance extend?" (3) "Is it lawful to resist a prince who ruins the state, and, if so, to whom should the organization of resistance, its means and limits, be confided?" (4) "Are neighbouring princes bound by law to help the subjects of princes who afflict them either for the cause of religion or in the practice of tyranny?"[47]

To the first question, the *Vindiciae* answers no. Since the king, as well as the people, is a vassal of God and by contract of vassal and Lord, is bound to obey and uphold divine law, he legally commands the obedience of his own vassals (whose duties are likewise sanctioned by contract) only so long as he conforms to divine will. Just as in the feudal contract, when the higher covenant is broken the lower also ceases to be binding. The answer to question 2 discloses the author's aristocratic orientation. It is society, not individuals, that is charged with resistance to a monarch who has defiled the church and disobeyed God. The private subject can do nothing against his king unless called upon by the representatives of society, the magistrates (meaning, in sixteenth-century France, the nobles). Question 3 is also answered in the affirmative, for, although monarchy is a holy office, the political powers exercised by it are received ultimately from society (through law), and the misuse of such powers or the usurpation of others can and should be openly resisted — by constituted authority. Thus, in the *Vindiciae*, of the two contracts which defined the monarchy, the one between God and king was essentially religious and the other, between king and people, was political. A violation of either contract justified society — which, according to Aristotelian premises, is superior to any part of it, including the king — in revolting against such a government. The answer to the fourth question is equally positive. The Church of God is one and universal; if any part of it should be harmed the damage would effect all parts; all elements of the church therefore share in the responsibility to protect and defend the whole. Thus Christian princes are bound to give aid to any segment of the religious kingdom being threatened or abused. It is likewise the clear duty of a Christian prince to succor a beleaguered neighbor state, just as surely as it is for any Christian to assist a sick or injured friend.

Two ideas, which dominate the thought of most of the Huguenot theorists (and of their medieval predecessors), emerge very clearly and emphatically in the *Vindiciae:* first, neither political nor ecclesiastical power originates in the monarch; they are delegated to him by society which functions ultimately in the name of God; secondly, it is not in the people that the authority to resist and depose the monarch resides, but in the constituted representatives of society, magisterial nobles and the Estates General. Calvinist democracy, as expressed by the Huguenots, was really a conservative theocratic and aristocratic oligarchy. Popular sovereignty was not what we think it is today, but the right (privilege) of the people to follow their aristocratic and ecclesiastical leaders in opposition to a government that those leaders have pronounced to be in violation of divine law.

FOUNDATIONS OF THE CATHOLIC LEAGUE

✦ ✦ ✦ ✦

Iɴ May 1574, Charles IX died, leaving the throne and the problems of France to his twenty-three-year-old brother, Henry III, who for a year had been the elected king of Poland. Henry enthusiastically renounced his Polish crown and in September "escaped" to France to accept the scepter of Most Christian King. Many princes of the time would have eagerly grasped both thrones, but Henry was no empire builder and had few real interests east of Champagne. Throughout France in the fall of 1574 hopes ran high that the wars would now be ended, religious and political unity re-established, and the economic hardships alleviated. Most of all, the French people hoped, and believed, that Henry III would reform the government and make the crown of France once more the proudest and most powerful of Europe. Had not the young king, while yet in his teens, led the royal forces brilliantly in their defeat of the Huguenots at Jarnac and Moncontour? Had he not proved himself on many occasions to be a leader, not a docile figurehead cowering under the more dominant wills and personalities of the Guises, Coligny, Catherine de' Medici, and Philip II, as had his two predecessors? Was he not truly a defender of the faith and a worthy spokesman for Christendom? Surely France would now resume its divine and ancient role as champion of the church, which had so recently been usurped by the Spain of Philip II.

Most of these hopes were based on the reasoned observations and sanguine wishes of those who had watched this talented prince develop from energetic boyhood to promising manhood. Henry did possess more real potential than any of his brothers. He gave the appearance of a polished cavalier, a colorful and opulent showman, and an eloquently moving speaker. His mind was quick and as a youth his body was agile. The outward appearances all pointed to a kingly bearing. But there was no majestic personality and even less of a constancy of character to accompany his showy and shallow façade. "Never did any prince," observes one of his biographers, "seem more worthy to ascend to a throne than did Henry, in the opinion of his orthodox subjects, and never did a monarch more thoroughly disappoint such expectations. . . . France imagined her king to be a hero, and found him imbecile." [1]

Henry's actions during his fifteen-year reign were unpredictable and irrational. At one moment he could be solemnly and pompously conducting his court; at another, dressed in sackcloth or the habit of a flagellant monk and bearing the marks of a penitent, he could be seen praying for hours at the little hermitage in the Bois de Vincennes; or at any time he might be observed with his rowdy companions dashing through the narrow streets of Paris on horseback in quest of excitement and diversion. The banquets and court festivals of Henry III's reign were notorious for their frivolity, debauchery, and lasciviousness. He was forever seeking new forms of pleasure in unusual ways and, although his indulgence in *la chasse de palais* (the amorous pursuit of court girls) seemed never to be satiated, his only consistent affection was toward his ubiquitous packs of lap dogs.[2]

The king completely alienated himself from the nobility and people of France when he appointed his mignons — perfumed and jeweled palace playmates — to the principal offices of government. Surrounded by these rowdy and licentious cohorts, Henry scandalized the crown of France almost irreparably. Among his most favored mignons were Anne, duke of Joyeuse, whom he made first Chamberlain and elevated to the governorship of Normandy; and young Jean-Louis de Nogaret de la Valette, to whom he gave the county of Épernon (after declaring it a duchy), and the office of colonel-general of infantry.[3] It was in reference to the duke of Épernon that Philippe Desportes penned these lines to Henry:

> Ce Mignon si frisé qui sert d'homme et de femme,
> A votre esprit léger nouvellement surpris,
> Il est votre Adonis, vous êtes sa Cypris,
> Il vous nomme son coeur, vous l'appelez votre âme . . .[4]

> This Mignon so curly locked as to be both man and girl,
> Who has so recently ensnared your mind,
> He is your Adonis, you are his Cypris,
> He calls you his heart, you call him your soul . . .

Occasionally Henry did show moments of wise decision and capable leadership, but unfortunately he could never bring himself to refrain from his pleasures long enough to maintain a consistent and positive policy. In times of crisis indecision was his salient trait. The strings of government were either left to dangle or be manipulated by his resourceful mother while his mignons and the leading nobles vied with one another for position and power.

THE POLITIQUES

It was in the early years of Henry III's reign that another important party began to exercise significant influence in France, at first in the provinces of the southeast and then throughout the realm. The Politiques, as they were popularly called since 1563, represented a political orientation based not upon religious tradition nor social contract, as with the Monarchomachs, but upon the political integrity and divine right of the monarch to establish and enforce the laws of the commonwealth.[5] To the Politiques, religious uniformity was of secondary importance; what mattered most was the unity, stability, and sovereignty of the state. Order meant more to them than liberty, and legality seemed more vital than resistance. The Huguenots, observes Laski, "saw only the direct evils of the tyranny beneath which they lived; the *Politiques* emphasized the cost of overthrowing that tyranny." [6] In their pursuit of political expediency, therefore, they theoretically favored the almost unlimited power of the king and thus helped pave the way for the royal absolutism and divine-right monarchy of the seventeenth and eighteenth centuries. In this they were in step with one of the long-range trends of the Renaissance, but at the same time they marked a break with the accepted notions of religious unity which at the time prevailed among Catholic and Protestant zealots. Religious toleration became a watchword of the Politiques, but it was a toleration by necessity, not by principle. Religious unity might well be preferable to diversity, but it was not worth the price of political upheaval and war resulting in the inevitable weakening and collapse of the state. The desire for peace and national unity, therefore, compelled the Politiques to advocate religious tolerance.

As the religious struggles prolonged, however, and as Spanish intervention became a more integral part of the Catholic strength, the Politiques became more and more hostile to the Spanish-League alliance, until it was finally they, more than the Huguenots, who were carrying on the patriotic war against the enemies of France. After 1590, the opposition to Philip II's policies grew stronger as thousands in France who previously had been indifferent to the Protestant-Catholic quarrel took up arms in defense of their *patrie*. The growing agitation of the Politiques and the increased involvement of Philip in France gradually converted the religious wars into an international political struggle which ended in eventual Spanish defeat.

The theoretical position of the Politiques was most ably stated in the speeches and letters of Michel de l'Hôpital and

Etienne Pasquier; in the legalist treatises of Louis Le Roy, Pierre Gregoire of Toulouse, Adam Blackwood, and Jean Bodin; and later in the apologetic works of Louis Servin, François Le Jay, Pierre de Belloy, and Jacques Hurault.[7] To these might also be added, in an indirect and very individual way, the *Essays* of Michel de Montaigne. Of all these, Bodin's political philosophy, particularly his statements on the nature of sovereignty, have had the greatest long-range impact. The change in Bodin's attitude toward the monarchy as expressed in his *Methodus*, published in 1566,[8] and his *République*, published in 1576,[9] is typical of the changing attitudes of the Politiques as the Wars of Religion dragged on. In 1566 many royalists believed peace and unity could be won by suppressing the Huguenots. Four years later they were convinced that whatever hope existed for political stability was being destroyed by the civil wars. After 1584 most of them were willing to give full support to the Huguenots and Henry of Navarre in defense of the monarchy against the tyranny of the League.

Monarchy, Bodin affirmed in the *République*, was not only the earliest and simplest form of political organization, it was also the best. Its prototype, and the unit from which it is built, is the family, with the king occupying the same authoritative and absolute role in the nation that the father holds in the family unit. The authority of the king is thus uncontested and unquestioned by the component parts of society whether they are institutionalized or not. This sovereignty was a fact of natural law and not a result of specific grants to the monarch from the people; it was perpetual and inalienable, and for its exercise the king was responsible only to God. The principal hallmark of royal sovereignty was the authority not only to administer and enforce the laws, but also to make them. Thus the king stood above the law and could be bound by no man-made rules.

According to Bodin, there were only three kinds of limitations on the lawmaking power of the king, and none of these were either personal or institutional: they were divine law, natural law, and the fundamental laws of the nation (such as the Salic Law and the inviolability of private property). Within this broad framework the monarch was free to exercise his will and authority. Like other organs of the government, the Estates General could submit reports, give advice and counsel, and hear cases; but all decisions were the prerogative and responsibility of the king, and he could not be held accountable for them by any magistrate or group of people. As for the right, claimed by the Hugenots, to revolt against a wicked or unjust ruler, Bodin concluded that "a subject is never justified under any circumstances in attempting to do anything against his sovereign prince, however evil and tyrannical he may be." [10]

The Politiques were more than royalist pamphleteers and political theorists, however. By 1572 they were a loosely organized and active political movement dedicated above all else to ending the religious wars and re-establishing the political unity of France. During the first years of Henry III's reign they affirmed their loyalty to the crown, but as the complete unworthiness of the last Valois became more and more apparent their enthusiasm for Bodinian royalism waned. But after 1589, Henry of Navarre became the new focus of their affection, and with his renunciation of Protestantism and coronation as king of France in 1593–94, the Politiques emerged as the real victors of the religious wars.

Yet in 1572 it would have been misleading to talk about a single Politique party, for several organized groups and many loose associations were included in the movement. At court, for example, a group (sometimes knowns as the Malcontents) organized by some of the principal commanders of France — Francis of Montmorency, marshals Biron, De Cossé, and D'Entragues, and periodically led by the king's brother Duke Francis d'Alençon (created duke of Anjou in 1576) — endeavored with some success to bring an end to the civil hostilities and a limited acceptance of the Reformed religion. At the same time in southern France the governor of Languedoc, Henry, count of Damville (duke of Montmorency after the death of his brother, Francis of Montmorency, in 1579)[11] led a similar array of "moderates" in an effort to obtain civil peace through the political uniting of Catholics and Huguenots, and at the same time win greater independence of action for themselves. Most of the early Politiques were Catholics, but some pacifist Huguenots (known as *Réalistes*) were also associated with the Malcontents and Politiques, making the "party" even more heterogeneous.[12]

In 1574 the Huguenots proposed a tentative alliance with the Politiques. Damville was amenable, and in November issued a proclamation confessing his loyalty to the crown but announcing his intention of combining with the Protestants in the common defense and good of the realm. In January–February 1575 a joint assembly of Huguenots and Politiques convened at Nîmes and drew up a set of resolutions which amounted almost to the establishment of a separate state within the state.[13] These "Articles of Union" declared that their purpose in combining was "for the just and necessary conservation both of the crown and public order of our common mother and native country, as well as our persons, families, and property," [14] and affirmed that this could be achieved only through religious peace. The treaty was signed by representatives of the Huguenots and, representing the Politiques, by Damville himself. While the alliance lasted, the dashing Huguenot captain, Francis de la Noue, was its most enthusiastic advocate.[15] Thus, in spite of the Politique claims of loyalty to the crown, Damville and his followers pursued a very independent course for many years, combining with the Huguenots whenever such a policy seemed expedient and throwing in with the government or the Catholics when that proved to be more *politique*.

THE LEAGUE OF PÉRONNE

Late in 1575 the situation in France became untenable for the government and it was forced into an embarrassing peace negotiation. The southern Politiques under Damville, after joining forces with the Huguenots, compelled the king to recognize a virtually independent government in southern France ruled by Damville and Condé (who at the time was in western Germany).[16] In September, Alençon fled from court, and in February 1576, Henry of Navarre, who had been held in custody since the St. Bartholomew massacre, also escaped. After renouncing his previous renunciation of Protestantism, Navarre was accepted as the real leader of the Huguenots and, jointly with Damville and Alençon, began the march on Paris. In terror Henry III sued for peace.

On 2 May 1576, at the château de Beaulieu, a remarkable treaty known as the Peace of Monsieur (in honor of monsieur, le duc d'Alençon), was signed. It granted concessions and privileges to the Protestants which were nothing short of revolutionary for that day. Freedom of worship was guaranteed to Huguenots in all parts of the kingdom—except in Paris or where specifically objected to by a lord or magistrate in his domain — including the liberty to perform the rituals and ceremonies of the Reformed religion and to instruct their children in Protestantism. Civil equality was to be guaranteed through the creation of bipartisan law courts, known as *Chambres mi-parties*, judicated by an equal number of Catholic and Protestant justices. Eight fortified towns were granted to the Huguenots for their protection, to be garrisoned by their own troops.[17] The government made public apology for the massacre of St. Bartholomew's Day, declaring that it occurred "against the will of the Crown." The treaty ended with a government promise to summon the Estates General within six months and to act upon the wishes of the people as represented by that body.

To the ardent Catholics in France this declaration had an ominous ring. It meant more than a recognition and acceptance of religious diversity; to them it was an opening of the protective floodgates before the onrush of heresy, and could mean the eventual inundation of Catholic Christianity. Among the sixty-three articles of the Peace of Monsieur was a pronouncement restoring the government of Picardy to the prince of Condé and granting him the city of Péronne as a Huguenot stronghold. The governor of Péronne, Jacques d'Humières, took an immediate and vigorous stand to prevent the city from falling into Huguenot hands. First he called together the "gentlemen, soldiers, and inhabitants of the cities and rural areas of Picardy" in a series of meetings for the purpose of forming a league of resistance against Protestantism.[18] Secondly he addressed an appeal known as the *Manifeste de Péronne*, to all the princes, noblemen, and prelates of the realm asking for their active participation in a "holy and Christian union of all Catholics in defense of their heritage and the exercise of intelligence and cooperation among all the good, faithful, and loyal subjects of the king, for the restoration of religion to the kingdom." [19] This action was justified, the manifesto maintained, because their enemies intended to "establish errors and heresies in the kingdom to annihilate the ancient religion, to undermine the power and authority of the king and introduce another and novel form of government into the realm."

The ultimate intention of this action appears to have been to make the Catholic League of Péronne the nucleus for a greater French Catholic union, and perhaps even to make it the beginning of an international organization against the encroachments of Calvinism.[20] The manifesto, supported by all those adhering to the Picard League, and which was later adopted by other groups, set forth three principal goals for the Catholic organization: the re-establishment of the Roman Catholic Church; the preservation of Henry III and his successors in the "state, splendor, authority, service, duty, and obedience due to him by his subjects"; and the restoration to the provinces of their ancient rights and liberties "such as they were in the time of Clovis, the first Christian king." [21]

At the outset this seems to be a typically conservative and rather expected Catholic reaction to the recent Huguenot victories and the concessions granted to them in the Peace of Monsieur, but a closer examination of the concluding articles of the Péronne League reveals a much deeper and more radical organizational break with tradition.[22] The inference was strong that even the monarch himself would be opposed if he failed to support the Catholic movement. The fourth article of the manifesto reads: "If there is any obstacle, opposition, or rebellion by anyone, or in the name of any body, to what has been stated above, the associates of this union will be obliged to employ all of their goods and means, even to the sacrifice of their own lives, to pursue, chastise, and punish those who desire and make such obstacles." Article VII affirms: "Associates will be judged by their prompt obedience and service to the chief, who will be their deputy, will follow and give counsel, comfort, and help, as well as support and maintain the said association against all of its adversaries. Partners who are too weak or unzealous will be punished by the authority of the chief according to his orders, which they all agree to obey." And Article VIII further declares that: "Every Catholic of the towns and villages will be advised of the association and will be secretly solicited by the leaders to join it and to furnish, according to their respective ability and power, arms and men for the furtherance of these goals." Article XII was an oath by which the participating member bound himself to loyalty to the League and promised to remain a member of it until his death.[23]

This League of Péronne was the most important association of Catholics against the Huguenots since the beginning of the religious wars, but it was not the first. Prior to 1576 a number of similar organizations, of a more limited nature, had sprung to life, principally in the south. The earliest of these provincial leagues appears to have arisen at Bordeaux in protest against the Protestant attempt to gain possession of the Château Trompette during the reign of Francis II.[24] This was followed in 1563 by a violent outburst of popular indignation over the assassination of Francis, duke of Guise, which resulted in the very active League of Toulouse.[25] This organization, composed of many clergymen, nobles, and bourgeois of Languedoc and Guyenne, and under the direct jurisdiction of the Parlement de Toulouse, actually took up arms and pledged itself by oath to march wherever required for the defense of the Catholic religion.[26] In 1563 leagues were formed in Guyenne and in bordering provinces for similar purposes.[27]

It is important to call attention to the fact that the nucleus of many of these provincial leagues was not the nobility, nor even the clergy (although they did play a key role), but the local guilds or fraternities of middle- and lower-class artisans. The urban craftsmen in sixteenth-century France, just as the rural peasants, were staunchly Catholic and resented any encroachments upon their religious traditions — particularly the Protestant attacks on their patron saints, relics, and rituals. The guilds offered an ideal institutional structure for the organization and coordination of Catholic opposition to the growing Huguenot forces.[28]

Now in 1576, Henry III, in a moment of clear thinking, saw the possibilities of the League of Péronne as an ally for the strengthening and glorification of the crown. He also realized that such an organization, backed by powerful nobles and supported by much of the population of France, could be a very dangerous force if used against him. He therefore seized the opportunity and declared himself head of the League.[29] He wrote to all of the provincial governors recommending the union and attached to the oath circulating among them an additional agreement safeguarding the rights and prerogatives of the crown. By placing their signatures on this document the princes and nobles agreed to "employ their goods and their lives to carry out the commands and orders of His Majesty, after having listened to the remonstrances of the assembled estates of the kingdom." [30] Henry believed this article would mitigate the inference in the League's manifesto that the Estates General could impose its will on the king. He felt also that it would improve his position in the more insecure provinces of Normandy, Languedoc, Province, Dauphiné, and Auvergne and give him a stronger hold in the Catholic provinces of Picardy, Burgundy, Lyonnais, Orléanais, and the Ile-de-France.

The December–January meeting of the Estates General at Blois proved Henry to have been overoptimistic about the security of his position and completely mistaken about his leadership of the provincial leagues.[31] The strength and independence of this newly mobilized Catholic power was immediately felt at Blois. All three of the orders demanded more frequent summoning of the Estates, and agreed that their will should be binding upon the king.[32] The first and third estates were adamant about financial matters and flatly refused to grant the increased taxes requested by the king. When it came to the vital discussion of the religious problem — in particular the question of whether or not the concessions granted to the Huguenots in the Peace of Monsieur should be maintained — opinion was divided. The clergy and nobility stood firm, though not unanimous, in their opposition to toleration, insisting that religious unity must be enforced. The third estate debated the issue hotly before also concluding that "all the subjects should be united in one religion by the best means which the King might decide to employ." Jean Bodin and other Politiques among the deputies made a strong appeal for nonviolence in settling the religious issue,[33] but the strength of the League adherents in the third estate was sufficient to override this proposed moderating amendment.

The immediate result of the Estates General of 1576–77 was the reopening of hostilities in France — coordinated with renewed violence of the organized Calvinist participation in the Netherlands revolt — and the breakup of the tenuous Huguenot-Politique alliance. In September 1577 a truce was once more reached between the combatants, and a new pacification announcement known as the Edict of Poitiers was issued.[34] Most of the more radical concessions to the Huguenots granted in the Peace of Monsieur were repealed, but they were still permitted to live unmolested in most parts of the kingdom (though without the public exercise of their religion, which was now restricted to the domains of those noblemen formally permitting it), and the *chambres mi-parties* were reduced to four in number and composed of two-thirds Catholic judges.

Realizing that another independent power in France, even though Catholic, if not controlled directly and intimately by the crown, would lead to a further disintegration of royal authority, Henry III ordered the immediate abolition and discontinuance of all Catholic leagues.[35] It was, of course, impossible to enforce such a pronouncement, but for the next seven years, until it was suddenly upset in 1584, the balance of powers in France remained relatively unchanged.

FORMATION OF THE NEW CATHOLIC LEAGUE

On 10 June 1584, while engaged in his reckless attempt to secure the sovereignty of the Netherlands which had been promised him by the Dutch estates, the unpredictable Alençon (now duke of Anjou) suddenly died. One month later William the Silent, prince of Orange and leader of the Netherlands revolt, was assassinated. The two events had no causal relation to each other, but they did have immediate and momentous repercussions. Anjou, the last surviving brother of the childless king, was heir to the throne of France. With the Valois dynasty approaching its end, the heir apparent was the Protestant prince of Béarn and king of Navarre, Henry

Bourbon, political and military leader of the Huguenots. The former relation between the Huguenots, the crown, and the League was suddenly reversed, and a new and vital period of the French religious wars began. The death of William the Silent threw the Dutch revolt into a new phase and caused a renewed effort on the part of Philip II to regain these valuable but rebellious states. It also forced a closer contact between Dutch and French Calvinists and helped produce a more tightly coordinated Spanish policy toward the Netherlands and France.

At this point Elizabeth, too, decided that the time had come for England to take a more positive stand in the growing controversy and to give open and vigorous support to the cause of Protestantism in the Netherlands, France, and Scotland. For several years Anjou had been the leading suitor for Elizabeth's hand; with his death there was almost as little hope for a continuation of the Tudor line as there was for the Valois. Elizabeth preferred not to become so involved in the Netherlands affair that it would lead to war with Spain, but now, led by Walsingham, Leicester, and even Lord Burghley,[36] the queen's council urged her to take the offensive against the king of Spain because, they reasoned, "It is better for Her Majesty to enter into war now, whilst she can do it outside her realm and have the help of the people of Holland and their parties." On 20 October 1584 the council proposed: (1) to send an envoy to the Netherlands in order, first, to determine what actions France planned to take, secondly, to propose to the Estates the offering of Flushing, Middleburg, and Brill to Elizabeth, and, finally, to determine how much the Netherlands could contribute in monthly payments and food and what forces of their own they could maintain; (2) to procure a good peace with the king of Scotland; (3) to grant financial aid to the bishop of Cologne "to make head against the Spanish forces"; (4) to have the Estates urge Duke Casimir (of the Palatinate) to occupy Spanish power in Guelderland; (5)

to induce the king of France to inhibit the selling of victuals to the Spanish; and (6) to "devise how the king of Navarre and Don Antonio [pretender to the crown of Portugal, which had been taken over in 1580 by Philip II] might be induced to offend and occupy the king of Spain." [37] After 1584 any state or group which was an enemy of Spain or the pope was now to be a friend of England.

The stage was set for that final and most crucial phase of the ideological conflict in France — and in Europe — which eventually was to witness the emergence of a new and virile France, the victory of royal absolutism, the submergence of Spain under the debris of a shattered Germany, and, after their further baptism of fire, the rebirth of England and Holland as the great maritime powers of Europe. From the passions and violence, the frustrations, skepticism, and failures of this period came the beginnings of a new concept of social life — religious toleration and freedom of conscience — the greatest heritage of the Wars of Religion, although it still took many years before it began to be realized. Men did not cease to hope for a re-establishment of religious unity, but, with occasional exceptions, they no longer sought it by the sword. That had been tried and found impossible to achieve.

The death of Anjou moved the French Catholics to a new realization of the precariousness of their position should Henry of Navarre become their king. The immediate result of this recognition was the formation of a new and revitalized Catholic League. This organization, the "Sainte Ligue perpétuelle pour la conservation de la religion catholique," was formulated on the general pattern of its predecessors, but with more decisive objectives, with a broader base of popular support, and with the active leadership of Duke Henry of Guise and his influential supporters. Its clearly defined political objective was to prevent the royal crown of France from falling to a Protestant heretic. Who then should become king upon the death of Henry III? Guise would not have been completely averse to taking the honor himself, but the legitimacy of his claim might have been difficult to assert. Therefore, in spite of his own great popularity among the people of France, Guise agreed to proclaim as rightful heir the aging cardinal of Bourbon, uncle to Henry of Navarre.[38]

This new league which came into existence in 1584-85 was organized on various levels, with the Paris structure being the most complete and important. The association there, predominantly self-governing and notoriously articulate, sprang to life quite independently of the previous provincial movements.[39] The leaders in its creation seem to have been Charles Hotman of Rocheblonde, brother of the Huguenot pamphleteer, and three clergymen of high ability: Jean Prévost, curate of Saint-Séverin, Jean Boucher, priest of Saint-Benoît, and Matthieu de Launoy, canon of Soissons. Three prominent Paris lawyers were also involved in the formation of the municipal league and they continued to play key roles in its bizarre history for the next few years. These were Michel Marteau (known generally as La Chapelle-Marteau), counselor to the Chambre des Comptes; Jean de Clerc (called Bussi or Bussé Leclerc), attorney of the Parlement de Paris; and Jean Louchart, commissary at the Châtelet.[40] To this core of determined devotees was soon added a half-dozen others, selected predominantly from among the priests and the bourgeoisie, to form the *Conseil des Seize* (Council of the Sixteen) — named for the sixteen political divisions of Paris. Although the actual number of persons in the Sixteen varied considerably, it remained a compact though protean bureau, headed usually by an inner committee of five men who formed the administrative nucleus of the League in Paris, and, through its guild and ecclesiastical connections with other cities, in the rest of France as well.[41] In their favorable position as a *comité de surveillance*, these five functioned as the eyes and ears of the council. Policies and decisions were communicated by them to League members through the associated merchant and craft guilds to the local committees organized throughout the country.

The Paris League was an amazing institution representing a surprising degree of democracy in its "precinct" organization as well as in political theory, yet being responsible for a fanatical reign of terror such as was not witnessed again until the French Revolution two centuries later. Membership in the League was drawn mostly from the commoners, merchants, artisans, and parish priests of Paris. They exercised their franchise through the local and district clubs organized at the grass-roots level in all parts of the city.[42] As soon as a club had grown enough to attain a quasi-constitutional status, other clubs were then formed inside of it which in turn went through the same metamorphosis. The infant clubs which were thus created generally contained the more radical elements of their parent structure and ultimately came to spark and control the larger organization. The numerous guilds and religious fraternities — particularly the Jesuit houses — served as meeting and rallying centers for the movement. In this way the *Confrèrie du Nom de Jésus* became the Jacobin Club of the Paris League, just as the *Seize* had become its Committee of Public Safety.[43] Members of the League took an oath of allegiance to God, His church, King Charles X (the title to be assumed by the cardinal of Bourbon) and his officers, and to the city of Paris. They vowed to love and support one another, to propagate the goals and ideals of the League and bring new members to its support, and to be on constant alert for activities prejudicial to their cause.[44]

As the controlling council of the Paris League, the Sixteen met frequently to coordinate the activities and manage the affairs of the organization. Sometimes they met at the homes of the various members, but more frequently at the colleges of the Sorbonne. Often they held their council sessions at the Jesuit house near Saint-Paul's church;[45] and Boucher's chamber at the Collège de Fortet was so frequently the site of meetings that it came to be known as the "Cradle of the League" (*Berceau de la Ligue*).[46] Close but very secret communications were maintained between the Sixteen and the duke of Guise, who, after 1584, was the effective leader of the French Catholics. François de Mayneville was the usual intermediary between Guise and the Sixteen, although a M. de Conrard and le sieur de Beauregard are sometimes mentioned in this role. Until 1589 there was no central coordinating organization for all of France except the personal role of Henry of Guise and the nominal head of the French League, the cardinal of Bourbon. Cooperation was achieved through the common actions and correspondence between the Paris Sixteen and the similar councils set up in most of the other League towns of France.

POLITICAL THEORY OF THE LEAGUE

The semi-democratic nature of the League as reflected in its municipal organization was expressed also in its philosophy of government. Following the death of Anjou in 1584 a remarkable transformation took place in the political thought of both Huguenots and Leaguers. With the realization that their leader stood an excellent chance of becoming king of France, the Huguenots shifted their ideological position with regard to the monarch to one of support and justification, while the Catholic League now adopted a position very similar to that previously held by the Huguenots.[47] Indeed, in its appeal to the masses, its insistence upon monarchical limitations, and its emphasis upon the intimate relation between government and religion, the League went even further than had the Protestants. The striking similarity between Huguenot theory before 1584 and League theory after that date has been noted by many historians and political scientists. J. N. Figgis' comparison of the two is particularly succinct and discerning:

> We cannot really separate between the principles of Ligueurs and Huguenots. Both assert the cause of civil liberty. Both do so on the basis of an original contract, and combat the notion of absolute power

responsible to God alone. Both develop their argument on religious lines and treat heresy or rather heresy combined with persecution as a proof of tyranny. The Ligueurs treat the national State as but a part of a larger whole. In this perhaps lies their main difference from the Huguenots, who go no further than to demand foreign princes' help in favour of "the religion." They did not and could not talk of a Protestant Christendom.[48]

Although Leaguer pamphleteers and Parisian preachers echoed many of the concepts expressed in the *Vindiciae contra Tyrannos,* they also reflected a greater reliance upon the will of the people and the popular law than did the Huguenot writers.[49] Just as with the Calvinists, there was always present in League theory a strong feudal element — particularly in its demands for the maintenance or revival of medieval rights and privileges which were being lost in the Renaissance — but there was also a very great emphasis in League writings on the newer notion of some form of popular sovereignty.[50]

But the central thesis of all League philosophy was the axiom that religious unity was the binding social foundation of any state. It follows that the head of a government, who cannot be in opposition to the basis of his own society, must of necessity be a Catholic.[51] This was a divine law and could not be abrogated by the decrees nor the doctrines of men. Acceptance of a non-Catholic king would be not only heresy and a mockery of God but treason against the state.[52] *Une foi, une loi, un Roi,* said the ancient maxim; and the League intended to uphold it. After all, added Jean de Caumont Champenois in one of his forceful pamphlets, the monarchy is not really a hereditary institution at all, but a gift of God bestowed by His Church through consecration. The Most Christian King, therefore, governs not as a sovereign ruler but as a lieutenant of the supreme head, Jesus Christ.[53]

Of the numerous League pamphlets and political tracts to appear after 1585, those of Louis D'Orléans, Jean Boucher, and Rossaeus were particularly effective. D'Orléans' vigorously written *L'Avertissement des catholiques anglais aux*

catholiques français, which appeared in 1586, became a hand-
book of the Catholic Leaguers. In it D'Orléans pointed to the
disorder and chaos caused by the Reformation in France, and
called upon the now awakened Catholics to unite and seize the
initiative in ridding the realm of this spreading sore. Using the
thesis of the Huguenot's own *Franco-Gallia*, he summoned
the people to reject the candidature of Henry of Navarre as
king of France, for, he protested, just as that "detestable
book" grants the right of election to the subjects of the king,
so now should all true Catholics refuse to accept the king who
is being proposed to them. "Who then will receive him, the
heretics? Who will shout, God save the King! the Catholic
Leaguers? Who will wish him health, the Machiavellians?
Who will support him, the Politiques?" [54] Later the same year
D'Orléans published another rousing call to the Catholics of
France (*L'Apologie des catholiques unis*),[55] this one aimed at
the Politiques rather than the Huguenots. The Salic Law, he
argued, was of pagan origin and was never meant to supersede
the Will and Law of God. The basic necessity of the royal
lineage is to be unequivocally Christian (meaning Catholic),
and if this requirement cannot be met in the male line another
must be chosen.

Jean Boucher, one of the fieriest of the Paris preachers —
also a doctor of theology at Paris, prior of the Sorbonne, and
active member of the Sixteen — not only rejected the idea of
Henry of Navarre as king, but with equal vehemence denounced the deceitful monarchy of Henry III. In his *De justa
abdicatione Henrici tertii*, published in 1589 following
Henry's murder of the duke of Guise, Boucher boldly asserted the doctrine of tyrannicide against this "enemy of God
and of man," and called upon the people — not the aristocracy
as in the Huguenot *Le Réveil-Matin* — to rise up and physi-
cally dispose of the tyrant. Monarchs, declared Boucher, do
not succeed to the throne by absolute hereditary right; they

are constituted by the people (and consecrated by the church) and can thus be lawfully deposed by the same authority.

The most elaborate statement of the League position on politics came, as did that of the Huguenots, from the pen of an unidentified writer. The sophisticated though somewhat incoherent treatise entitled *De justa reipublicae christianae* was signed simply "Rossaeus," a name which has eluded positive identification to the present day, although it is now generally believed to have been the pseudonym of either Guillaume Rose or William Reynolds.[56] Rossaeus constructed his intricate argument for popular sovereignty on the twin foundations of benevolent divine nature and human rationality. Governments came into existence originally through the will of God and of the people because of the social needs of man, he affirmed. Thus, since monarchs exist in order to fulfill specific duties, their authority extends only to the limits of these obligations. If the boundaries of royal prerogative are exceeded, the people are justified in defying the king. One of the primary conditions of kingship, and its most fundamental *raison d'être*, is to maintain and defend the true and divinely established religious traditions of the nation against all threats of heresy and treason. This duty cannot be flouted with impunity, and its complete denial by Henry of Navarre invalidated his claim to the throne of France.

The result of this philosophy might well have strengthened the assertions of the Holy See, had it not been for the aroused antagonism between the League and the new pope, Sixtus V, who ascended to the papal throne in April 1585.[57] The radical League theorists had no intention of supporting the claims of papal supremacy in France, and many of those who associated the League with the idea of a revived Christian commonwealth looked not to Sixtus V but to Philip II. "God has delivered us from a wicked and politique pope," shouted one of the Leaguer priests on the death of Sixtus V, "Had he lived

longer, people would have had a fine surprise in Paris in hear-
ing us preach against the pope, for we should have had to do
it." [58]

From its very inception, League opinion was sharply divided into two camps on this important issue of loyalty. As
long as the duke of Guise headed the League he was able to
focus its energies and reconcile its factions, for he was equally
popular among the masses and the Catholic nobility; but after
the early months of 1589 the division between *Maheustre*
(nationalist-oriented "politique" Leaguers) and *Manant* (the
more radically democratic and "catholique" Leaguers) wid-
ened into an irreparable breach. Some League writers — like
Boucher, D'Orléans, and Jean Porthaise and many influential
Jesuits, among them the great polemical writer, Robert Bellarmine, and in the 1590's Luis Molina — held to the essentially medieval idea of a great commonwealth of Christendom,
the *res publica Christiana*, united by fundamental bonds of
heritage, culture, faith, and law. This notion died slowly in
western Europe and had its last great burst of influence during
the period of the League. To those holding this view, the
Holy League was not concerned with territorial boundaries or
political matters of state; it was concerned with maintaining
the traditions, doctrines, and institutions which gave form and
life to the Christian commonwealth. Between 1585 and 1589
this argument held great force among the Leaguers. Mendoza
never let Guise forget that they were fighting in a common
cause, that all private, class, or national interests and ambitions
must be subordinated to a greater goal, and that Philip II had
no other design in France than the promotion of this ideal —
the restoration of the unity of Christendom.

But to many of the Leaguers the immediate problems of
heresy and royal succession in France were the League's
only reason for existence and the only motive for soliciting
Spanish aid. To them the idea of a Christian commonwealth
had little appeal. Their real interest was in establishing re-

ligious unity in France, for only by ideological unity could social stability be assured. They were equally suspicious of papal pretensions and Spanish subsidies, and when the immediate problem of French succession was solved they felt no further obligations to the League or to Spain. It was this split within the League itself, opened wide by Henry IV's adjuration of Protestantism in 1593, that undermined and finally destroyed the League and insured the ultimate victory to the Politiques.

THE LEAGUE AND SPAIN: TREATY OF JOINVILLE

By the autumn of 1584, Henry of Guise was well aware that a closer alliance with Spain would have to be made if the League were to become strong enough to oppose the expanding force of the Huguenots, whose ranks and coffers were now being recruited and provisioned from England, Switzerland, and Germany. The League was active and growing in size, but it lacked military strength and money. It became increasingly obvious that more than pamphlets and pulpit oratory would be needed to convince Henry of Navarre and his followers that he was not welcome to the throne of France.

Guise's overtures to Madrid did not go unheeded. Philip readily perceived the advantage of a close ally in France, an ally more dependable than Henry of Valois and more forceful than his pensionaries at court. He had for some time encouraged the idea of the Catholic leagues in France and had reiterated his willingness to support any group actively engaged in fighting heresy. In the early 1560's, while Philip was still maneuvering for possession of Navarre, he had his ambassador to France, Thomas Perrinot de Chantonnay, establish close relations with the Guise faction at court for the purpose of increasing his own voice in French affairs through the party which at the time had the upper hand. There is evidence that proposals were actually put into motion for the creation of a Catholic league with Philip at its head.[59] With his newly ac-

quired French queen, Philip might already have been toying
with thoughts of placing one of his children on the tottering
French throne. Nothing more concrete than this seems to have
developed, however. At the same time, Philip was negotiating
with Antoine of Navarre to get him to repudiate his Protestant
wife, Jeanne d'Albret, and lead the Catholics of France
against the Huguenots.[60] Obviously the cautious Spanish king
had limited confidence in the Guise reliability, since that
family was not without dynastic ambitions of its own.

In 1565, Philip made another bid for allies in France by
trying to win over Catherine de' Medici through the famous
Bayonne interview between the queen mother and her daughter, Philip's wife.[61] That these efforts, just as the previous
ones with Navarre and the Guises, were largely unsuccessful
there is no doubt, but it is likewise obvious that Philip was
vitally interested in the French situation and was not averse to
negotiating with any faction promising an advantageous alliance against the Huguenots. Nevertheless, it should be carefully noted that Philip approached these arrangements with
great caution, for he was not yet ready psychologically or
militarily to launch a great enterprise against the Protestants.
From his point of view, the situation was not nearly so
desperate as it was eventually to become.

Twelve years later Philip found himself in deepening difficulties. His relations with England were growing worse; the
massacre of St. Bartholomew's Day had only aggravated the
Huguenot menace in France instead of eliminating it; and he
had on his hands a costly and dangerous revolt in the Netherlands, which was being fed both by the Huguenots and by
Elizabeth of England. In 1577, Philip — somewhat apprehen-
sively, for he did not want to promote a Scottish-Guise venture
that would carry with it no benefits to him nor the Catholic
cause — acceded to the persistent entreaties of the Scottish
ambassador of Mary Stuart, and began to pursue a more intimate relationship with the young Duke Henry of Guise.

Through his resident ambassador in France, Juan de Vargas Mexia, Philip took the initiative in opening negotiations with Guise for a closer coordination between him, the Spanish ambassador, the Scottish ambassador (Archbishop of Glasgow), and Philip's governor general in the Netherlands, Don Juan of Austria.[62] Again no binding commitments or alliances were made (although Philip did begin sending money to Guise), but closer relations were maintained for several years, and something of a rehearsal for the later Spanish-League entente was enacted.[63] Certainly it prepared the way for the more active participation of Philip in French affairs.

The sudden death of Anjou in May 1584 made it imperative that some decisive action be taken. Henry of Guise was convinced that the League needed Spanish help if it was to prevent Navarre and the Huguenots from controlling France. For the next few months the letters that passed between them and the communications between Guise and the Spanish ambassador were steered toward a common goal. In December, Philip dispatched one of his agents from Paris to the Château of Joinville, the ancestral home of the house of Guise, where he met with leaders of the League to work out suitable arrangements for an active alliance between the king of Spain and the Catholic League.

Jean Baptiste de Tassis, one of Philip's most faithful career diplomats, was assigned to negotiate the accord with the League. At Joinville, Tassis met Juan de Moreo, knight commander of the Hospitalers of Malta, who was sent from Madrid with powers to assist in drawing up the agreement. The League was represented by Henry of Guise (who was also empowered to act in behalf of his brother Louis, cardinal of Guise, and his cousins the dukes of Aumale and Elboeuf); by François de Mayneville, representing the cardinal of Bourbon (who had been selected by the leaders of the League as their claimant to the throne); and Charles, duke of Mayenne, Guise's younger brother.[64]

The Treaty of Joinville, completed on the last day of December 1584, was a very comprehensive document and remained the basis of relations between Spain and the League for the next decade. It set up the following points as the basis for Spanish-League cooperation:

(1) A heretic could not be king of France and therefore the cardinal of Bourbon was recognized as heir to the crown.

(2) Upon his accession, the cardinal was pledged to strengthen the union by ratifying and observing the Treaty of Cateau-Cambrésis.

(3) The two participants were to work toward the complete abolishment of Protestantism in France and in the Netherlands.

(4) The French princes and the future king renounced all alliances with the Turk.

(5) They promised to disavow piracy and any other activity which might jeopardize Spanish navigation and trade with the Indies.

(6) The decrees of the Council of Trent were to be published and accepted in France.

(7) The League was to assist Philip in recovering the cities belonging to him which were being held by the king of France. Specific mention was made of the city of Cambrai.

(8) Philip promised a yearly subsidy for the expenses of the war, payable in monthly installments of 50,000 escudos. All payments made up to the time of the accession of the cardinal were to be repaid by him at that time.

(9) After the heresies had been eliminated there was to be a continued alliance between the two parties for the mutual defense of France and the Netherlands. Philip agreed to provide men and money for this enterprise as the need arose.

(10) Any nobles, gentlemen, cities, or groups that might in the future ally themselves with either party to the treaty were to be regarded as comprehended in it.[65]

In addition to these main terms of the compact there were two special articles, one promising to assist in apprehending Don Antonio, prior of Crato and bothersome pretender to the Portuguese throne (occupied since 1580 by Philip), and the other a guarantee that Henry of Navarre's territories beyond the French frontier, namely, Lower Navarre and Béarn, would pass to Philip.[66]

Philip had not as yet committed himself to sending armed forces to France, but his apparent willingness to subsidize his new allies attests to the gravity of the crisis and manifests his deep concern over the growing strength of Navarre and his Protestant followers. Paris now became the focal point of Philip's foreign policy.

Chapter III

MENDOZA AND FRANCE

✤ ✤ ✤ ✤

Philip II's policy in regard to France had been one
of caution and forbearance prior to 1584. The situation there,
though chaotic and uncertain, had not caused undue apprehension before the death of the duke of Anjou. France's political decline after the middle of the century had reduced the
threat of any direct attack on Spain, and as long as it remained
a basically Catholic country Philip had no strong desires to
involve himself in the domestic disruption of this northern
neighbor. Numerous French enterprises, both on the continent and on the seas, and certain individual French subjects
had caused the Spanish king frequent irritation, but his policy
remained one of cautious deferment.

Certainly the civil wars in France had caused great concern
in Madrid, but not to the extent of active intervention. As
long as the French crown was able, and willing, to contend
with the Huguenots on more than equal terms there was no
immediate cause for alarm. The intervention of Anjou in the
Netherlands, however, compelled Philip to realize the key
position France occupied in his conflict with the Dutch rebels.
France could be a very valuable ally in supressing the revolt,
or she could be a most dangerous foe if enlisted on the side of
the enemy. Previously Philip's only worry had been the
strength of Navarre and his Huguenots, but with the sudden
success of Anjou it became apparent that the Valois dynasty
itself could not be trusted in such a crucial spot. The success

of his entire foreign policy, and, as he believed, of Christendom itself, depended upon suppressing heresy and revolt in the Netherlands. This in turn was contingent upon isolating the Dutch from either England or France.

The basis, therefore, of Philip's policy toward England and France in relation to the Low Countries was threefold: stop English aid to the rebels; prevent close cooperation between the Dutch and the king of France; and strengthen his own and the Catholic position (while at the same time reducing the growing Huguenot menace) by a close tie with the League and the Catholic princes of France. The first of these, Philip soon found, could only be accomplished by force of arms; the second and third might be achieved by diplomacy. The "Invincible" Armada and the indomitable Mendoza were to be Philip's chief agents in this all-out attempt to crush the revolt and "re-establish the religious unity and tranquillity of Christendom."

MENDOZA'S DIPLOMATIC MISSION TO FRANCE

Near the middle of October 1584[1] the new Spanish ambassador to France arrived in Paris, quietly and unannounced, and took up temporary lodging at the home of Jean Baptiste de Tassis. Don Bernardino de Mendoza's precise activities for the next month are uncertain, but it can be assumed that he was busily laying the structural foundations for his six-year embassy. As early as the spring of 1584 it was known in official circles that he would replace Tassis at that crucial post,[2] and by August his *lettres de créance* were being drawn up. Between August and October he was in Madrid making final arrangements for the mission. Of his many instructions on handling the diplomatic affairs in France (and with England too for, since his own expulsion from London earlier in the year, Spain had had no resident ambassador there), one of the priority matters was the immediate negotiation of a treaty with Guise and the League.[3]

On 23 September 1584, Philip wrote to Tassis informing him of Mendoza's forthcoming arrival and telling him to re-assure the duke of Guise that they would soon have a "solu-tion to their anticipations." [4] This may account for the secrecy of Mendoza's entry into Paris and for his close association with Tassis prior to the signing of the Treaty of Joinville. But shortly after Mendoza's departure from Madrid, Philip changed his strategy and decided to have Mendoza remain in Paris and send Tassis to negotiate the treaty.[5] Orders to this effect were quickly made and rushed to Paris with Juan de Moreo. The reason for this change is not entirely clear, but Moreo's sudden trip to Madrid in September, from his pre-liminary negotiations with the League, might suggest either a desire of Guise to negotiate with Tassis, whom he already knew, or an early disclosure of Moreo's later antipathy toward Mendoza.

The announced purpose of Mendoza's mission to France was to offer official condolences to the royal family on the death of the duke of Anjou,[6] but there were some at the Valois court who knew of Mendoza's ability and energy as a negotia-tor and they therefore suspected that he had come for more significant reasons. Mendoza tried to allay their suspicions by giving "confidential" hints to many different people about his "real" objectives; but, among others, the English ambassador in France, Sir Edward Stafford, was not so easily deceived. "Bernardin gives out divers causes of his coming," reported Stafford to Secretary Walsingham, "To all he says it is to condole on Monsieur's death, but for the rest, to some, that it is to redemand Cambray, to others, to release it to the King, to others, to demand it first, and if he cannot obtain it, then to offer its release on two conditions, viz. that the Queen Mother release her whole pretension to Portugal, and that the King promise neither to help or allow his subjects to help the Low Countries." [7] Philip hoped that nobody would suspect Men-doza's part in the Joinville negotiations nor that he was to become Philip's liaison with the League, but even before his arrival many observers knew that this was more than a routine change of ambassadors. Mendoza was in France for all of the reasons indicated by Stafford, but the one requiring the greatest secrecy he did not divulge. Armed with plenipotentiary powers and 6000 escudos in gold (a useful weapon in that day as well as in our own), the ambassador started out to build up a solid foundation for the effective operation of Spanish diplomacy in France.

MENDOZA'S BACKGROUND

Don Bernardino was perhaps as well-qualified for the responsibilities being placed on his shoulders as anyone in Philip's service. He was not only a career diplomat and soldier but also a very well-educated scholar with significant talents as an author. It appears, from the scattered sources available,[8] that he was born in Guadalajara, home of the head of the illustrious Mendoza family, in 1540 or 1541, tenth child of Don Alonso Suárez de Mendoza, count of Coruña, and Juana Jiménez de Cisneros, niece of the Great Cardinal.[9] It can be assumed with a fair degree of assurance that Bernardino's early life was not without trials and excitement, for he had a total of eighteen brothers and sisters, all children of the same marriage. His oldest brother, Lorenzo, who inherited his father's title, served in many military campaigns under Charles V and Philip II. In 1580 he was sent to the New World as viceroy of Mexico. Another of his brothers, Antonio, entered the diplomatic service and was instrumental in obtaining free and safe passage through Lorraine for Alba's troops en route to Flanders in 1567. A third brother, Dr. Alonso de Mendoza, became a professor of Holy Writ at the University of Alcalá.[10] At a very young age Bernardino began his studies at Alcalá, and on 11 June 1556 he received the degree of Bachelor of Arts and Philosophy. Sixteen months later he was awarded the Master's degree (*Licenciatura*) in the same faculty and then entered the College of San Ildefonso at Alcalá where he was elected boardholder of the Colegio Mayor. Mendoza continued with his academic profession for only a few years, before he abandoned it, sometime after May 1562, to embark on a military career.

The chief source for Mendoza's years with the army is his own *Comentarios*, first published in France in 1590.[11] This lucid but rambling military history shows that, prior to serving with the duke of Alba in the Netherlands, Mendoza saw combat against the Berbers in North Africa, took part in the expeditions of Oran and Peñon de Velez in 1563 and 1564, and was with Don Juan of Austria when he brought relief to the besieged outpost of Malta in 1565.[12] In the spring of 1567, as Alba assembled his forces for the long march into the Netherlands, Don Bernardino received his first diplomatic assignment. The duke sent him to Rome to obtain a papal benediction on the great enterprise and to clarify the interests of the Catholic religion in regard to the expedition.[13] Mendoza fulfilled this assignment with relative dispatch and then rejoined Alba's army in Flanders.

During the next ten years Mendoza's life was linked inseparably with the war in the Netherlands. He saw action in most of the major campaigns in the early years of that struggle — Mons, Nimwegen, Haarlem, and Mook — and distinguished himself more than once for his valor and stamina. His loyalty and ability did not go unnoticed, for soon he was advanced to captain of light cavalry where he proved himself both capable and willing to lead the most dangerous attacks against the enemy positions. It was widely recognized that the deciding factor in the strategic victory at Mook was the audacious charge of Mendoza's unit on 14 April 1574.[14]

It was while campaigning with Alba's army that Mendoza's talents as a diplomat came to be recognized, both by the duke and by the king. Early in 1573 he was sent to Madrid to solicit funds and troops of Philip; a mission requiring a considerable amount of tact and ingenuity, since Alba had already used up far more money, time, and manpower than was considered necessary to subdue the rebel uprising. In less than six weeks, Mendoza was back in Flanders with the requested subsidy and with the promise of a sizable number of reinforcements.[15]

In July 1574, after Luis de Requesens, grand commander of Castile, had replaced Alba in Flanders, Mendoza was sent by Philip on a special diplomatic mission to England. At the court of Queen Elizabeth, which Mendoza was soon to know so well, the emissary was to obtain the promise of refuge and subsistence in English ports for the armada which Philip proposed to send against the Dutch.[16] Mendoza achieved amazing success in this assignment and within a month was again in Flanders at the head of his cavalry. The next two years were devoted to military activities under Requesens and Don Juan of Austria, and in February 1576 he was rewarded for his years of service by acceptance into the highest order of Spanish knighthood, the Order of Santiago.

Mendoza's intimate knowledge of political and military affairs in the Netherlands and England and his demonstrated competence in diplomatic negotiation soon prompted the Spanish monarch to establish him as resident ambassador to England, a post which had been vacant for more than six years. The following instructions, dated 8 January 1578, indicate the scope and some of the purposes of Mendoza's mission:

What you, D. Bernardino de Mendoza, my Captain of Light Cavalry, have to do in England where you are being sent:

Because the state of affairs in my Low Countries has been put in such conditions since the last upheavals there that it has become necessary to take up arms again in order to pacify, hold, and maintain the Roman Catholic religion and obedience to the king, it has seemed advisable to clarify this situation to the queen of England, our neighbor and ally. We therefore have resolved to send you to this post with this commission, and also with the information you have of the said Low Countries where you have served me for many years. I do this because of the satisfaction and confidence I have in your judgment and good wisdom, and also because I believe you will be just as acceptable to the said queen as you were when the grand commander of Castile, my former governor of the said Low Countries, sent you, in my name, to negotiate with her over certain matters which have subsequently been favorably carried out . . .[17]

Early in February Mendoza left Madrid, crossed the border into France at Irún-Hendaya, and proceeded to Paris where he had been instructed to make a friendly visit of state.[18] From Paris, Mendoza traveled to Flanders and thence to London, and on 16 March 1578, in his first audience at the English court, presented his credentials to the queen. For the next six years Mendoza threw himself wholeheartedly into the complexities of diplomatic life in England. Believing in a forceful approach to matters of diplomacy as well as to military affairs, Mendoza carried with him to the embassy post the same aggressiveness which had won him so many encounters in the field. In some matters he carried out Philip's policies with even greater energy and forcefulness than his master had anticipated. The essence of Mendoza's orders was to support Spanish policy and the cause of Catholicism wherever and however he could, but at the same time he was required to maintain the traditional peaceful relations with England. With English privateers harrassing the Spanish sea lanes, plundering colonial towns, and attacking stragglers from the returning plate fleets and with the Spanish government seizing English ships and crews when they put into Spanish ports for trade, Mendoza's task became almost insurmountable.

From early in his ministry, Mendoza met innumerable obstacles to maintaining the conciliatory policy which had been assigned to him. The hostile atmosphere in England by 1578 was not at all conducive to normal diplomatic relations, and Mendoza made no hesitation in resorting to more "effective" methods. The English Catholics bombarded the ambassador with stories of their sufferings at the hands of the heretic queen. Exiled countrymen stoked the fires of hatred which were building up, and the activities of the Jesuits further strained relations between the two countries.[19] Mendoza protested violently, but in vain, when Drake returned in September 1580 from his lucrative voyage of pirateering and circumnavigation. Not only did Elizabeth refuse to give up any of the rich plunder but some of her counselors insulted the ambassador further by offering him a share of it if he would tone down his indignant report to Philip.[20] Tensions were increased even more when Don Antonio, pretender to the Portuguese throne, made a direct appeal to Elizabeth for her assistance in his behalf. Walsingham supported the prior, but Mendoza's persistence was eventually rewarded when Don Antonio was shunted off to France. No sooner was this threat minimized when Anjou arrived in London to woo the queen and to solicit her support for his enigmatic projects in the Netherlands.

Mendoza became convinced before his master did that coexistence with Elizabeth was no longer a desirable or even a feasible policy and that before the Netherlands could be restored to peaceful obedience their lifeline to the troublesome Tudor government would have to be severed. For this reason he let himself become involved in the Throckmorton Plot to overthrow the queen. By November 1583, however, Walsingham's intricate web of counterespionage had discovered almost every move of the conspirators, and the forced confession of Francis Throckmorton in that month clearly implicated the Spanish ambassador.[21] In January 1584, Mendoza was declared *persona non grata* at the English court and ordered to leave the country immediately. His parting retort to the queen was the ominous threat that she would yet learn that "Bernardino de Mendoza was not born to disturb countries but to conquer them." [22] His exit from England was via Flanders, where he stopped for some days to confer with the duke of Parma before traveling on to Paris. On 10 April 1584, Mendoza left Paris in the company of a courier furnished by the French king, and he arrived in Madrid near the end of the month.

Mendoza's responsibilities in Paris as the spearhead of Philip's diplomatic offensive were numerous, varied, and difficult, but he attacked them with vigor and persistence. Arriving amid strained international conditions and a chaotic domestic situation, his welcome was far from hearty. Not only that, his unpopularity at the English court had been transmitted to the French by courtesy of the English ambassador, who did all he could to influence the royal family, against Mendoza. On his first audience at court Mendoza presented those credentials authorizing him to convey official condolences from the king of Spain to the royal family on the death of the heir. At the same time he also delivered two letters to the queen mother from her granddaughter, the infanta of Spain, for which Catherine expressed sincere gratitude.[23] Sir Edward Stafford, the English ambassador in Paris, reported that Mendoza's audience with the queen mother on November 16 was short and cold. He also indicated that his "priming" of the queen mother prior to the meeting probably had something to do with it. "I was bold to tell her," he reported to Walsingham, "that I was sorry to see the King of Spain had no more respect for the King and her than to send so bad a Spanish relic, retired out of England, to be here, to work as bad effects as he had done with us." [24]

On his second audience, a week later, Mendoza again delivered his message of condolence and also made known the purpose of his presence there as permanent resident ambassador. On the following day he delivered his *lettres de créance* to the king. In a communication to Philip II, dated November 25, the queen mother acknowledged Mendoza's credentials and officially accepted him as ambassador.[25] Shortly after this second interview Tassis took his leave of Paris and proceeded to Joinville to negotiate the treaty with the League. From there he went on to Tournai to assume his new duties as inspector-general of the armies in Flanders.

After the beginning of the year Mendoza launched his official ministry. His first audience with the king in 1585 was a stormy affair ending in high tempers and a hot exchange of words.[26] A delegation, sent by the estates of Brabant, Gelderland, Flanders, Holland, Utrecht, Friesland, and Mechlin, was in Paris to offer the king of France sovereignty over the Netherlands in return for his political and military support in the expulsion of the Spanish armies.[27] Mendoza was furious! He insisted that the king of France should not even give audience to rebels of the king of Spain, and that to do so was an open affront and would be regarded by his government as an unfriendly act. Henry rose in a sudden fit of anger at this rebuff and shouted that he was nobody's subject and would be commanded by no one — including the king of Spain. He assured the ambassador that he would give audience to whomever he pleased.[28]

In the long run Mendoza's persistence was rewarded, for Henry, after listening carefully to the propositions of the delegation, decided to decline the enticing Dutch offer. His refusal, he explained, was due to "having too many problems and affairs of his own to worry about without entangling himself in the affairs of others."[29] This development was followed on February 26 by a very friendly and constructive meeting of Mendoza with the king and the queen mother in which he further admonished them of the dangers in negotiating with an unrecognized state.[30] He reported to Parma at the time that, contrary to court rumors, Henry thought very highly of him and had praised his frankness and initiative to the royal council. It is unlikely that Henry had much respect for Mendoza, but he was at times impressed by the ambassador's self-confidence and he recognized Mendoza's influence with the king of Spain. In a series of carefully ciphered dispatches, dated from February 6 to March 9,[31] Mendoza kept Philip closely informed of the purposes and activities of the Dutch delegation and of his own endeavors to prevent Henry from accepting their offers.

In the meantime, Elizabeth dispatched a delegation of her own, headed by the earl of Warwick, to the vacillating French king, exhorting him to accept the Dutch proposals and offering him knighthood in the venerable Order of the Garter. Never refusing the chance for glory or prestige nor the opportunity to throw a lavish party, Henry accepted the English honor with the most extravagant pageantry the frivolous French court had seen in years. The great ceremony was held at the church of the Augustinian Canons where all of the court nobility as well as the foreign ambassadors participated.[32]

TESTING THE LEAGUE

For the present Mendoza had succeeded in keeping Henry III from making any kind of commitment, either with England or with the Netherlands themselves, for the protection of the Low Countries. But the situation was still volatile and the king's thoughts and actions were completely unpredictable. Opposing forces and issues faced him from all sides, so the success of the Spanish ambassador in preventing him from one line of action was no guarantee that he would not seize upon another.

Henry's distrust of the League mounted to contempt and fear, even though he was not yet aware of the full extent of its affiliation with Spain. Mendoza had skillfully convinced the king, by showing him letters from Philip, that Spain had no part in the activities of the League. If carried out swiftly and carefully, Henry mused, here was a threat to the crown which might now be successfully attacked without bringing reprisals from the Catholic king. With this in mind, he issued an edict on March 9, outlawing all unauthorized assemblies within the realm and forbidding the formation of armed units.[33] This decree applied both to Huguenot and League alike, but could hardly have been taken very seriously, even by Henry himself. It was probably more an attempt to keep the League in check by bringing to bear the moral sanctions of legality.

The League's answer was not long in coming. On March 31 a manifesto was issued in the name of the cardinal of Bourbon, defining the numerous grievances from which the nation was suffering under the corrupt rule of the Valois and directed especially against the pampered mignons who had almost taken over the administration of the state.[34] The manifesto emphatically declared that a heretic should never become king of France, and insisted that if the crown did not end its favors to the Huguenot nobility and take more vigorous action against them the League itself would intervene. It also demanded that persons previously holding offices for meritorious service should not be deprived of these offices to make room for the king's favorites unless they had functioned illegally and were convicted by the Parlement de Paris. It furthermore denounced excessive taxation and demanded long-range financial reforms. The manifesto reaffirmed the functions of the Estates General and called for its regular meeting every three years. It ended with an appeal to all the towns of France, while abstaining from all but defensive hostilities, to refuse admission to royal garrisons until the king agreed to meet their demands.[35]

It is difficult to assess Mendoza's role in this League action. He probably remained in the background as much as possible but, according to his own testimony and that of others, he did go to Joinville earlier in the month to discuss the situation with Guise.[36] There he urged the duke to be firm with the king and not permit the initiative to be lost through "cowardly dissimulation." In a dispatch dated 18 April 1585, Mendoza reported to Philip the full contents of the League manifesto. He also added his own observations on the increasing activity of the League towns and the marked defiance demonstrated by the Leaguers of Paris. He announced the adherence of eighty-eight important towns to the League and the creation of a strong line of fortifications extending from Verdun to Orléans, with Châlons as Guise's temporary headquarters.[37] The time for testing the League was at hand.

In Paris, League emissaries were consolidating their position among the municipal officials, and they lost no time in making contact with the Spanish ambassador. Mendoza was careful to avoid taking any active part in the plans of the Sixteen at this time, but he was apprized of their movements by Guise's principal agent, François de Mayneville, and he promptly relayed the information to the Spanish government in carefully ciphered and closely guarded dispatches.

Henry III was surprised by the swiftness and apparent strength of the League and by the growing popularity of the duke of Guise. He attempted a counterstroke by moving Swiss and German mercenaries into eastern France, but these were intercepted and detained by Guise's brother, Mayenne. Effectively thwarted and completely confused, Henry withdrew to the Louvre palace behind the protection of his newly commissioned private guard, the *Taillagambi* (consisting of forty-five armed knights, mostly Gascons, of the Order of the Holy Spirit),[38] while his aging mother, tired and sick, took steps to end the crisis and avoid a three-way civil war.

All through April, May, and June, Catherine was at Épernay desperately negotiating with the heads of the League to bring about an acceptable *modus vivendi*.[39] Close contact was maintained with the court through the king's personal physician, François Miron, who was apparently also Mendoza's chief news source for these negotiations. Catherine de' Medici's early letters to her son disclose an optimistic belief that firm action against the League would cause its leaders to back down, but this hope was soon displaced by the fear that the League actually did have sufficient strength to press its demands. Mendoza kept Philip informed on the progress of the negotiations, and in doing so revealed his own misgivings about the eventual success of the talks. On May 4 he reported (as a result of Miron's account of a stalemate at Épernay) that Henry threatened to sue for peace with the Huguenots if the cities and villages of France continued joining the League. Such an eventuality, he affirmed, must be avoided at all costs,[40] for keeping the king of France resisting the Huguenots was one of the cardinal aims of Mendoza's mission. On June 5 he held a secret session with Secretary of State Villeroy, at which time plans were supposedly discussed for an alliance between France and Spain for the auspicious purpose of a joint enterprise against the Calvinists of France, England, and Scotland. Mendoza reported that he was assured by Villeroy that the king favored the enterprise, but this seems rather doubtful.[41]

In the meantime, negotiations between the League and Catherine de' Medici continued. In June, Guise and the cardinal of Bourbon met with her at Châlons-sur-Marne and, after many weeks of fruitless talks, Catherine finally capitulated to most of the League demands and advised the king to grant the main points of the manifesto.[42] She was aware that forbidding the practice of Protestantism in France and officially allowing none but a Catholic to become heir to the throne would precipitate another war with the Huguenots. But in making these concessions she believed the Catholics of the League would remain loyal to the government and would support a campaign of sufficient strength against Navarre that the twenty-three-year civil strife might be ended.[43]

The prospect of religious peace and unity persuaded Henry to yield to his mother's advice, and on 7 July 1585 she concluded at Nemours a settlement of peace and alliance with the heads of the League. This Treaty of Nemours was ratified by the king on the following day and was registered by the Parlement de Paris on July 18. Mendoza advised Philip that

Henry was extremely anxious about the Spanish reaction to the treaty, and even sent Villeroy to inquire of him whether word had yet come from Spain about it. Villeroy's visit was on July 15, which was at least a week earlier than Mendoza could possibly have heard from Madrid. He had, however, received Philip's previous comments of concern and apprehension in response to his own reports of the negotiations. Mendoza said the French king expressed hope that this would bring their two kingdoms closer together since it was "such a holy and just enterprise" (una empresa tan santa y justa). He added that he feared Henry had other things in mind than "the service of Your Majesty." [44]

The principal terms of the treaty were the following:

(1) All previous edicts of pacification were superceded.

(2) The practice of any other religion than the Roman Catholic was forbidden in France.

(3) All ministers of any other religion should leave the kingdom within one month.

(4) Heretics were not allowed to hold any public office.

(5) Within six months all subjects of the king must make profession of the Catholic religion or leave the realm.

(6) The *chambres mi-parties* were to be abolished.

(7) Surrender of the fortified places conceded to the Huguenots in the Peace of Monsieur was demanded.[45]

In addition to taking the Huguenot's strongholds, Catherine granted Verdun, Toul, Saint-Dizier, and Châlons to Guise. Soissons went to the cardinal of Bourbon, and a number of fortifications in Burgundy, Brittany, and Picardy went to Mayenne, Mercoeur, and Aumale.[46] Also in the treaty was a subtle promise by Guise to renounce all foreign alliances. Guise probably had no serious intention of abiding by this commitment, but the article did worry Philip, when he heard about it from Mendoza, and renewed his distrust of Guise's aims and methods. Part of Philip's irritation was caused by the sudden termination of the negotiations and the signing of the treaty without corresponding with him about it.[47] On July 16, Mendoza sent a copy of the treaty to Philip with the added comment that it appeared "the Leaguers are motivated more by their own interests than they are by religious zeal." [48] Mendoza's suspicions were not unfounded, for the evidence is ample that Guise did have personal ambitions and was not above using this treaty as well as the one with Spain to help further his own cause.[49]

It was Mendoza's job to remedy this condition. Philip's gravest fears were that Henry III and Guise, if they succeeded in crushing Navarre, might become strong enough to unite the divergent forces of France and become hostile to Spain. On July 23, Philip instructed his ambassador to get some positive assurance from Guise that he would never bear arms against the king of Spain and never attack Spanish territory.[50] Mendoza communicated this demand to the duke and soon received a reply assuring him of Guise's loyalty to their treaty agreements and to their common religious cause. Guise declared that when he renounced foreign alliances he had in mind those which might be injurious to the kingdom of France, not those which contributed to its advantage as the one with Spain did. At the same time Guise reminded Mendoza of the 50,000 escudos for that month which were overdue and sorely needed.[51]

News of the Treaty of Nemours reached Rome just as Louis de Gonzague, duke of Nevers, was terminating his controversial and unofficial visit to the pope in behalf of the French League.[52] Sixtus V, newly established on the papal throne after the death of Gregory XIII in April, was a headstrong, autocratic, and practical ruler who took his political position very seriously. He disliked Philip II and his policies and openly opposed him on many occasions; he was equally suspicious of the Catholic League in France. He favored the uprooting of heresy in that kingdom, but distrusted the ambitions of the house of Guise and feared the independent nature of the League.[53] The Treaty of Nemours gave the pope new confidence in the *Sainte Union* and he elected to enter the conflict in France on the side of the alliance. On 9 September 1585, Sixtus V issued a bull of excommunication branding the king of Navarre and the prince of Condé as relapsed heretics and declaring them incapable of succeeding to the throne of France. The decree also deprived them of their estates and absolved all of their vassals from allegiance to them.[54]

The papal bull created excitement on all sides and precipitated a renewal of the war in France. To Philip II it brought a glimmer of hope that the pope might decide to support his efforts in France and perhaps even in the Netherlands.[55] In France the decree brought cheers from the League, but Catherine feared it had dealt a death blow to her tenacious faith that Navarre (who, it should be remembered, was still her son-in-law) would soon renounce the heretical sect and return to the mother church.[56] The Politiques were strengthened by their stand against foreign intervention, and their members were increased through the reaction of previously neutral "patriots" and uncommitted moderates. The Parlement de Paris looked on the papal pronouncement as a gross intrusion into the domestic affairs of France and refused to publish or register it.[57] Henry of Navarre denounced it boldly and appealed to the Sorbonne, to the nobility, and even to the Third Estate of France, against "Monsieur Sixtus, self-styled Pope" (although contemporary gossip held that Navarre was so disturbed by the papal bull that half of his mustache turned white).[58] Mendoza believed that the turning point for the church in France had now been reached, that the people would unite in their opposition to heresy, and that it would soon be rooted out. He called upon Philip to send money quickly to assist the League in this enterprise, "for you know," he reminded the king, "how just is the cause." [59]

Chapter I V

MENDOZA AND GUISE

✤ ✤ ✤ ✤

F OLLOWING the publication of the bull of excommunication war flared up in several parts of France; soon it
involved almost every province of the kingdom. In the north
and east League and royal forces under Guise, Mayenne, Épernon, Joyeuse, Biron, and others began a slow war of sieges to
reduce the Huguenot strongholds one by one. As Navarre
busied himself with guerilla tactics in the south, Condé moved
into League territory, defeated Mercoeur at Fontenay, and
began laying siege to royalist and League outposts in Poitou
and Touraine.[1]

TEMPERING THE SPANISH-LEAGUE ALLIANCE

During the so-called War of the Three Henrys (whose
military operations will not be discussed except insofar as they
directly affected the diplomatic negotiations) the Spanish-
League alliance had its first real tempering by fire, and from
the exposure of its weaknesses and limitations it emerged
stronger than before. Philip and Guise had many conflicting
interests which had to be reconciled before they could succeed
in their common goal. This took time and required patient and
skillful negotiations. Mendoza had the onerous task of har-
monizing Philip's phlegmatic circumspection with Guise's
impetuous arrogance and making the alliance between them
not only secure but active and serviceable. This task was
rendered even more difficult by Philip's increasing preoccupa-

tion with the problem of English aid to the rebels and his gradually ripening decision to oppose Elizabeth with armed force.

The first test came in the summer of 1585. News arrived early in July that Marguerite of Valois, sister of the king and wife of Navarre, had left her husband to join the Catholic cause. Defiantly she raised two companies of infantry and fortified herself in the city of Agen in the heart of Protestant Guyenne. In the next few weeks the queen of Navarre increased her force to twenty-two companies and opened negotiations with both Guise and Philip for aid against the attack of her husband. On August 17 the Spanish king communicated this information to Mendoza and asked for his recommendations in the matter, adding that he was skeptical of Marguerite's action achieving any long-range good.[2]

In the meantime, Guise also wrote letters to Philip and to Mendoza, confessing his own lack of funds and proposing that the king of Spain assist the beleaguered queen with "40,000 or 50,000 écus of gold." This he asserted would enable her to hire and equip enough men to hold this strategic salient until stronger League or royal forces could reach her.[3] On September 23, Mendoza replied to Guise's note, expressing his admiration for Marguerite's stand but supporting Philip's skepticism about the ultimate value of risking either men or money in her behalf.[4] Intervention, he pointed out, could lead to a breach in the alliance between the League and the French crown if pressed too far. He further reminded Guise that Catherine de' Medici had sanguine notions that her daughter would someday reconcile Navarre to the Catholic church and that the crown of France would thus be maintained among her children. This latest of many quarrels between Marguerite and Henry, however, brought Catherine's denunciation of her daughter's actions and strengthened the sympathetic ties between herself and her son-in-law. If Spain, or even Guise, should take too strong a stand on such a family matter in defiance of Catherine's personal concern, Mendoza maintained, it would probably end the Nemours alliance.

Guise accepted Mendoza's explanation, though the negotiations over this affair continued on into the next year. Philip finally decided that a little help could do no harm so he sent her a gift of 20,000 escudos when Marguerite's messenger, M. de Duras, returned to Agen.[5] After a terrible bloodshed, the city was finally taken by Navarre, and Marguerite was incarcerated in the fortress of Usson. Through the help of Lignerac, an agent sent by Guise to assist her, she was able to escape, only to be recaptured shortly thereafter. Mendoza attributed the fall of Agen and the capture of Marguerite not to Navarre but to Henry III who, he said, ordered the attack. He also reported that the French king had accused Philip not only of assisting the queen of Navarre with money but also of sending Aragonese soldiers to her aid.[6]

Of even greater importance to the ultimate success or failure of Spanish policy in France was the delicate negotiation of Philip, Mendoza, and Guise to bring into the conflict the powerful independent governor of Languedoc, Henry, duke of Montmorency-Damville. Henry III and Navarre were also making concerted efforts to win the support of this cautious Politique, for the strength which he could throw into the balance would probably be decisive. In 1585, Philip began a vigorous campaign to attach Montmorency to his cause, while Mendoza and Guise endeavored to create a situation which might bring him into active support of the League.

According to the Venetian agents, both in Paris and Madrid, Philip had made considerable progress in winning Montmorency's friendship by mid-1586, in spite of the fact that the Politique leader had already reached a formal agreement with Navarre (the "Contre-Ligue du Bien Public"). Giovanni Dolfin reported on July 17 of that year that in a conversation with Mendoza he discovered that the king of Spain enjoyed a good amount of authority with Montmorency.[7] And, from Madrid,

Lippomano testified that "The French agent here [Longlée] assures me that the King has lately sent, by way of Besançon, 50,000 ducats to Guise, and 50,000 to Montmorency by another route." [8] By December, Philip indicated to Mendoza that his efforts with Montmorency were beginning to show signs of success, and that the Politique leader appeared also to be inclining toward an understanding with Guise.[9]

During the following year, Philip, realizing the importance of Montmorency's position, made even greater efforts to bring him into the Catholic League.[10] As a last resort, Philip proposed, in true sixteenth-century style, the uniting of the Montmorency and Guise families through the marriage of their eldest children.[11] Details of the proposed alliance were transmitted to Montmorency by Philip's special agent, Alexandro Constantino, who was authorized to promise him a generous dowry in return for his written consent to the marriage. Constantino was also instructed to request that Montmorency abandon his association with Navarre within four or five months and take an active part in reducing heresy in France. As a *quid pro quo* Philip promised attractive financial rewards for him and his wife.[12] Mendoza was given full notification of these negotiations and instructed to make the specific arrangements with Guise.[13]

As the good duke was never averse to improving his material well-being, this proposal had a fair chance of success, until the decisive break, later in 1588, between Guise and Henry III made the arrangement untenable. With the breakup of the Nemours coalition in May, Montmorency's only plausible alternative was to follow his original course and court the favor of the most likely successor to the Valois throne, Henry of Navarre. On the "Day of the Barricades" southeastern France was lost to the Catholic cause.

OVERTURES TO NAVARRE

Paris during the War of the Three Henrys was in a constant whirl of negotiations and intrigues over party loyalties and

military advantage. Henry III had not allied himself with the
League because he favored it or because he liked the duke of
Guise but because his hand was forced and he had no satisfactory alternative. Influenced by his mother, he still persisted in the notion that Navarre might yet be induced to
renounce the heretical sect and return to fellowship in the
Roman church. He had done so once before, why not again?
If Navarre could be persuaded to abjure, Henry III would
have no further objection to his succeeding to the throne;
for, apart from religion, Henry of Valois trusted Henry of
Navarre more than he did Henry of Guise.[14]

Throughout 1586, Mendoza worked tirelessly to prevent a
conciliation between the two monarchs or any faltering on
the part of Henry III in his alliance with the League. Then
in March, since the war was not going well, Henry attempted
to persuade Guise to agree to a general peace with the Huguenots. Guise peremptorily refused to negotiate, in spite of his
lack of money and supplies, and sent word to Mendoza telling
him of the king's intentions and asking for assurances of
Philip's support. Mendoza's reply to Guise was the discon-
certing assurance that, as far as the assistance from Spain was
concerned, he could be "just as certain of its willing and
prompt arrival as on past occasions." [15]

In the meantime, Henry had given secret instruction to
Biron, marshal of France and commander of the royal army,
to try to make contact with Navarre and persuade him to
negotiate a truce.[16] Biron was not privy to all of Henry's
schemes, but he did know enough to make him a valuable
contact man; so Mendoza, aware of this and alert to the likelihood of deceit on the part of the Valois king, carefully
cultivated his friendship and confidence. The ambassador's
personality was generally adjustable to the demands of a
situation, whether it required congeniality, sympathy, and
charm, or haughty vituperation.[17] With the marshal he was
most persuasive and soon the two had developed a mild friendship for one another.

By May 1586, Mendoza had learned from Biron that something was in the wind and that Henry III was plotting secretly with some of his closest advisers against the interests of the League. On May 11, Mendoza wrote an urgent dispatch to Philip, carefully coded in a new cipher, disclosing what he had learned about the dealings of the French king. "Biron has assured some of his friends," reported Mendoza, "that the king is hatching a secret plot which no one has been able to understand, although, he says, it must come out within the next six months since things cannot last as they are with the army mobilizing while peace negotiations continue. . . . There is in fact no person of good judgment here who doubts that the king is plotting something with Secretary Villeroy, and that Bellièvre is in with them." [18] Some of those involved in the plan assured Mendoza that the cause of Henry's mysterious actions of the past few weeks was due to his growing "mental disturbance" and nothing more:

> The grand chancellor and other ministers complain also that for the last two months the king will not listen to business of any sort and, although he sits up nearly every night writing memoranda in his own hand until two in the morning, he burns them all the next day. They say that all he writes is about the religious orders. . . . As he changes every hour, and from many other indications, Mucio [Guise] tells me that the chancellor assures him that the king's reason is unhinged, and it is feared he will shortly lose it altogether.[19]

Mendoza had cause to believe that there was more to Henry's peculiarities than absent-mindedness. By continuing to press his informants for further details and from his own public and private observations, Mendoza was able to discern the main outline of Henry's intentions.

> When his mother questioned him the other day about the marriage of the princess of Lorraine [to Navarre], he told her not to trouble herself further about the matter as he had obtained what he wanted and would now very shortly be able to overthrow some of his enemies and avenge himself upon others. . . . The English ambassador, in audience the other day, warned him in the name of his mistress that the Guises and the Catholic princes were in close com-

munication with Your Majesty, and that if he did not prevent them by making a peace they would take his crown from him. He replied that he knew it well, but that things had gone too far and he could not stop them now. He said there was no better remedy than for Béarn [Navarre] to become a Catholic, by which all his claims would be assured.[20]

During the summer campaign it became obvious that Biron's orders were to play Navarre into a position more favorable for negotiation and then sue for a truce.[21] But Henry had also prepared Navarre for the situation through his secret meetings with the latter's personal envoy, Rosny (later duke of Sully).[22] In August a truce was concluded between Navarre and Biron, and the queen mother hurried to resume her well-worn role as arbitrator.[23] Negotiations dragged on into the winter before Catherine finally conceded defeat.[24] Navarre became even more adamant in his refusal to abjure Protestantism, in spite of Catherine's willingness to consent to a divorce between him and Marguerite,[25] and early in 1587 the war was again resumed. Philip's policy in France continued to prevail.

MENDOZA, GUISE, AND THE SCOTTISH CATHOLICS

Much of Mendoza's negotiation with Guise during the summer and fall of 1586 was concerned with affairs in Scotland where an important phase of Philip's foreign policy was being implemented. It was no secret that, by associating himself so completely with the Counter Reformation, Philip was becoming involved in the political affairs of most of the states of Europe and was called upon by Catholics everywhere to support their activities and organizations.

For several months Guise had been corresponding with the Catholic nobility of Scotland over the possibility of an armed revolt against young James VI (son of Mary Stuart) and the re-establishment of Catholicism in that kingdom. It was first proposed to seek assistance from Henry III because of the long tradition of friendship and alliance between France and

Scotland, but in view of the languid attempts of Henry to eliminate heresy in his own realm it was decided not to call upon him to fight the Calvinists of Scotland.[26] Therefore, negotiations were reinitiated with the Spanish ambassador to solicit Philip's support in the enterprise, an undertaking which the Paris Politiques and others had expected for some time.[27]

After many unsuccessful preludes, the leaders of the Scottish Catholics — the earl of Huntly, the earl of Morton, and Claude Hamilton — submitted completely to Guise's terms and propositions and sent him a signed letter which he was to complete as he saw fit and send on to the Catholic King. On 16 July 1586, Guise communicated his negotiations to Mendoza in the following letter.

> I have asked the ambassador of Scotland to communicate to you an enterprise, the foundations of which I have been laying for a long time with great pains, but which I have hitherto been unable to effect. I have now brought the principal Scottish lords around to the resolution which will be disclosed to you, and which I am certain you will heartily endorse, knowing the attachment you have to the advancement of the Catholic religion. . . . I have made an ample exposition of the matter to His Majesty in a dispatch carried by a Scottish gentleman [Robert Bruce] who had been sent to me by the said lords. I sent him directly from here because of the safer road, and to avoid his being discovered while passing through Paris. I beseech you to also send a letter of your own with the recommendation and assistance which you judge to be necessary for such a just and holy enterprise.[28]

This communication reached Mendoza just as his courier was setting out for Madrid with his latest reports; it prompted him to delay the dispatch until he had heard what the Scottish ambassador was instructed to tell. The proposed enterprise was presented orally to Mendoza by the resident Scottish envoy in France and by a written memorandum from the duke of Guise. It contained the following points: (1) 6000 troops for one year were requested, to be used to guard against an English expedition against them (within the country itself

the Scottish Catholics felt they were strong enough to overcome any Protestant opposition); (2) a grant of 150,000
escudos, to be deposited for withdrawal when needed, was
requested; (3) any other aid which the king might be willing
to give them for the next two years would be appreciated;
(4) no levies against the king of Spain should ever be made
in Scotland; and (5) two good Scottish ports near the English
border were to be turned over to Spain.[29] Mendoza relayed
this document to Philip and enclosed his own favorable recom-
mendation with the following observations:

> I send enclosed the points of the instructions which he [Bruce]
> has received from the ambassador, from whom I will ascertain
> whether the 6000 soldiers to be maintained for a year are to be for-
> eigners or not; a point which he was unable to elucidate. I will also
> inquire into whose hands the 150,000 escudos should be entrusted.
> He told me that the Scots promised to begin the execution of the
> business whenever Mucio gave word that the 150,000 escudos were
> ready, and they were assured of receiving aid. He made me take a
> note of this point, which seems to infer that the Scottish nobles
> expect the aid to take the form of foreign troops, since no others
> could be sent from abroad. Mucio probably did not like to state this
> in writing to Your Majesty until he heard your intentions.[30]

Philip's reply to this matter, dated September 28, was cautious. He admired the intentions of the Scottish Catholics, but
expressed serious doubts as to their hopes of reconverting the
country, as permeated as it had become with heresy. He withheld a final decision on the matter, however, until he had
heard from the duke of Parma in Flanders and could consider
his and Mendoza's recommendations more carefully.[31] On the
same day Philip communicated his views to Parma, recommending extreme caution and advising him to remain in close
contact with Mendoza and Guise.[32]

Mendoza also contacted Parma by direct courier and laid
before him the proposals of Guise and the Scottish nobles,
along with the observations of the king and his own proceedings and suggestions. He strongly urged Parma to support
the enterprise because of its worthiness, because it was the

opportune time and had great chance for success, and because of the importance of "maintaining the friendly relations and cooperation of Guise and the League of France." [33]

A month later Parma replied to Mendoza's note and joined the king in recommending discretion and prudence to the ambassador in his handling of this matter. He agreed that "Such a rising in Scotland. . . . or any other diversion, would be most opportune, and the sooner it is effected the better," but, he cautioned very emphatically, "if the affair is not solidly based it will turn out as former attempts have done, and maybe worse, for it should not be overlooked that even if they should take hold of the king, the greater part of the country is heretical, and with help (which they will surely receive from the queen of England) they will always remain the stronger party." This fear led Parma to conclude that the entire enterprise might fail and would cause greater damage to their cause than good. Furthermore, Parma was at the time in the midst of some very crucial negotiations with Queen Elizabeth,[34] and could ill-afford to have them upset by a hasty maneuver in Scotland. He therefore suggested to Mendoza that he postpone action for the present while continuing to maintain a close diplomatic understanding with Guise and the Scottish Catholics. "In the meantime," he advised, "keep the Scots in hand with good words and in the discussion of the questions you have pointed out as desirable to have answered. They should be dealt with, as you say, in a way which will not alienate them or give them any cause for complaint. You understand these matters well and will be able, with your usual dexterity, to keep them friendly." [35]

MENDOZA AND THE QUEEN OF SCOTS

The Scottish problem did not end at that point for Mendoza, it merely became more tightly entwined with the English affairs which came to occupy even greater importance with each passing month. Early in 1586 a line of communication

Henry of Lorraine, duke of Guise

Philip II, king of Spain

Henry III, king of France and Poland

Catherine de' Medici, queen mother of France

Charles X, Leaguer king of France

Ball at the court of Henry III

A League procession in Paris

Charles of Lorraine, duke of Mayenne

Henry IV, king of France and Navarre

was finally opened between Mendoza and the imprisoned
Mary Queen of Scots through the French ambassador to England and agents of Mary in Paris and London.[36] The two key
links in this channel were Gilbert Gifford in England and
Thomas Morgan in Paris.[37] Morgan, who had been imprisoned
in the Bastille in 1584 as a result of his participation in a plot
against Elizabeth, had carefully maintained his contact with
the Scottish queen. Now with Gifford's help (and others in
England, including a cooperative brewer who conveyed the
letters on their final lap to Mary in a keg of beer) he opened
a way of communication between Mary and the Spanish ambassador in Paris. On 20 May 1586, Mary began her vital and
risky series of negotiations with Mendoza with a letter which
has since become highly controversial. After acknowledging
receipt of two previous messages from Mendoza, one of which
was nine months in transit, she begins her note with the following lines:

I was very pleased to learn of the good choice made by the
Catholic King, your master and my good brother, in sending you as
resident to France, in accordance with the request which I made of
him at one time. I have been so closely guarded for the past eighteen
months that all attempts at secret intelligence have failed me until
last Lent when Morgan managed to open the present one. Since as
yet I have received nothing else, I do not know how he might have
proceeded in the promotion of our previous designs. Thus I find
myself in a quandary as to what course to pursue here. I have instructed William [Paget] to communicate certain overtures to you,
about which I pray you will impart freely to him whatever you
think might be obtained from the king, your master, in order that I
will not importune him for something which you deem would be
unsuccessful.

Then, in a despondent vein of resignation, she divulges the
chief purpose of her letter to Mendoza and urges him to handle
the matter carefully.

There is another matter about which I preferred to write to you
privately so that you could pass it on to the king for me, if possible,
without anyone else knowing of it. That is, considering the great

obstinancy of my son in regard to heresy (about which I assure you I cry and lament day and night, more than for my own calamity), and foreseeing the eminent damage which would come to the Catholic Church if he should succeed to this [the English] throne, *I have resolved that in case my son does not submit to the Catholic Church before my death* (which I see very little hope of as long as he stays in Scotland), *I will cede and grant by Will my right to the succession of this* [the English] *crown to the king, your master,* on condition that he take me entirely into his protection from now on, and likewise the state and affairs of this country.[38] For the discharge of my own conscience I could not place this responsibility in the hands of a prince more zealous in our religion, or one more capable in every respect to re-establish it in this country, as the best interests of all Christendom require. I feel most obligated in this respect to regard the universal welfare of the church above any particular aggrandizement of my posterity.

I beg you again to keep this matter very secret in as much as it would cause the loss of my dowry in France if it were known to the rebels there. In Scotland it would bring a complete breach with my son, and in this country my total ruin and destruction.[39]

This was indeed a valuable document, and Mendoza handled the matter accordingly, dispatching a courier immediately to the Escorial with his own reports and with the reciphered letter of the Queen of Scots. He urged Philip to take decisive action, and reviewed for the king his own position of long standing on the matter of aid to the Stuart queen. Because of his fear of elevating the house of Guise, who were Mary's nearest relatives, or of improving the French position in Scotland and England, Philip had hesitated many times when the ambassador advocated supporting Mary. This danger was allayed with Mary's political adoption of the Spanish king, so Philip began for the first time to take steps in her behalf against the Tudor queen. On July 18 he made the following reply to Mendoza concerning the letter from Mary:

I was happy to receive the copy of the letter written to you by the queen of Scotland, along with your own of June 26. She has certainly risen a great deal in my estimation as a result of what she says there, and has increased the devotion which I have always felt for her interests — not so much because of what she says in my favor (though I am very grateful for that too), but because she subordinates her love for her son, which might be expected to lead her astray, for the service of our Lord, the common good of Christendom, and that of England. You may write and tell her all this from me and also assure her that if she perseveres in the path she has rightly chosen, I hope that God will bless her by granting her rightful possessions. You will add that I shall be very pleased to undertake the protection of her person and interests, as she requests. Be careful to keep this matter secret, in accordance with her wishes.[40]

Philip also agreed to grant her 12,000 escudos, which would be paid in three installments of 4,000 as soon as Mendoza could arrange for a method of transmitting it to her. He also promised, in response to a suggestion made by Mendoza in his letter of June 26, a stipend of forty escudos to Morgan. This amount was to be paid out of Mendoza's own expense account.

Mendoza, seeing the possible fruition of one of his most persistent ventures, quickly transmitted Philip's favorable reply to Mary and increased his own efforts to bring about a successful solution. In July he received a visit from an English priest named Ballard who informed him of a plan being laid at that moment to assassinate Elizabeth and liberate the English throne from heresy. Ballard's mission was to inquire of Mendoza whether or not the Spanish king would come to the assistance of the English Catholics if they rose against the queen.[41] The plot was apparently being carefully conceived right under the nose of Elizabeth's subtle sleuth, Sir Francis Walsingham, into whose household one of Mary's agents, Robert Poley, had secured a position as financial secretary to Walsingham's son-in-law, Sir Philip Sidney.[42] Anthony Babington and five others of the queen's household were at the center of the plot and intended to rescue Mary and spark a general Catholic rebellion in England, coordinated with a simultaneous uprising in Scotland. It was at this point that help from the Spanish king was needed to insure a quick and decisive victory.

Shortly after Ballard's arrival, Gilbert Gifford was also sent to Paris by the English conspirators to get a definite commitment from Mendoza.[43] Mary knew of this daring plot to overthrow the regime when she wrote the following letter to the Spanish ambassador.

It has given me singular contentment to see how the Catholic King, my good brother, is beginning to counteract the plots and attempts of the queen of England against him, not just because of the good I hope to receive from it, but principally for the maintenance of his own reputation in Christendom, for which I feel particular concern. You cannot imagine how the news of the exploits of the earl of Leicester and Drake elevates the hearts of the king's enemies throughout Christendom, and also how his patience and long suffering with this queen of England killed the confidence which Catholics here had in him. I freely confess to you that I too was so discouraged about entering into any new attempts, because of the failures of those of the past, that I have closed my ears to several overtures and propositions that have been made during the last six months on the part of Catholics here, because I had no way of giving them a reliable response.

But now that I understand the good intentions of the king toward us here, I have apprised the leaders of the Catholics sufficiently of the plan, which I have sent along with my opinions on each point of resolve, together with its execution. And to save time I have ordered them to dispatch in all haste one of their numbers who is sufficiently instructed to treat with you, according to the general offices which you have been given, and to make all such requests concerning the affair to the king, your master. You will be pleased to know that on behalf of their faith and promise given to me, they guarantee to faithfully and sincerely accomplish — even at the risk of their lives — whatever is promised you by their deputy [Gifford]. Therefore I beg you to give him full recognition as though I had sent him myself. He will inform you of the means for my escape from here, which I will endeavor to effect on my own if I have been given the assurance of armed support.

Thank heaven my health is now better than it has been for three months. I am very grateful to you for your good turn in reaching the best side of the king, your master, for the 12,000 écus . . . Please help me express to the king, my good brother, the obligation that I owe him for it, and the good intentions I have to try to repay it whenever I have the means, and I hope not to prove ungrateful to you, personally . . .[44]

But, the best laid plans . . . ! Walsingham was far too clever to be duped by such a grandiose enterprise. Philip's warning to keep the plans within a smaller circle had gone unheeded, yet even in the smallest body Walsingham had his ubiquitous spies. He knew every step the conspirators planned, and generally before they knew it themselves. In fact, not only did his agents follow every move of the plot, they helped make it! Robert Poley, planted by Mary in Walsingham's house, turned out to be one of Walsingham's own agents, as did Gilbert Gifford, the vital and trusted liaison between the English Catholics and Mendoza.[45] Poley and Gifford transmitted a copy of every important message between the conspirators to Walsingham's adroit "Black Chamber" where Thomas Phelippes and other expert cryptanalysts easily broke their cipher and provided Elizabeth with a running account of everything taking place.[46] The result was the seizure of Babington and his associates, their prompt execution, the trial of Mary, and her execution on 8 February 1587.[47]

THE ALLIANCE STRENGTHENED BY ORDEAL

As long as Guise remained unaware that Mary had bequeathed her inheritance to the king of Spain the Anglo-Scottish affair served as an additional bond between Philip and the house of Lorraine. But there were other factors during 1586 and 1587 which came between them and threatened to disrupt the Spanish-League alliance. According to the terms of the Treaty of Joinville, Philip had agreed to pay Guise and the League 50,000 escudos per month during the time they were actively engaged in fighting the Huguenots or in recovering the Spanish cities held by the king of France.[48] After the signing of the Treaty of Nemours (in which, to Philip's annoyance, there was no mention of Cambrai), Guise de-emphasized the Joinville agreement in order not to alienate his new-found friend, the king of France. This, Philip felt, justified his being late at times in making the promised payments, and in occasionally overlooking them entirely.[49] Now Philip's additional preoccupation with the Armada prevented him from giving Guise the attention and support he expected, and made Mendoza's difficult task almost insuperable. As early as September 1585, Philip had begun to default in his aid, forcing Guise, according to Mendoza's report, to sell much of his own land and property to meet the growing needs of the League. In a long communication from Rheims, dated 1 October 1585, Guise sent his complaints to Mendoza and asked for his assistance in securing the overdue payments, now that hostilities had opened against Navarre.[50] Again, on October 22 and on November 1, Guise pleaded with Mendoza to urge Philip to comply with their treaty agreements.[51]

During 1586 and 1587 the needs of the League continued to mount, and it appears from numerous letters that Mendoza worked unceasingly to keep Guise supplied with enough money to promote the war, which both he and Philip insisted must go on. In November, Guise proposed to Mendoza that 30,000 écus was the minimum requirement of the League in order to counter the designs of the king — but to be of any use it was needed immediately.

You can see clearly the state of our affairs and can judge, by the laudable intentions which are manifest there in Paris on behalf of the resolution to serve God, how necessary it is to ready our means in order that we may be prepared at any hour to support with all our strength a worthy enterprise in behalf of the faithful towns [des bonnes villes] which have everything staked on the Union. I beseech you to try to promote affairs in this direction in order that our means may match our resolution, . . . for our strength (a necessity which could not be avoided) is unmistakably conditioned upon your aid, and the absence of our strength would bring a setback to all of our affairs.[52]

Philip refused to be rushed. In September he sent 50,000 ducats to Guise via Tassis in Flanders, and ordered Mendoza to grant some from his own account. But these were far short of the reported needs. In place of material grants, Philip favored the duke with a bit of his own homespun philosophy, which remains as a monumental commentary on Philip's personality and on his forty-two-year reign. "Have patience, help will arrive. Don't shout in protest until you are sure you have been refused. Mucio [Guise], the cause of religion is on the threshold of its greatest triumph, but it requires time, and prudence." [53]

From late in 1586 there was growing concern expressed in the negotiations between Philip, Guise, and Mendoza over the latest Protestant reinforcements to the Huguenot armies. With new and considerable grants of money from Elizabeth in the summer of 1586,[54] Navarre was able to hire a considerable number of Swiss and German mercenaries to augment his own army.[55] The negotiations between Navarre and various German princes began in September and continued on into 1587 before final agreements were reached. On 11 January 1587, John Casimir, who since the death of his brother in 1583 had been regent of the Palatinate, agreed in the Treaty of Friedelsheim to provide some 8,000 German *reiters* (cavalry) and 14,000 *landsknechts* (mercenary infantry), to be ready to move into eastern France by early summer.[56] Much of the financial burden of this mobilization was met by Queen Elizabeth who, according to Mendoza, granted Casimir 100,000 crowns for taking up arms against the Catholics, and the king of Denmark who contributed 100,000 talers for the same cause.[57] This levy was also to be augmented by 15,000 Swiss pikemen, furnished by the Protestant cantons,[58] and a smaller contingent of French infantry promised by young Guillaume-Robert de la Marck, duke of Bouillon.[59] Navarre also planned to send 4,000 of his own musketeers and arquebusiers under the command of François de Châtillon, son of Gaspard de Coligny, to join the invading army after it had crossed the borders of Lorraine.[60] This latter move was not so much to strengthen the force, Mendoza later asserted, as it was to insure its adhering to the objectives of the invasion.[61]

On November 20, Guise wrote to Henry III to remind him of the seriousness of the situation and to plead for financial and other material support for the troops under his command. He also corresponded with Mendoza to solicit help from Spain and with Colonel Ludwig Pfyffer to raise troops among the Catholic cantons of Switzerland.[62] Mendoza took up the affair energetically and through a series of letter exchanges obtained an additional grant of 150,000 escudos from his master, 300,000 escudos from Parma (along with a company of light cavalry and 1,000 Italian lances), and a gift of 6,000 écus from the duke of Savoy.[63] At the same time he reported to Philip that he believed it was Henry's perfidious intention to sacrifice Guise to the Germans, which, timed to coincide with the duke of Joyeuse's projected assault against Navarre, would leave the king at last master of France. The ambassador further accused Henry of refusing to give Guise proper and sufficient reinforcements, and reported that the king replied that he had offered to give Guise additional troops, but that the duke had refused to accept them.[64] Mendoza estimated Guise's total strength at the time of the invasion at six companies of *gens d'armes* (heavy cavalry who sometimes fought as mounted infantry), two regiments of Italian infantry, and 4,000 light cavalry.[65]

Toward the end of August the invading mercenary forces crossed the borders of Champagne south of Lorraine and slowly moved westward toward the heart of France. Meanwhile, Joyeuse, at the head of a lustrous and well-equipped royal army, rushed southward to take up a position on the outskirts of Coutras where he could deal the final blow to Navarre. The crucial moment in the War of the Three Henrys had arrived. But on October 20 the first part of the Valois' dream of re-establishing the royal power became a nightmare. In the short but intense battle of Coutras, Joyeuse's army was literally cut to pieces by the determined charge of the Huguenot cavalry and the disciplined furor of their infantry. Navarre was overwhelmingly victorious, and Joyeuse lay dead on the field of battle.[66] The road lay open for a junction of the Protestant forces under Navarre with those swarming into France from the east.

But Navarre, overestimating the reliability of his mercenaries and not wishing to extend his own lines too far north while Catholic patrols still foraged in the southeast, made no attempt to rendezvous with the Protestant army moving leisurely into France. The invading force was led by an almost completely unorganized council of war, composed of the leaders of each of the contingents: Baron Fabian von Dohna for the Germans; Claude-Antoine, sieur de Clervant, the Swiss; and the twenty-four-year-old duke of Bouillon for the French; with two envoys from the king of Navarre, and Michel de la Hueguerye completing the perfunctory sextet. As they plundered their way across eastern France, disease spread rapidly among them and they died by the hundreds each day. La Hueguerye estimated that by September 10 they had lost some 12,000 men.[67] Prevented by orders from Navarre from following the Loire (he feared they would meet Henry III's army, encamped at Gien), the undisciplined troops turned back into ravaged Champagne, then northwest toward the richer plain of La Beauce. Soon the Swiss, becoming dissatisfied with the motives of the venture and unwilling to violate their treaty agreements by fighting the king of France, began deserting en masse. They dispatched a delegation of their leaders — Ulrich von Bonstetten, Michel Beley, head of the Bern regiment, Ulrich Breuel of the Zurich regiment, and Conrad Martin, chief of the Basel regiment — to negotiate with Henry III for their capitulation.[68]

On October 26 the German force, still outnumbering Guise's harassing cavalry by at least four to one, was surprised and shaken at Vimory, some nine miles from Dohna's Montargis headquarters, by an audacious night attack. The reiters rallied and drove off the assault, but not before considerable damage had been done to German strength and morale. The invaders, growing more discontented as they learned that Navarre had no intention of joining them, turned westward toward the riches of Chartres. On November 24, Guise fell upon them again at Auneau, this time routing and scattering the remnants of Dohna's once formidable army.[69] Those who were not killed fled in disorder toward the Swiss frontier.

Châtillon was able to rally some of the French for a momentary stand at La Bussière, but Bouillon ordered a general retreat and for the first time he was obeyed.[70]

In an apparently desperate effort to deprive Guise of an overwhelming victory, Henry III sent Épernon to make peace with the retreating Germans. Guise reported that Épernon had been in position to strike the enemy, but, faithful to Henry's scheme, had held back. In the following note to Mendoza, he accused Épernon of unpardonable treachery.

Not merely has Épernon placed himself between the reiters and me, in order to favor them during the fine treaty he has concluded with them, but he has also given them money so as to maintain the credit of the heretics with the strangers, and a thousand arquebusiers of the king's own guard, and ten companies of gens d'armes to accompany their retreat. It is strange that the forces of the Catholics must be employed to recompense the heretics for the evils they have inflicted upon France. Every good Frenchman and true Catholic must feel himself offended.[71]

Then, while the Germans were camped in Burgundy disagreeing over the terms of peace, Guise, at the head of an indignant host of Burgundian peasants, attacked them once more and scattered their remaining forces.

The turning point had truly been reached, just as Henry III predicted; but, far from bringing him the glory and power he had expected, it brought failure and disgrace. Guise, not the king, was hailed as the hero and defender of France. The way was cleared and the stage set for an open revolt of the League against the crown. Mendoza's detailed reporting of the campaign to Philip convinced the Catholic King that Guise was a worthy steward for promoting his and the Lord's work in France. Philip decided that the time had come for the final and decisive *coup de main* which would return Western Europe to the Universal Church. Mendoza's handling of the major affairs of 1585–87 had convinced Philip that his ambassador was a reliable servant and could be counted on to maintain the Catholic cause.

Chapter V

DIPLOMATIC PROCEDURE, I:
GATHERING DATA

✤ ✤ ✤ ✤

Before continuing with the development of Spanish-League relations following the repulsion of the German invasion, it seems advisable to devote a few pages to the actual mechanics of the Paris embassy during the tenure of Don Bernardino. Paris was the key post in Philip's foreign policy and the principal agency through which Spanish diplomacy functioned between 1584 and 1593. This in itself would be sufficient justification for further inquiries into the diplomatic machinery, but the operation of the Paris embassy during this period also sheds light on the nature and manifestations of the ideological dogmatism which dominated the times.

MENDOZA AND HIS STAFF

Mendoza took up his duties at Paris in November 1584 with no misgivings about the difficulties ahead nor the importance of his mission. He was singularly qualified and well-prepared for what lay ahead. He was familiar with the domestic situation in France and acquainted with most of the leading personalities at the French court, including the king and the queen mother, as well as many of those who seldom made an appearance in Paris, such as the dukes of Mercoeur, Lorraine, and Nemours. Even more significant is the fact that he had met Guise and Mayenne, and knew the cardinal of Bourbon. In an age of personal diplomacy, acquaintances such as these can scarcely be overemphasized. He also had first-hand experience in the related affairs of England, the Netherlands, and Scotland, and was not without awareness of conditions in Rome. The Spanish ambassador at Rome, Enrique de Guzmán, count of Olivares, was of the same mettle as Mendoza, and the two kept in regular contact through couriered dispatches. Alexandre Farnese, duke of Parma, Philip's able commander in the Netherlands, was another of Mendoza's closest diplomatic associates, and, although they failed to agree on many points of tactics, they coordinated Philip's policies in France and Flanders surprisingly well.

Mendoza had the benefit of noble birth (which, though not an absolute necessity for sixteenth-century diplomats, was certainly an advantage), and the erudition gained from a sound education at one of the leading universities of Europe. He wrote well — sometimes even eloquently — in both Spanish and Latin, and had a reading and speaking knowledge of Italian, French, and Portuguese. Despite his seven years in England, however, he did not speak English[1] — but, then, few people did except Englishmen. Mendoza's knowledge of military affairs served him well in France, for much of his time was spent in gathering and assaying information of a military nature.

Perhaps even more significant was the fact that Mendoza went to Paris with an adequate supply of money and the full confidence and support of Philip II and the Spanish government. "I see," wrote the king to Mendoza in March 1584, "that you have acted with the same good sense and courage in the manner of your departure [from England] as in all else that has happened during your stay in that country. I am entirely satisfied with you and with your good services, and will take care that they are duly remembered." [2] Mendoza understood Philip's foreign policy and, except for the king's extreme circumspection in implementing it, was in harmony with it. He was a pious and devout Catholic, convinced that

God's voice was manifest in the decrees of the church, and that the maintenance of the unity and purity of Christendom was the highest duty incumbent upon sixteenth-century Christian patriots. And to Mendoza, no less than to Philip, the responsibility for the leadership of this crusade lay primarily with Spain.

Mendoza's personality had numerous facets. Many who knew him personally spoke very favorably of his amiability and cordial manners; and some were impressed by his generosity.[3] There is evidence that he disclosed occasional cheerfulness with a considerable sense of humor, and he appears to have been a very interesting conversationalist.[4] Others, of course, found him to be domineering and bigoted, with an insufferable arrogance in all matters involving Spain or himself. But not even his enemies doubted Mendoza's ability as a persistent and shrewd negotiator.[5] Toward his friends he was unswervingly faithful, and toward his foes uncompromisingly severe.[6] He was always loyal to his king, and completely subordinated himself to the service of Spain, which he genuinely believed was the service of God.

This zealous devotion and subordination to a cause made him haughty and intolerant toward anyone not supporting the same principles and ideology, and unscrupulous at times in his support of anything which he thought would contribute to its success. For Mendoza, the foes of Spain and of Catholicism were not honorable adversaries; they were the enemies of God and Mankind. Against such seditionists there are no rules of good conduct, he maintained; they must be destroyed by whatever means is available. Mendoza did not lack integrity, but it was integrity based upon the belief that the cause he represented was superior to any individual or group which composed or opposed it.

Information about Mendoza's personal and embassy staff is exceedingly difficult to ascertain. He has left very few hints as to its size, and with rare exceptions makes no reference to any of its members by name. The ambassador was in possession of many of the papers and files of his predecessor, but this is insufficient proof of the presence of a permanent staff secretary since Tassis himself remained in Paris for more than a month after Mendoza arrived and could very well have personally turned over many of his papers to Mendoza (as he did 6000 escudos of embassy expense money.)[7] The additional fact that all embassy papers were considered the property of the ambassador, and his personal responsibility, suggests the absence of any permanent functionary assigned or controlled by the Spanish government.

It would appear from scattered references to Mendoza's secretaries as his *domésticos*[8] that whatever staff he had was small and was composed of his own household servants rather than royal civil servants. The mobility of the embassy in France during the unsettled war years would also support this conclusion. Furthermore, the fact that Mendoza paid his entire staff out of his own salary and not from his expense account suggests its limited size and its personal attachment to the ambassador. The only servants who receive mention by name in his correspondence are Hans Oberholtzer, who previously had served with Mendoza in Flanders and continued as his secretary during his London embassy,[9] and Herman Cartelegar, a highly trusted servant who was more than once sent on difficult assignments, including the carrying of top secret materials to Flanders or Madrid, when the demands of secrecy and safety precluded the normal lines of post or courier service.[10] Presumably these were the men who handled the bulk of the clerical work attached to the embassy, including the ciphering and deciphering of dispatches.

FRIENDS AND ENEMIES AT COURT

Because of the secrecy connected with negotiating the Treaty of Joinville, Mendoza's debut in Paris was considerably lacking in the pomp and ceremony of the usual sixteenth- and seventeenth-century ambassadorial entry and reception.[11] As soon as he officially took over his duties, however, the expected dignities and honors due a representative of His Most Catholic Majesty were insisted upon. At his first formal audience with the king, Mendoza made it clear to Henry III that, although he was charged with reaffirming the friendship and good will of his master toward the king of France, he was also expected to do this only so long as His Most Christian Majesty maintained his ancient duties as supporter and defender of the church.[12] Henry was angered by Mendoza's impertinences, but was restrained by his mother from making a scene at such a solemn ceremony. Not until 1588 was there an open breach between Mendoza and Henry, but even before that time their interviews were generally disagreeable and sometimes violent.

Throughout his ministry, Mendoza's relations with Catherine de' Medici were much more cordial than with Henry. At his first interview with the queen mother, he delivered a well-chosen and almost tenderly phrased message from Catherine's beloved granddaughter, the infanta Isabel Clara Eugenia of Spain, oldest daughter of Philip II and Elizabeth of Valois. Many times during the next five years, news of the infanta, brought to her by the Spanish ambassador, caused Catherine to forget her anger or dissatisfaction with Mendoza and impelled her to thank him for his thoughtfulness and regard for her family.[13]

Mendoza was no recluse in Paris. He made it a practice to be seen in the right places and with the right people. He frequently "chanced to meet the king and queen mother coming from church," or while walking in the parks, and used this "accident" to exchange more than just a formal greeting or to pay an appropriate tribute.[14] His most frequent official contacts with the French court were with Henry's chief ministers and secretaries of state. Most routine communications which Mendoza wished to make to the king were sent to Secretary Villeroy, who either passed them on to

Henry or else handled them himself.[15] Personal interviews between Mendoza and Villeroy were quite frequent and represented the chief source for the ambassador's knowledge of the official thoughts and decisions of the king, for Villeroy was the chief of protocol and handled all procedural matters with the foreign ambassadors. Although he was Henry's principal secretary of state, he never fully respected the king (which could also be said of many of the ministers), and by the beginning of Mendoza's ministry he had become more truly Catherine de' Medici's minister than Henry's. Mendoza was quick to notice this situation and soon made every effort to cultivate Villeroy's friendship and confidence, as he also did with the other ministers and secretaries, especially Pomponne de Bellièvre and Pierre Brulart.[16] Whatever the occasion or situation, Mendoza could be counted on to be one of the first and usually best informed men at the Valois court. His ears were constantly alert to the scantiest bit of gossip or to the softest innuendos of a public oration which might contain information of value to his government. With some exceptions he was also able to evaluate his sources and weigh the data so that whatever was passed on to Philip was, for that time, of unusual reliability. Very little of political importance transpired in Paris — or in France, England, and the Netherlands, for that matter — which Mendoza was not quickly aware of and able to inform his government of in the shortest possible time.

Among the foreign ambassadors Mendoza had both friends and enemies. His closest public collaborator in affairs dealing with England and Scotland was the Scottish ambassador to France, James Beaton, archbishop of Glasgow. The archbishop was a devoted follower of Mary Queen of Scots and served her very faithfully in Paris. Even after her execution he was, surprisingly enough, confirmed in his embassy by James VI, and he continued to work closely with Mendoza and with Guise. The following paragraph from one of Mendoza's letters to Philip, concerning the archbishop, witnesses to his importance in Mendoza's work.

I have also asked the Scottish ambassador for someone for a similar task, and he has promised, with the same diligence which he always displays in Your Majesty's interests, to find me one. He sends me instant advice of everything, sometimes even at midnight. In acknowledgment of this, and of the fact that every interview that Iñiguez [Juan Iñiguez, sent by Philip as a special agent to Guise] and I have had with Mucio [Guise] has been arranged by him (the letters all being sealed with his own hand), I did not think it too extravagant to give him a little present. However, since he is a man who could only be offered a very large sum in money, I took the occasion of his having greatly admired a tapestry bed of mine and had it dismounted and sent to him. The value of it is 380 escudos, and I have considered it advantageous to Your Majesty to thus signify your approval of his services. . . .[17]

For a time one of Mendoza's most influential friends among the diplomats in Paris was the papal nuncio, Fabio Mirto Frangipani, archbishop of Nazareth. Nazareth had been sent to Paris by Sixtus V, shortly after the latter's accession to the papacy, without any notification to the French king.[18] Henry III, strongly influenced by Luigi d'Este, the cardinal protector of France, sent a decree to the nuncio as he reached Lyon, ordering him to leave the country at once. The French ambassador in Rome, Jean de Vivonne, sieur de St. Gouard and marquis de Pisany, was thereupon instructed to remind the pope that by the Concordat of Bologna (1516) a papal nuncio could not be sent to France unless he was acceptable to the king; and Nazareth was not acceptable to Henry because he was a Neapolitan subject of the king of Spain.[19] Pisany spoke to the pope in stronger terms than had been anticipated in Paris and was promptly ordered out of the Papal States by an angered curia. In a rage, the French ambassador stomped off to the baths at Lucca where he unleashed his vituperation against the pope in a lengthy epistle to Secretary Villeroy. In the meantime, Henry III, frightened by Pisany's embarrassing demonstration, capitulated almost unconditionally to the pope, and ignominiously pleaded for Nazareth's return to Paris.[20]

During his active twenty months in Paris Nazareth was one of Mendoza's closest co-workers in bolstering the Catholic position in France, and he played a leading role in trying to gain the reluctant papal approval of Spanish assistance to the League. Nazareth's death on 16 March 1587 dealt Spanish influence with the papal legation in France a serious blow. The chief remaining advocates for Spanish-League policies in Rome were Olivares, the Spanish resident ambassador, and Cardinal Sanzio, principal agent of the League at the Vatican. The duke of Nevers also occasionally represented the League at Rome, but his patronage was languid at best, and after 1588 he became an open supporter of Henry III. Gian Francesco Morosini, bishop of Brescia, was Nazareth's successor and served as papal legate in France until 1589; but he was never very close to Mendoza. Not until the arrival of Cardinal Cajetan in December 1589 did the ambassador again have a sympathetic and active collaborator from Rome, and his support was largely neutralized by the schism within the League.

Not all of the diplomatic influence at the Valois court was favorable to Mendoza. The Venetian ambassador, Giovanni Dolfin, distrusted Mendoza's motives and methods and expressed a low regard for his arrogance, although the two did remain on cordial terms throughout their ministries.[21] The Florentine, Dr. Filippo Cavriana, disliked Mendoza heartily, but his colleague (whom he replaced in November 1585), Giulio Busini, thought rather highly of the Spanish ambassador.[22] Mendoza's most implacable enemy at court seemed to be the English ambassador, Sir Edward Stafford. Stafford's hatred of Mendoza dated back to the latter's ministry in London, which ended in his ignominious expulsion in January 1584. When Mendoza arrived in Paris, Stafford was the only ambassador who refused to extend the customary amenities to the envoy.[23] He even refused Tassis' invitation to an introduction, insisting that he would only speak to Mendoza if ordered to do so by the queen herself.[24]

Stafford was even more embittered by the frequent examples of partiality in matters of diplomatic preference which he protested were being shown against him in favor of the Spanish ambassador. In February 1586, for example, he was greatly offended when at an interview with the king, at which both he and Mendoza sought an audience, Mendoza was summoned to the royal chamber first. "When I passed through the room where he was seated," reported Mendoza, "he turned his back on me, looking daggers."[25] In September of the same year a more serious problem of precedence arose. The court was located at Saint-Germain, where all of the ambassadors had been summoned for an audience. Lodging was to be provided for them at Poissy. When Stafford sent his valet ahead to secure his accommodations, he was told that he would have to wait a day or two until the papal nuncio and the Spanish ambassador had chosen their lodgings, then he would be welcome to choose his own. Stafford was so infuriated by this insult that he refused to take any lodging at all. He stayed, so he reported to Walsingham, at a "borrowed house of Simier's nearby."[26]

At official functions and ceremonies Mendoza usually participated along with the other foreign emissaries, but seldom with any great show of enthusiasm. At the gala presentation of the Order of the Garter to Henry III in March 1585, Mendoza, in spite of his mounting anger and indignation over Elizabeth's sham bargaining for Henry's support of the Dutch rebels, retained his composure and ambassadorial dignity throughout. But ceremonies were not Mendoza's forte; he much preferred the personal contact of closed-door negotiation. As his health became worse, this preference became greater. But even in the best of physical condition Mendoza could hardly bring himself to like the ostentatious ribaldry of a Valois party.

MENDOZA'S INTELLIGENCE SYSTEM

Mendoza's contacts with official circles of the French court and his alert ear for the usual Paris gossip provided him with the ordinary information which every ambassador was expected to glean for his government.[27] But the late 1580's were not ordinary times. The additional responsibilities falling to Mendoza as a result of the absence of resident Spanish embassies in many of the other key states, and the extreme importance of coordinating the many different parts of Philip's foreign policy, necessitated additional sources of information and greater security in transmitting it to the home government. As the hatreds and suspicions of the religious wars mounted, it became increasingly difficult to obtain reliable information by the older methods. The hardening of ideological lines even endangered the security of the ambassador himself. In the early spring of 1587 he reported that he had been turned out of the house which he had occupied since the beginning of his embassy because his landlord was a staunch royalist and feared the king would suspect him of belonging to the League if he continued to house the Spanish ambassador. When he tried to arrange for other lodging Mendoza was astonished to find that three other landlords also refused to admit him as a tenant for the same reason. This indignity to himself and to the king, he protested, was one of the greatest humiliations he had ever suffered.[28] The event is significant for it illustrates a trend that was becoming ever more evident: the increasing awareness, particularly among the Politiques, of the Spanish-League connections, and the mounting hostility against Spaniards in France as a result. Not only did public insults and physical clashes increase after 1587, the Parlement de Paris even organized its own counterespionage operation against Spaniards, League, and Jesuits.[29]

The intelligence system which Mendoza inherited and greatly expanded was based upon the accepted sixteenth-century practice of pensions and gifts. There was little or no distinction between a bribe and a gratuity, or between political seduction and economic assistance to friends. "Should he [an ambassador] lack friends and ability to discover the truth and to verify his suspicions," comments the anonymous seventeenth-century author of *Embajada española*, "money can help him, for it is, and always has been, the master key of the most closely locked archives."[30] Because of his six years of diplomatic service in London, with the connections he made there, and the numerous English Catholic refugees in France and the Netherlands, Mendoza had a wide circle for gathering information on English affairs.[31] During 1586–1588 this service was of extreme importance to Philip in supplying him with notices of English naval strength, port facilities and armaments, movements and preparations of the English fleet, and so forth, although the information received was not always up to date or reliable. The English exiles were mostly staunch and sincere Catholics who looked forward to the eventual re-establishment of Catholicism in England. Most of them also looked to Philip as the agent through which God's Will would be realized, and they therefore supported his policies in France, England, and the Netherlands.[32] Others were mere opportunists.

Philip looked kindly upon these religious refugees and for many years had granted some of them monthly stipends. Often they reciprocated by providing him with information or other services of value to Spain and to the Catholic cause. Particularly helpful to Mendoza in his intelligence network were Lord Thomas Paget (Baron Beaudesert), Charles Paget his younger brother, and Charles Arundel. Lord Paget, who had been imprisoned by Elizabeth in 1579 for his Catholicism, fled to Paris in November 1583 where he began active participation in the Catholic missionary effort. Early in 1584 he went to Rome and thence to Spain, where he was granted a monthly stipend of 100 escudos. Charles Paget left England in 1572 and took up residence in Paris, where, along with his fellow refugee, Thomas Morgan, he became secretary to the archbishop of Glasgow. Paget and Arundel had been receiving their 80 escudos per month for several years before Mendoza arrived in France. Arundel and the younger Paget worked very closely with Mendoza, and through them the ambassador was able to enlarge his contacts even further.[33] By early 1586 he had secured an unidentified agent to function as head coordinator of information in London. On May 11, Mendoza wrote the following note to Philip concerning this mysterious correspondent.

As confirmation comes from all sides on the armaments in England, I have decided to obtain information about them by sending to London an Englishman who was recommended to me by Paget as being thoroughly trustworthy. He has already departed and takes with him letters of credence for friends of mine in London and also other letters from Charles Paget requesting them to send men to all the ports to inquire fully into the armaments and report the results secretly through the French ambassador in London. If they cannot do this they are requested to send this man back to me fully informed verbally.[34]

This arrangement was made in response to Philip's urgent request that Mendoza supply him with more reliable information from England:

I can well believe the difficulty you will find in obtaining trustworthy reports from England . . . as you say, but now it is a matter of such great importance for these reports to be obtained, that I must urge you again not to be satisfied with the news you are able to glean from the French embassy in England (although that too is a good source), but try by every other means to seek information. If you are intimate with the Scottish ambassador, as I think you are, send men [to England] by the intervention of Mucio and through the ambassador. They will surely have men whom they can trust, and some pretext for sending them, without the men who go even knowing that they are being sent at your request.[35]

Claude de l'Aubespine, sieur de Châteauneuf, the French ambassador referred to by Mendoza and Philip, was a sympathizer of the queen of Scots and the English Catholics, and proved to be a most vital link in Mendoza's communications to England. In September 1586, Mendoza explained the function of the French ambassador in the following terms:

> In order to have a safer channel for my correspondence with England I had him approached secretly by religious persons and told how great would be the service he would render to the cause of God if he permitted letters and money from Catholics here to pass under cover of his dispatches. He willingly consented to this and has punctually fulfilled it without opening a single letter. The secretary whom he has sent here is the one who supposedly does it, so that the ambassador will not be personally involved.[36]

Other English exiles who played important roles in Mendoza's service were Charles Neville, earl of Westmorland, Dr. Nicholas Wendon, Thomas Throckmorton, and Thomas Morgan. Westmorland had been receiving a Spanish pension since 1569 when he fled from England to the Spanish Netherlands after failing in his attempted rebellion with Northumberland. According to Mendoza's records he received 100 escudos per month. Throckmorton, brother of Francis who was involved in the 1583 plot against Elizabeth, had been in Paris since 1582 as an active agent of the king of Spain.[37] Of lower birth but equally valuable in supplying hard-to-get facts were Pedro de Zubiaur, a prisoner in England, William Bodenham, a Dunkirk shipowner, and an English merchant named Copcott. The wealthy Genoese merchant Augustin Griffin, resident of London, also supplied Mendoza with occasional news from England and even appears to have been hired by the ambassador as a special confidential agent.[38] Mendoza's relations with André de Loo, the Flemish merchant of London who was the regular emissary between Elizabeth and the duke of Parma, are less certain; but it appears that information, other than the official notices authorized by Walsingham, passed between them on occasion.[39] Added to these rather prominent persons were a great number of nameless informants located in various parts of England (mostly in the ports) and in France, who are summed up in Mendoza's expense accounts under the heading "Correspondientes y perssonas que me dan y traen avissos importantes al servicio de Su Md. y inteligencias que tengo en este Reyno" (Correspondents and persons who, for the service of Your Majesty, bring me important notices and information about this country).[40]

The situation in Portugal, which since 1580 was part of Philip's empire, also required careful observation as a result of the persistent efforts of Don Antonio, prior of Crato, to place the Portuguese crown on his own head. The pretender resided alternately in England, France, and the Netherlands, but his movements were carefully observed and reported by Mendoza's agents. The principal factotum in this affair was Antonio de Escobar, a Portuguese subject living sometimes in Paris, sometimes in London. "Sanson," as Escobar is cryptographically known in all of Mendoza's correspondence, was ostensibly a partisan of Don Antonio and as such received frequent and intimate news about him from those attached to his household. Sanson was also in a position to acquire valuable information on English affairs.[41] In addition to this efficient channel of communication, Mendoza also received irregular reports from Antonio de Viegas, a Portuguese confident sent to London by Philip to help keep an eye on Don Antonio.[42] Viegas wrote to Mendoza under the pseudonym Luis Fernandez Marchone, although in Mendoza's letters to Philip he is sometimes referred to simply as Viexas. Also working on the Portuguese matter in Spain were Diego Borello and even the youngest son of Don Antonio himself.[43]

Supplying valuable information on the activities of rebel leaders in the Netherlands was Godfrey Foljambe, hired by the duke of Parma at thirty escudos a month, and two of Mendoza's employees: M. d'Estrelles, a former rebel but since his distinguished service at the defense of Tournai in 1581 a loyal subject of the Spanish king, and a certain Hugo Frion.[44]

In addition to the informants previously mentioned at the

French court, Secretary Villeroy was Mendoza's most frequent contact; but there is insufficient evidence to establish any surreptitious relationship between them. Mendoza did, however, have in his employ a number of minor court functionaries and servants of the royal family, including several of Catherine de' Medici's maids and retainers and some of the court musicians.[45]

One of the strangest and most involved relationships in Paris was that between Mendoza and the English ambassador, Sir Edward Stafford. In spite of Stafford's personal hatred of Mendoza, it appears from many of the Spanish ambassador's letters, and from other sources, that early in 1587 Stafford began selling information to Spain through the mediation of Mendoza and Charles Arundel.[46] Whether Stafford's information was reliable or not, whether it was delivered with treasonable intent, and whether or not it was actually material vital to English interests and useful to Spain are problems which have been debated extensively (though inconclusively) by several well-known scholars.[47] In spite of the contradictory nature of the available evidence, and the labyrinth of deception and intrigue in sixteenth-century espionage, it does appear quite certain that, in April 1586, Guise gave Stafford 3000 écus in return for some bits of information, which were passed on to Mendoza and thence to Madrid with Charles Arundel.[48] But Mendoza became suspicious of Arundel and advised Philip to keep a close eye on him in Madrid. It was feared by both the king and the ambassador that Stafford had feigned friendship to Guise in order to get Arundel into Spain on some valuable mission for Elizabeth.[49] Arundel was kept under close surveillance, but he convinced Philip that he was not engaged in counterespionage for the queen. Thereafter, when he returned to Paris, Arundel became very active in Mendoza's service and began working on Stafford to get his assistance in selling information. Stafford's numerous debts and recent gambling losses increased the ambassador's receptiveness.[50]

Thus, after February 1587, Stafford, if it is correct to identify him as Mendoza's "new confident," became one of the chief sources for Mendoza's news from England.[51]

At first Stafford was apparently unaware of the destination of the information after he delivered it to Arundel. On February 28 Philip advised Mendoza:

> The new confident, whom you have obtained to keep you informed on English affairs, is very appropriate. You may thank the intermediary from me and encourage him to continue his good service. Give the other one the 2000 escudos, or the jewel you suggested of similar value, although it may be more confidential and preferable to give it to him in cash, through the same intermediary. If the correspondent does not know that the news passes through your hands you can arrange with the intermediary what to say to him about the course which has been adopted for sending it. You should manage it as you think best and tell them that you do not doubt that the reward will be commensurate with the service. This will encourage them to do their best.[52]

Later, when Mendoza's identity was known to Stafford, Philip cautioned his ambassador, "You must do your best to maintain the new confident, with whom you are now on such good terms, but your communications must be kept extremely secret, for if this medium should fail us we would lose a most valuable source of information, and there are undoubtedly people there who watch you closely."[53]

By the middle of 1587 it was obvious that he was being watched closely for, early in July, Philip learned that Longlée, the French ambassador in Madrid, knew of Stafford's visits with Mendoza and was probably aware of something going on between them. On July 6, Philip sent Mendoza a long letter to this effect and advised him on the actions to be taken.

> At any event, it is quite certain that Longlée here knows that he [Stafford?] often meets you at night, and he is more likely to have learned it from the other side [France] than from here. Nevertheless, you must keep this fact to yourself and arrange your communications with him in the greatest of secrecy. At the same time, convince him, for the sake of his own safety, to stay in his present position as long as he can. . . . But do not hint to him that his communication with

you has been discovered by anyone who might use the knowledge
to his damage, for fear that he take alarm and forsake the good path
he has hitherto followed. If he must change his place, persuade him
to enter the council, but if he cannot do that he should not refuse
the other post [of viceroy to Ireland]. Urge him wherever he may
be, to continue his good services, for which he will be adequately
rewarded. In any case, keep his friendship and get as much information from him as you can, and from the others, reporting all things
to me.[54]

Stafford did remain in paris, in spite of direct charges made
against him by Walsingham, and it appears that he continued
to supply Mendoza with information until after the Day of
the Barricades.

CONTACTS WITH THE LEAGUE AND THE JESUITS

Negotiations between Mendoza and the heads of the League
were carried out with the utmost caution and deliberation.
Correspondence passing from Guise to Mendoza was sometimes ciphered and was always carried by a private courier
who had proven his trustworthiness and who had the full confidence of both men. Most of the letters and even verbal
negotiations carried on between them were handled by the
duke's chief officer and aid, François de Mayneville. Mayneville
maintained close contact with Mendoza most of the time
and was also a familiar figure at sessions of the Paris Sixteen.
When not in Paris or en route between the capital and Guise's
headquarters, Mayneville was usually engaged in some other
assignment for the League.[55] He was so completely in the confidence of Guise that he was entrusted with the most secret
matters which could not be risked to writing. He met frequently with Mendoza, discussed the most vital issues of
strategy with only verbal orders from Guise, and at times even
drafted proposals and agreements on the basis of these oral
instructions.[56] Other persons sometimes named as intermedi-
aries in these negotiations are a Monsieur De Bray, who was
also a private confident of Guise, and Pericart, the duke's
secretary.[57]

Personal interviews between Mendoza and Guise were infrequent, but extremely important, and were generally arranged by the Scottish ambassador. These meetings sometimes took place on the rare occasions when Guise appeared in Paris, or when Mendoza left the city to meet him at some other designated spot. Mendoza has left one very interesting account of such a meeting outside of Paris on the night of 15 July 1585. He tells that he was taken by coach to a place seven leagues from Paris, called Villame, where he met with Guise in a small private house. The place was lightly guarded, he said, by cavalry from Bassompierre's regiment. The interview which took place there concerned the details of the Treaty of Nemours, which had just been completed, and its relation to the king of Spain.[58]

Another important person involved in the contacts between Mendoza and Guise, and also between Mendoza and members of the Sixteen, was Madame de Montpensier, sister of the duke of Guise. Madame de Montpensier was not only one of the political leaders of the Paris League but was also a woman of vehemence and action. She worked tirelessly for the promotion and strengthening of the League and endeavored, by whatever means available, to fight Protestantism in France. Michelet called her "La furie de la Ligue." On more than one occasion the duchess met with Mendoza, secretly of course, to discuss affairs involving her brother and the League,[59] and it appears not unlikely that she was in very close communication with him after 1587. Philip considered her to be of great importance in coordinating Spanish decisions with the activities of the Paris Catholics, so, in order to reduce the risk of having her name appear in Spanish correspondence, he ordered that her name be coded to read "Silvio" in all future dispatches and reports of the ambassador.[60]

The first mention of a personal interview between Mendoza and members of the Paris Sixteen appears as a postscript to Mendoza's dispatch of 1 July 1587. This notice tells of a meeting he had with one of the members of the Sixteen who was sent to him to discuss the vital issue of the forthcoming German invasion and the defense measures to be taken by the League in Paris. "One of them was sent to me in the name of all in order to ascertain my views concerning some of the points about which I shall inform Your Majesty." [61] The full details of this meeting were not sent to Philip immediately but they were included shortly thereafter in Mendoza's dispatches of July 12. [62] This undoubtedly was not the first time Mendoza had negotiated directly with the Sixteen, and it was certainly not the last. After the Day of the Barricades they exchanged counsel often and openly, and in 1589 Mendoza became their *de facto* head. Before 1588 members of the Sixteen met many times at the cabaret of an old Spaniard named Sánchez, who received a small stipend from the League and was kept in clothes by Mendoza in exchange for his services as an intermediary between the council and the ambassador. [63]

The exact relation and activities between Mendoza and the Jesuits are also difficult to establish, but the sources give adequate support to the suggestion that the Jesuits were much more active in the affairs of the League than the official histories of the Order would have us believe. [64] Most of this activity was unofficial. The governing hierarchy of the Jesuit Order, including General Claudio Aquaviva, were either openly opposed to Jesuit participation in the League or else tactfully uncommunicative about their affairs in France.

One of the most indefatigable agents of the League was the Jesuit Claude Matthieu of Lorraine, who, because of his numerous diplomatic missions and special traveling assignments, came to be known as the "Courier of the League." [65] He journeyed to Switzerland to engage troops for the League cause; performed liaison duty on many occasions between Paris and Madrid; and carried the League banner to the Holy See, gaining for his efforts the support of Pope Gregory XIII. There is also evidence that he was instrumental in the arrangements for the Spanish-League Treaty of Joinville.[66] Perhaps Matthieu's most successful yeoman duty for the League was his mission to Rome in 1585 to solicit Pope Sixtus V's support of the League by excommunicating Henry of Navarre.[67] There is little doubt that he performed his assignment with skill and persistence, but the sight of such wholehearted devotion of a high-ranking Jesuit (Matthieu was the provincial of Paris) to the League cause — which Rome was not at all assured was the cause of Catholicism — brought serious alarm to both Aquaviva and Pope Sixtus V. When Matthieu returned to Paris he found that he had been relieved of his office and was ordered to retire to Pont-à-Mousson. Early the next year, however, he again undertook a mission for the League, but from this one he never returned. Aquaviva ordered him to remain in Italy, where he died early in 1587.[68]

Matthieu was succeeded as Jesuit provincial of Paris by another ardent Leaguer, Odon Pigenat, who for a short time was also *visiteur* of the Jesuit colleges in France. Of all the Jesuits belonging to or supporting the League, Pigenat was probably the most important, for it appears that he was not only in regular contact with the Council of Sixteen but after January 1589 was a member of that body.[69] He appears on occasions as one of the more radical voices in the Sixteen, although many Jesuit sources argue that he joined only to moderate and tranquillize them.[70] There is evidence that Mendoza had frequent and intimate contact with Pigenat, for the ambassador often met with members of the Sixteen at the Jesuit Collège de Clermont on the rue Saint-Jacques, and at the *Maison Professe* on rue Saint-Antoine. Pasquier affirms that every Sunday, Mendoza gathered with members of the Sixteen and with Jesuits of the *Confrérie du Chapelet* (which, along with the *Confrérie du Nom de Jésus*, formed revolutionary bodies within the membership of the League) at the *Maison Professe*.[71] The Jesuit house near St. Paul's

Church was another frequent point of rendezvous for Mendoza and the Sixteen.[72]

One of the most outspoken Jesuit preachers in Paris was Jacques Commolet who, because of his ceaseless barrage of sermons against all enemies of the League, gained the title of "Orator of the Sixteen." [73] With the split between Meyenne and the Paris League in 1589, Commolet sided with the Parisian radicals in advocating the surrender of France to Philip II.

Other Jesuits, both French and Spanish, who in various ways and in diverse capacities were also actively associated with the League, and therefore with Mendoza, were fathers Varades and Sanguenot, both rectors of the Jesuit Collège de Clermont; the preacher Guignard, who was librarian of the college; Henri Samnier, another League courier; and his confederates Bernard Rouillet and Antoine Possevin; the chronicler Barny; along with the less prominent Bernardin Castor, of Lyon; and Père Clement.[74] As early as 1584, according to Forneron, the Jesuit father Innocent Picquet received 12,000 écus from Philip for his assistance in the Spanish machinations against Elizabeth,[75] and was later assisted in this area by the Scottish Jesuit, Alexandre Hays.[76] Another prominent foreign Jesuit was Filippo Pigafetta, who arrived in France in 1589 in the entourage of Cardinal Cajetan.[77]

Many of the Jesuit confessors in France seem also to have favored the League, and in their influential positions were probably a very effective weapon against "rebels and politiques." Stafford had something pertinent to say about these confessors in 1585, and if proper allowance is made for his own bias in reporting the event, it can throw some light on this Jesuit activity in relation to the League.

There occurred an event here yesterday which has made the king look about him and I think frightened him more than anything, though he dares not show it. A gentleman went to confession to a

Jesuit, and after telling his faults, the Jesuit said he could give him no remission unless he promised to defend the League of the duke of Guise "to the last drop of his blood." He told the king of it, who was greatly amazed and sent him and two others to other Jesuits, but all preached the same thing.[78]

Nevertheless, not all of the Jesuits in Paris were Leaguers or even League sympathizers. Henry III's confessor, the Jesuit Edmond Auger, remained an outspoken critic of the League and all its activities, and, along with the *visiteur* Lorenzo Maggio, was a vigorous personal antagonist of Matthieu and Pigenat.[79]

Aside from the contacts already shown between Mendoza and the Jesuit Leaguers, we learn from Stafford that the Spanish ambassador's own confessor in Paris was a Jesuit, and, from the same source, that after 1587 Mendoza sheltered an unnamed English Jesuit in his house, later sending him to England as a special agent.[80] There can be no doubt that the Jesuits, even though the official stand of the Society was non-involvement, were actively and effectively participating in the League from the lowest to the highest levels, and that their ultramontanism (Pyrenees, not Alps) made them willing and useful supporters of the policies of Philip II.

DIPLOMATIC PROCEDURE, II:
COMMUNICATION

✦ ✦ ✦ ✦

THE transmission of diplomatic information from Paris to Madrid was fraught with many difficulties, especially during the crucial years of Mendoza's residency, and required a high degree of ingenuity as well as persistence. The urgency of the ambassador's mission compelled the exercise of caution and accuracy in reporting news to Spain. Many times Philip reminded Mendoza to be very careful about gathering his information and extremely cautious in transmitting it, "because of the great importance of the negotiation and the many dangers." [1]

MENDOZA'S DISPATCHES

The news and opinions gathered by Mendoza from France and all parts of Europe were relayed to Madrid in a multitude of notes, dispatches, and reports which were written up almost daily. These official communications with the home government form the major part of sixteen large *legajos* (bundles) in the Sección del Estado of the Simancas Archives, and comprise the principal source data on Mendoza's embassy. Most of his letters followed the commonly accepted form for diplomatic correspondence in the sixteenth century: acknowledgment of letters received, date of last dispatch, place and date of the present, and so forth, [2] and were addressed directly to the king of Spain. There are also good indications (by the prevalence of his marginal notations) that Philip read most of them. Many items of less importance, and matters of embassy routine, personal health, and interesting sidelights were generally sent to the king's secretary or to a member of the Council of State. Don Juan de Idiáquez, who was secretary of state and of war until the end of 1586 (when he became counselor of state) was perhaps the closest to Mendoza in the councils of the home government. He wrote to the ambassador often and handled many of the technicalities of the embassy. Mendoza corresponded frequently with Martin de Idiáquez, cousin and successor of Don Juan as secretary of state — in charge of affairs in Flanders, France, and Germany — and secretary to the king.

Mendoza was conscientious about keeping his government informed at all times, and to do this he had to write often. During the first three years in Paris he averaged over fifteen letters a month, and in 1588 and 1589 he wrote even more. Noticing that these letters were each between five and ten pages in length (some were as much as twenty-two pages), that they were many times written in duplicate or triplicate, were carefully ciphered before sending, and were accompanied by voluminous supporting data, it becomes obvious that Mendoza and his aides must have been very busy. Yet, in spite of this need for haste, many of these letters have considerable literary merit and give evidence of the author's early training in the classics. He frequently included well-chosen biblical quotations and occasionally made reference to a passage from Cicero, or other favorite from the Roman "golden age," to illustrate a point.[3]

Mendoza did not send dispatches every day, but about once a week, at which time he included all information of interest to his government since the dispatch of his last pouch. He usually broke down the subject matter into geographical areas and sent a separate letter for each. This breakdown normally consisted of one letter for English affairs, one for Scottish, one for Portuguese (although this generally took only a few paragraphs and was added to one of the foregoing), and two, three, or more on affairs in France. In this latter group he included the negotiations with Guise and the League and affairs in the Netherlands. Frequently the information on Guise and his *coligados* made up the greater part of the dispatches on French affairs. When a week passed without very much news to report, the number of letters was reduced and the different subject categories condensed into one. Sometimes the letters were written each day then saved until six or seven had accumulated before they were sent. The main reason for this practice was the lack of adequate and continuous carrying service.

POST AND COURIER

Philip gave precise instructions for the ambassador to send his dispatches by different channels for added security.[4] Three principal methods were used by Mendoza in doing this: the French government post; the merchant post (including individual merchants traveling to Spain); and private courier. The first method involved the greatest risk of the three, but was the least expensive. It was never used for important matters, and after mid-1588 appears to have been discontinued entirely. The merchant post was on the whole quite reliable and economical and was used more and more after 1586.[5] In a report of June 9 of that year Mendoza informed Philip, "In accordance with Your Majesty's orders that I am to write by various channels, I send the present letter by the merchant post which leaves from Rouen. Although it is slow, I have not yet lost any dispatches sent by it."[6] The greatest number of Mendoza's dispatches were sent by diplomatic courier, for which he spent almost 3000 escudos during the first nine months of 1587.[7]

Of Mendoza's many couriers the most frequently referred to by same was Pierre Blanchet, who many times made the hazardous journey overland, past Huguenot strongholds and troublesome patrols, from Paris to Irún.[8] Blanchet was a French Leaguer and ardent Catholic who served Mendoza faithfully as long as the Paris embassy lasted. He was also the most frequently used courier on the Flanders run, where the route was less dangerous, but where speed was a premium. Others frequently referred to by Mendoza as couriers to Flanders were Charles de Escala, Tussayn, Chatelart, Andrea van Metecoben, Pieton, and Ridel.

The usual compensation for carrying a packet of dispatches from Paris to Brussels was thirty-five *escudos pistoletes;* equivalent in metallic content to approximately eighty-five dollars but when equated with a comparable purchasing power today would vary all the way from fifty to one-hundred and fifty dollars, depending upon the nature of the purchase.[9] This fee differed slightly at times according to the political and military conditions, the urgency of the message, the point of delivery, and the proven competency of the courier; but the base price remained stable throughout Mendoza's ministry. Tussayn seems to have consistently been paid forty escudos, and on one occasion Blanchet received seventy escudos for delivering a vital communication to Parma from Philip. Some of the French couriers, Pieton and Ridel for example, delivered dispatches to Lille for as little as fourteen *écus soleils* (*escudos del sol*, equivalent in Spanish money to fourteen escudos pistoletes and six *sueldos*),[10] but the usual rate was twenty-five écus. As a comparison, it is interesting to note that the rate for sending a packet of dispatches from Paris to Brussels by the French government post was only one écu (one escudo, two sueldos), or about two dollars and fifty cents.

The exchange of mail with Spain was considerably more complicated, involving as it did greater distances and much greater risks. The most common route followed by couriers carrying dispatches from Paris was via Limoges and Bergerac to the Spanish border at Irún.[11] The last lap of this route, from Limoges to Irún, was the most dangerous part of the journey, and taxed the natural and acquired skills of the couriers to their limit. At Irún the ambassador's pouches were transferred to the regular Spanish post which carried them directly to Madrid (or to the Escorial). The entire Spanish postal system at this period was remarkably well-organized and effective in spite of almost insurmountable obstacles.[12] The section between the capital and the French frontier, headed by its postmaster general (*correo mayor*) at Irún, Juan de Arbelays, was one of the most efficient.[13] When the overland courier route from Paris to Irún became too hazardous, diplomatic pouches were frequently sent to the port of Nantes (not yet a Huguenot stronghold) where they were transported by boat to Bilbao, on the Spanish Catabrian coast, and thence to Madrid.[14] Although slower than the more direct route, it was considered by Mendoza to be much safer, and therefore more satisfactory for highly confidential dispatches.

The length of time required for a letter to travel from Paris to Madrid varied a great deal, depending mostly upon the courier's knowledge of the terrain and his ability to evade the hostile Huguenot patrols in southern France. The fastest delivery recorded in the Mendoza correspondence was eight days,[15] but the average time from Paris to Madrid was more like twelve days. Many times, of course, it took two or three weeks for a dispatch to reach its destination, and some never arrived at all. Mendoza's important report of 5 August 1587 on the question of salt exports to Flanders did not reach Philip until October,[16] and his communication of 7 July 1588 about the peace negotiations between the League and Henry III was thirty-one days en route.[17] Interestingly enough, the average length of time for letters going in the reverse direction, that is, Madrid to Paris, was slightly greater, perhaps due to the frequent delay at the frontier waiting for a courier. Whatever the reason, a letter sent by Philip would normally be in

Mendoza's hands about fifteen days after it was sent. The record time was eleven days.[18]

On this hazardous run from Paris to Irún, Blanchet and the other couriers received the sizable sum of eighty escudos pistoletes. The only person recorded as having carried this route for less was a Pedro de Santa Cruz, who agreed to do it for seventy-five escudos. He delivered his first pouch at Irún three weeks late and was never heard from again by the Spanish embassy.

Of Mendoza's many diplomatic couriers, one of the most capable was Pierre el Basco, who worked exclusively on the Paris to Irún run. Pierre el Basco, evidently a native of the western Pyrenees region, knew his way around in southern France and more than once proved himself an equal match for Navarre's alert outposts. Mendoza's negotiations in France would have been considerably more secure if there had been more Pierre el Bascos in the Spanish diplomatic service. The names of three other couriers appear often in Mendoza's papers; they are Piquet, Arnet, and Pierre Babin. All three were French Catholics either belonging to or sympathetic with the League, and all seem to have been reliable and skillful couriers. Sometimes Herman Cartelegar, Mendoza's own trusted servant, carried messages of extreme importance requiring the utmost secrecy and security. Other couriers mentioned by the ambassador were Henrique Trapetier, Pierre Bribet, Pierre de Hechaurri, Juan de la Heuta Greffier, Ramos de Leguia, Luis de Pace, Antonio de Guares, Pierre de Amendeaux, Jeronimo Lopez Sapaerio, Antonio Payne, and Jacques de la Rue.

On rare occasions a courier took a dispatch all the way to Madrid,[19] for which he was compensated one hundred and twenty escudos, but it was more common, whenever couriers were scarce, merely to carry the ambassador's pouch to Bordeaux where it was entrusted to the armed protection of the French postal system for delivery to Irún. The postmaster (*maestre de poste*) at Bordeaux, Monsieur Cardera, was a conscientious functionary who provided fairly good service between Bordeaux and Irún at the nominal fee of eight écus. For carrying the dispatches from Paris to Bordeaux a courier was generally paid sixty écus, which made the whole trip to Irún amount to seventy escudos, twenty sueldos, that is, thirty-eight sueldos (one dollar and sixty cents) less than by straight courier. This combination of courier and government post was also used in communications to the duke of Parma. Couriers from Paris would deliver Mendoza's pouch to a station of the Spanish postal system in Flanders, which was capably directed by Correo Mayor Leonardo de Tassis, where it would then be rushed to Parma's headquarters.[20]

Mendoza also made use of at least three merchant posts in following Philip's instructions to "write by various channels": Andrés de Burgos, a prosperous Spanish merchant living in Paris; Issoardo Capelo, an Italian of Paris and Rouen; and the Balbani brothers, Matheo and Christoforo, living in Lyon.[21] Rates charged by these merchants to carry diplomatic pouches were not high (Matheo Balbani's rate for taking dispatches all the way from Paris to Madrid was fifty escudos), and the dispatches were generally quite safe. Traveling speed, however, was much slower than either government post or courier, and their schedules and routes were not designed for the accommodation of ambassadors. Seldom did a merchant caravan travel straight from one capital to another, and very rarely between Paris and Madrid. Therefore, the use of the merchant post meant slow delivery and sometimes many transfers en route.

The road from Paris to Bordeaux lay on a well-traveled trade route of the sixteenth century, and Mendoza sometimes made use of the merchants between these points to get dispatches to Postmaster Cardera at Bordeaux. For this service Capelo usually charged Mendoza only eight écus. Frequently Mendoza sent his pouch by merchants to Poitiers and thence to Bordeaux by courier, and occasionally Capelo took it all the way to Bayonne (at a standard rate of twenty écus). The Balbanis were the chief carriers for letters between Mendoza and the Spanish ambassadors in Italy and Germany.

DIPLOMATIC CIPHERS

To increase the factor of security in communicating with their home governments, foreign ambassadors in the sixteenth century (as in the twentieth) wrote their dispatches in diplomatic cipher.[22] This was not so much to keep an expert cryptanalyst from breaking the code and deciphering the message as it was to prevent "dishonest embassy servants or officious frontier captains" from discovering the content of a dispatch.[23] When ciphering and transmitting messages of top secrecy the greatest care was exercised in order to prevent, or at least delay, their discovery by hostile governments. Prior to the general European adoption of the Vigenère table and system of cryptography, or variations of it, in the seventeenth century, Europeans experimented with many comparatively unsystematic methods, most of which used some form of simple substitution cipher.[24]

Under Philip II, Spain developed a number of cryptographic methods, some of them easy to use and to break, others much more cleverly conceived and extremely difficult to decipher without a key. Philip was very concerned about diplomatic security, and at his succession ordered all the ciphers used by his father's government to be changed.[25] At the beginning of an ambassador's term he would be given a general cipher which he was to use whenever he felt it necessary to obscure the meaning of a dispatch. For more confidential communications he was also given a *cifra particular* which he employed alternately with the general cipher or, if he felt it was necessary, in place of it. Prior to Mendoza's Paris embassy it was customary for an ambassador to use only these two ciphers during his ministry but Mendoza, due to the importance Philip placed on the Paris negotiations and affairs in France after 1584, used five different ciphers.

Most of the Spanish ciphers of the late sixteenth century consisted of numerous arbitrary signs which were substituted for the letters of the alphabet according to a prearranged chart.[26] In order to increase the difficulty of breaking such a cipher two other precautions were taken: an additional number of signs was included to represent the vowels and the more frequently used consonants, thus making it extremely hard to break by a letter-frequency analysis; and several more signs were added as nulls, having no letter value at all, for the purpose of confusing an unwelcome peruser. Occasionally Spanish diplomats used a simple amplification of the ancient blocked alphabet cipher used centuries earlier by the Greeks. Jean Baptiste de Tassis, Mendoza's predecessor in Paris, employed this method as often as he did the "general" and "particular" ciphers assigned to him.[27]

When Mendoza went to Paris in October 1584 he took with him a new kind of cipher, similar to the symbol and number substitution ciphers of his co-workers, but with additional compounding through the use of *syllabic* representations and an increase in the number of whole-word symbols. This cipher, which Mendoza used for about 90 percent of his dispatches between November 1584 and June 1586, although very simple to read with a key, presented the reader with a baffling combination of numbers, letters, and signs, representing not only letters and words but now syllables as well.[28]

Mendoza's cipher worked smoothly for some time before it became obvious in the summer of 1586 that some of his dispatches were being read, not by Henry III and his ministers but by Secretary Walsingham in London. As early as the spring of 1585 a spy of Maurice of Nassau had stolen a pouch of Mendoza's letters to Parma and, after having the cipher broken and the letters deciphered, sent them on to Walsingham with the following note: "There having fallen into my hands certain letters from D. Bernardin de Mendoza to the Prince of Parma, by which appears part of the negotiation in France, I send them to you, but as they have been deciphered and as we must keep this cipher secret, for reasons which you know better than I do, I beg that this communication may not tend to our prejudice as regards other like letters." [29]

By the spring of 1586 Philip deemed it too dangerous to continue using the same cipher for all of Mendoza's correspondence, so in March he adopted another cipher which was used alternately with the old one until April 1587. This new cipher was almost identical to that of Tassis, two years before, except that the alphabet started with different coordinates, thus altering the numerical value of every letter. This cipher did not replace the other one, but was used in conjunction with it at a ratio of approximately one dispatch written in the new for every six or seven in the old.

The chief disadvantage of Mendoza's syllabic cipher was the constant necessity of a written key, especially for the long list of whole-word signs, which multiplied the risk involved and increased the chance of ciphering and deciphering errors. On 9 April 1587, therefore, he presented to Philip and Idiáquez a proposal for another new cipher, this one to combine the advantages of both the Tassis block and the Mendoza syllabic ciphers, with the added feature of being simple enough and systematic enough to commit to memory. This versatile cipher used only numbers as substitutes for the alphabet instead of signs but employed them in combinations forming syllables, as in his earlier cipher.[30] Along with a letter to Juan de Idiáquez recommending the use of this cipher, Mendoza also sent a copy of the cipher key and a short explanation of how it worked. He claimed that ciphering and deciphering time would be cut in half by employing this system and that accuracy would not be sacrificed.[31] It is difficult to determine just how often this cipher was used, since most of the dispatches after 1586 have been deciphered, but it was employed after May 1587 along with the two that have just been mentioned.

Late in January of 1588, some of Mendoza's and Philip's letters (as well as communications with agents) began to appear in yet another cipher. This one again resembled Mendoza's first (1584–1586), with a different set of number substitutes and completely new syllable endings.[32] It was used quite extensively during the spring and summer of that year, but after November was alternated with the others.

In November 1589, one of Navarre's patrols intercepted a pouch of Mendoza's and Moreo's ciphered dispatches to Philip. These documents were submitted to François Viète, the celebrated mathematician, who had been employed by Henry of Navarre for the express purpose of reading the Spanish dispatches, and after some length of time he succeeded in breaking the code.[33] In a letter from Tours, dated March 15, 1590, Viète made the following interesting comments to Henry IV about the Spanish ciphers and enclosed the deciphered letters and their key for the king's future use.

No doubt this will move our enemies to change their ciphers, to keep them more hidden, and cause them to try to impede those who serve you. They have already changed and re-changed them many times, and one is ever amazed at their astuteness. But our cause is just and theirs is evil. Therefore, God will dispel their counsels and bless our own, illuminating those spirits in our service whom he loves, according to their task.[34]

Philip knew the dispatches had been taken and, although he had no evidence as yet that the enemy had broken the cipher, he knew it would only be a matter of time before they did. Therefore he instructed Mendoza, in a letter of 30 January 1590, to change his cipher once more and not use the old ones again.[35] This time Philip sent Mendoza a new cipher — with a more conventional substitution pattern but with the addition of a great many more symbols representing vowels, and with some added short-cuts for faster ciphering, suggested by Mendoza[36] — and advised him to use it exclusively until he was instructed otherwise. This cipher, the last of the five utilized by the ambassador during his six-year term, was apparently used until he returned to Spain in 1591.

EMBASSY FINANCES

Money matters were a major problem for Mendoza, as for every ambassador, although he was much better off in this respect than many of his predecessors had been.[37] Mendoza's annual stipend was usually six thousand escudos pistoletes ($14,700), from which he was expected to pay for his rent in Paris, his food, clothing, and personal items, his household servants and secretaries, and any other expenses related to the normal operation of the embassy. Some idea of the purchasing power of this sum might be imagined from the following prices, picked at random from a lengthy report sent by Mendoza in May 1590.[38] A cow was worth twenty escudos ($49.00), a pig brought eight escudos ($19.60), and a sheep ten ($24.50). A pound of beef sold for five sueldos (twenty cents), mutton nine sueldos (thirty-six cents), and pork ninety-two dineros (thirty cents). Butter was seventy-two dineros a pound (twenty-five cents), Dutch cheese one hundred and two dineros (thirty-five cents), and French cheese twelve dineros (four cents). "One hundred apples from last year" sold for one hundred sueldos ($4.00), a sack of charcoal for two escudos (eight cents), and a cart of firewood (sixty pieces) for three escudos (twelve cents).

Since Mendoza's salary seldom fully met the demands made upon it, he was forced many times to rely on the income from his own land and various other personal resources in Spain.[39] In addition to his salary, he was allowed an expense account for extraordinary embassy expenses such as courier and postal service, donations to Catholic charities, grants to the English Catholic seminary at Rheims, gifts to the royal family, pensions to the English exiles, and compensations to members of Mendoza's intelligence organization.[40] These *gastos extraordinarios* were carefully itemized once a year by Mendoza and sent to the secretary of the Council of Finances (Consejo de Hazienda) for reimbursement. Most of the payments to Guise, as agreed upon in the Treaty of Joinville, were handled through Parma and Moreo in Flanders to reduce the risks involved in doing it from Paris.[41]

The arrival of the ambassador's salary did not coincide either quantitatively or chronologically with the receipt of his expense reports. Money was applied to his account at irregular intervals and was expected to roughly balance his expenses and salary. It seldom did, and with the infrequency of the payments financing the embassy became a perennial headache. "I have not asked Mucio to provide me with the messenger and letters," complained Mendoza to Philip early in 1586, "for I have not a cent to give them, and I am quite sure that neither Mucio's man nor the other one will be satisfied with a trifle. I therefore again humbly supplicate Your Majesty to send me funds for my expenses, as I have not been paid a single penny [*dinero*] for the whole ten months." [42] Only once (1 January 1587) in the six years at Paris did Mendoza's receipts actually exceed his expenses at the time he submitted his report.[43] But by the time the next report was sent, in October, this favorable balance had been eaten up and a 234-escudo deficit accrued. By June of the following year this deficit had grown to 2693 escudos.[44]

Mendoza did not receive his money in cash directly from Madrid. Spanish escudos were deposited with the banking firm of Francisco and Pedro de Malvenda in Rouen from which the ambassador drew out the equivalent in French écus. This account was guarded and taken care of by Diego Hernández de Miranda, a resident of Rouen.[45] Mendoza also had credit with Gonzalo de Salazar and Juan de Carmona, merchant bankers of Lyon. This account was supervised by a

EXTRAORDINARY EXPENSES (July 1, 1586 to December 31, 1586)

Date		To	For	Amount		
				escudos	sueldos	dineros
July	24	Pierre Blanchet	Dispatches to Irún	80		
Aug.	5	Courier with urgent dispatch to Parma from Philip		35		
	13	Pierre de Santa Cruz	Dispatches to Irún	75		
	20	Tussayn	Dispatches to Parma in Flanders	40		
Sept.	13	Courier with disp. to Gen. of the Order of S.T. in Metz		8	16	
	20	Sanson	Agents in England	400		
	21	Charles de Escala	Dispatches from Philip to Parma	35		
	26	Earl of Westmorland	Services to His Majesty	250		
	30	Thomas Morgan	Pension for August & September	80		
	30	Charles Arundel	Pension since Sept. 1584 (80/mo.)	980		
Oct.	2	Pierre Blanchet	Dispatch carried from Philip	70		
	2		Dispatch to Irún via Limoges	80		
	8	Arnet	Annual gift and alms	2,000		
	8	Seminary of Rheims		94		
	15	Courier to Parma with dispatches from Mend. & Philip		520		
	18	Thomas Throckmorton	Pension since Sept. 1584	1,300		
	18	Milord Paget	Pension since Sept. 1584	80		
	24	Pierre Bribet	Dispatches to Irún via Limoges		12	
	27	Charles Paget	Pension since Sept. 1584	900		
Nov.	3	Charles de Escala	Dispatches to Parma in Flanders	35		
	20	"Un Flamenco" on way to Spain carried dispatch (6 écus)		6		
	23	Andrea van Metecoben	Dispatch to Parma	35		
Dec.	30	Pierre Blanchet	Dispatches to correo mayor, Irún	80		
"		Various poor and sick Spaniards in France		66	49	
"		Receipt of various letters (11 écus, 21 sous)		11	43	
"		Henrique Wanghely and Leonardo de Tassis for mail		194	40	

" Issoardo Capelo for carrying letters by merchant post	40	49	6
" Andrés de Burgos for carrying letters by merchant post	5		
" Paper, ink, etc. for the embassy	17	17	
" Diego Maldonado Assistance at embassy	94	25	6
" Sanson Additional stipend for info.	150		
" Correspondents, agents and other informants	448	10	
" To secret agent mentioned in letter of July	4,000		
" Earl of Westmorland Services and information	50		
" Thomas Morgan Services and information	80		
" Officials, servants, musicians of king's house, etc.	100		
Total expenses (July 1–Dec. 31, 1586)	12,443	20	
Owed to Mend. from last report	516	34	5
6 months salary at 6,000 per year	3,000		
Total	15,959	54	5

Credit received, August 11, 1586	8,000	
Credit received, September 20	8,275.	50
Total received	16,275.	50

	16,275	50	
Balance on hand, Jan. 1, 1587	315	53	7

lawyer of Lyon whose name is not given in any of Mendoza's papers, but who is always referred to as the "Attorney for the heiresses of Luis Caponi" (*Procurador de los Herederas de Luys Caponi*).

The abbreviated summary, on the preceding two pages, of Mendoza's ten-page report of extraordinary expenses covering the six-month period from July 1 through 31 December 1586 will perhaps give a more succinct and clearer view of his financial activities than many pages of text.[46]

The year 1587 began auspiciously for Mendoza, with a balanced budget and a few escudos extra to go on, but by its end he was faced again with a growing deficit and a tightening income. The ambassador was once more forced to plead for money to liquidate his growing expenses and to provide his government with the services and information required from the Paris embassy. As 1587 drew to a close it became increasingly evident that 1588 would be a year of crisis.

Chapter VII

THE REVOLT BEGINS

✤ ✤ ✤ ✤

Mendoza had been very active during the winter of 1587–88 in support of the League's efforts to raise arms and money for Guise's campaign against the German invaders. Now, as the king returned to Paris expecting the plaudits of a grateful population for delivering them from danger, Mendoza reported to his master that Paris and most of France was seething with discontent and disorder. If a well-organized movement were launched against the weakened king, conjectured Mendoza, it would be sure to succeed, especially if it were done in the name of religious unity and led by the duke of Guise.[1] But Philip was not to be rushed into taking some rash or foolish action in France which could lead to certain discredit and to possible disaster. At the time he was much more concerned about the increasing influence of Épernon over the king, and so his first instruction to Mendoza in 1588 was to warn Henry of the danger he had subjected himself to by placing such reliance upon Épernon, "who, being so inclined toward the Prince of Béarn [Navarre], could bring great harm to them and to Christianity in the matter of the future succession to that throne." [2]

In the meantime, the general feeling of impending doom which seems to have grasped France in the late months of 1587 was changing to a belief that God was beginning to pour out his wrath against the heretics. The sudden death of both Condé and Bouillon in early 1588 only strengthened their

superstitious faith and gave credulous meaning to the mysterious predictions of Nostradamus, Roggieri, and others, and to
the strange manifestations of nature. On the 24th of January,
reported Pierre de l'Estoile, a dense mist settled on Paris, the
like of which had never before been witnessed. So black was
this mist that torches had to be carried in midday, and two
people walking side-by-side could not see one another. Even
animals could not find their way about, he insisted, and many
birds, losing their directions, plummeted into courtyards,
struck chimneys, or flew into other obstructions.[3] But before
the year ended it had carried with it into oblivion two of the
greatest hopes of the Catholic world.

UNEASY PEACE

When the winter campaign closed, Guise proceeded to
Soissons where he was joyously received with gifts and celebrations by many of his friends. Even the pope honored him
with a blessing and a handsomely engraved sword.[4] Guise intended to go on to Paris from Soissons, but was expressly forbidden by the king to enter the capital. Suspicious of Henry's
intentions, Guise wrote the following note to Mendoza, ana-
lyzing the existing situation between himself and the king:

The king, having suddenly realized what forces we have within
this kingdom, and having also perceived the support we have beyond
it, has tried to deprive us of both by every means except force, which
he judges useless. . . . You know with what persuasions he has
worked with the pope, with what edicts his subjects have been
nourished, and what offers have been made for the advancement of
religion. Now he wants to get the jump on us, to convict us of ambition and insolence if we take up arms, and, if we do not, to wait
until our means are overtaxed, our adherents scattered by his disfavor, and ourselves oppressed by the most careful and ingenious
artifices he can invent; as during this war when people were afraid
to join us, and all those who did had to serve at our expense. . . .
Either we shall be driven to make open war on the king, or else His
Majesty will make war upon us so covertly that we shall not be able
to resist without appearing to put ourselves in the wrong and thus
losing all our friends. Or else he will wait a while and begin when

six times as much money will not place us in as good a position as we are now in.[5]

Late in January, Guise proceeded to the city of Nancy where a family council of the heads of the houses of Lorraine was held. The result of this gathering was the notorious Eleven Articles of Nancy, presented formally to the king early in February. These articles proposed the conditions which must be met by the king if he desired a continuation of the Nemours coalition. They made the following demands:

(1) The king should declare himself more openly in support of the League and for the suppression of heresy.

(2) He should remove from his council certain persons who are suspected of heretical inclination. (Épernon).

(3) The decrees of the Council of Trent to be published in France and put into force.

(4) The Inquisition to be established in the capital of every province.

(5) The Catholic clergy must be allowed to buy back the lands which they had been forced by earlier treaties to sell.

(6) All who had been heretics since 1560 to give one-third, and all Catholics one-tenth, of their property in order to carry on successfully the war against the Huguenots.

(7) All Huguenots' property to be sold. (Catholic relatives to be given the first chance to buy it at a reduced price.)

(8) All Huguenot prisoners of war who refused to recant their heresy to be put to death.

(9) Prisoners embracing Catholicism to pay a fine and serve up to three years in the army without salary.

(10) The money thus accumulated to be used to pay the debts contracted by the League to support the war.

(11) The heads of the League not only to hold the

towns already specified by the Treaty of Nemours but also to be given permission to build fortifications and garrison them with troops raised by taxes on those towns and on the surrounding territory.[6]

In order to defer action on these articles as long as possible, Henry promised to consider the petition carefully and slowly. In the meantime he tried to entice Guise away from his friendliness toward Spain with "a world of extraordinary offers," promising material benefits and unprecedented honors which, in a note to Mendoza, Guise compared with those used by Satan in tempting Jesus in the wilderness. "And I trust," added Guise, "that I too shall be supported by good angels." [7] Enthusiastic over the Articles of Nancy, Mendoza expressed satisfaction with Guise's work and with the activity of the League, and reported to Philip that "I have had no further need of making them feel the spur." [8]

While Guise was engaged in negotiation with the king, Mendoza and the Paris League began preparing the capital for what might become an open show of force. Since the preceding summer the municipal organization had rapidly grown in strength and influence, and Henry's discreditable handling of the German invasion had caused hatreds to mount. The Council of Sixteen was now fully organized with representation from every urban class. Drouart was a lawyer, Rolland worked in the royal mint, La Bruyère was a nobleman (the only one), Michel was an attorney in the Parlement de Paris, Louchard was an auctioneer, Michelet a guard at the Châtelet, Le Lou was a process server, Poccart a tinworker, Senaut a clerk, Gilbert a butcher, and Ameline a merchant and "gentleman of affairs." [9] These eleven men along with Compans, Cruci, La Chapelle-Marteau, Bussi Le-Clerc, and Louchart, presidents of the old five quarters of Paris, formed the Sixteen in January 1588. Sometimes considered also as members of the council and sometimes as a separate organ of directors were Prévost, Boucher, Launoy, and the prominent churchmen, Hamilton, Lincestre, and Santeuil.[10]

Mendoza began working more closely with this group and guiding their planning toward the common goals he envisioned for Catholicism. He remained very alert to the dangers, however, and kept his negotiations with the Sixteen as clandestine as possible. In his dispatches Mendoza referred to the Sixteen merely as the "consejo" and never mentioned any of them by name except for an occasional reference to La Chapelle-Marteau who, because of his civic office could be addressed without causing suspicion. Personal contact with them was usually made through Mayneville, or in secret meetings of the council.

These men, with their direct communication with the populace through the Paris guilds and also through the parish priests, constantly stirred up the people against the king and his court mignons. Contact was also maintained with Guise and Mayenne, so the Paris League was always kept abreast of the latest planning. Since November, Madame de Montpensier and the cardinal of Guise had reinforced the League attack on the crown with their own tireless harangues. In February, because of her activities the duchess was officially exiled from Paris, but she refused to pay any attention to "the king's impertinences." [11]

The likelihood of a security leak in an organization involving so many people on the planning level was very great. One of the most trusted functionaries of the League was Nicolas Poulain who, as Lieutenant de la Prévôté de l'Ile-de-France, was a prominent and respected city official. Poulain was in a position to know the instructions passed down from the Sixteen to the guilds before they were publicly made known, and his presence at meetings of the Sixteen allowed him to become fully informed on matters of highest secrecy. No spy could have been more astutely chosen or more strategically located. Since January 1585, when Poulain became a member

of the Paris League, he had also been a personal informant of
Henry III. He had done his job well, and at a great risk to his
own person; even the astute Mayneville had apparently not
suspected him.[12]

In March 1588 the Paris League began to make plans for
action against Henry. Guise had returned to Soissons and
seems to have been lulled into a feeling of security by Henry's
apparent acquiescence to the Articles of Nancy. But Paris
suspected the king of ulterior motives, and when they learned
that 4000 Swiss infantry, who had been stationed at Lagny,
were moving toward Paris, they elected to act without instructions from Guise. Among other things, the Leaguers apparently intended to seize the king and take him to Soissons as
a prisoner, although details of their plans are not entirely
clear.[13] Mendoza's role in this surreptitious plot is equally
enigmatic, but it is quite certain that he was aware of the
League's intentions if not instrumental in planning their
moves. The Paris League also drew up a list of grievances
against the king and communicated it to other League cities
along with a call for men and money.[14]

Poulain immediately carried these important and disturbing
notices to Henry; but the king, confused by the abundance
of rumors, threats, and decisions, refused to believe the story.
He preferred on this occasion to listen to Villequier, governor
of Paris, who told him that Poulain was really in the service
of Navarre and the Huguenots and that his latest disclosures
were devised by Navarre to bring about a definitive split
between the king and Guise.[15] Poulain pleaded with the king
to believe him. He even tried to prove his loyalty by asking
Henry to arrest him along with several members of the Sixteen; then, if the facts did not prove correct, the king might
hang him. But Henry's only action in the face of this dilemma
was again to order Guise to stay away from Paris. What
Henry shrank from admitting, the Florentine ambassador,
Filippo Cavriana, recognized as the brewing of "one of the

largest revolts and rebellions ever heard of, which will, I fear, compel me within a month to write you of most extraordinary events." [16]

By late April the clamorings of the League against the king finally frightened him into action. On April 24 he sent Pomponne de Bellièvre, counselor in the Privy Council, along with Philibert de la Guiche, sieur de Chaumont and governor of Lyonnais (who was also grand master of artillery), to Soissons to persuade the duke of Guise that he should not come to Paris. Bellièvre assured Guise that the king did not believe the calumnies circulated against the duke, and preferred to arrive at some mutual understanding with him — but not in Paris.[17] On the following day Henry dispatched Épernon into Normandy to take possession of that vacated governorship, to make sure of the loyalty of Rouen, and to collect troops "for any eventuality." [18] Shortly thereafter the rumor spread among the Catholics of France that Épernon had instigated a plot with the Huguenots to set fire to Paris on the day before Easter.

In spite of Bellièvre's pleas and threats,[19] Guise left Soissons on Sunday, May 8, and arrived in Paris around noon the following day. The events of the next five days are general knowledge to students of sixteenth-century French history and can be found retold in numerous books on that period. What is not so widely known is that the Day of the Barricades was not instigated by Guise, nor Henry, nor the Paris League, but was part of the over-all plan of attack made in Madrid by Philip II in conjunction with the sailing of the Armada.[20] Guise's delay in February, which had created such consternation among the Paris Leaguers, was caused by the untimely death of the marquis of Santa Cruz, commander of the Armada, and its accompanying delay of the sailing. Perhaps Guise might not have ventured to move at all if he had not been ordered to do so.[21] He had a great deal to lose if the venture failed, and a somewhat less than certain reward if it succeeded.

The relation between France and England at the time was ambiguous yet too important in Philip's plans to be left unattended. Henry and Elizabeth had been on better terms than any previous monarchs of these two states for years, and their respective designs on the Netherlands tended to crystallize into mutual sympathy for the rebel cause (as long as the only real power there was neither French nor English, but Spanish). Henry even went so far as to promise aid to the English if they were attacked by Spain.[22] Whether this promise would be fulfilled, or whether it was made simply to flatter the queen, Philip could not afford to find out.

Philip needed two things from France in order to insure the success of his Armada: ports with supplies for refurbishing any ships damaged by the treacherous Atlantic waters and for protective harbors; and assurances that the king of France would be unable to fulfill his promise of aid to Elizabeth.[23] Parma also insisted that his flank would have to be protected before he could take his main army into England.[24] Mendoza's exaggerated fear that Henry would actually aid Elizabeth caused him in the early months of 1588 to work unceasingly for a neutralized France.

Philip's long preparations were almost complete. In March he sent Guise 300,000 escudos with orders to do something in May to occupy Henry's attention.[25] At the same time Mendoza prepared the Paris League for a general demonstration against the king, to be coordinated with the sailing of the Armada. On April 14 he reported:

If the project in question is carried out as planned, the king will have his hands so full that it will be impossible for him, either by words or by deeds, to give aid to the English queen. It is for this reason that I have thought it wise to delay the execution of the project until the moment Your Majesty's Armada is on the point of departure.[26]

With this evidence little doubt can remain that the activities in Paris associated with the Day of the Barricades were minutely planned by Philip and put into operation by his enterprising ambassador. The exact details of the plan are not disclosed in Mendoza's papers, but it is apparent that he was in constant touch with Guise and that every move of the latter was governed by instructions from the ambassador.[27] Even in March, when Bellièvre arrived at Soissons to dissuade him from entering Paris, Guise first dispatched his courier, De Bray, to inquire of Mendoza the kind of answers he should give the king's secretary and how much longer he should delay before he should make his move.[28] By the middle of April, Mendoza could report to Philip that "Arrangements here [in Paris] are already well advanced and a considerable number of gentlemen have arrived to combine in its execution."[29] Ten days later Philip informed Parma of Mendoza's "démarche auprès d'Henri III," which, with Guise's cooperation, would enable Parma to rendezvous with the Armada without fear of the French troops which were at the time massed in Picardy.[30]

To make certain that Guise understood his part well and to insure his loyalty in carrying it out Philip dispatched a personal representative to him at Soissons. Commander Juan de Moreo, who had also assisted at the signing of the Treaty of Joinville, promised Guise that, as soon as he had control of the king, Philip would sever relations with Henry III, withdraw his ambassador from the French court, and accredit him (or another) to Guise and the League, who would be considered the provisional government of France until the cardinal of Bourbon was crowned.[31] He also offered Guise a stand-by force of 6000 infantry and 1000 to 1200 horse, which would be waiting at the frontier for Guise's disposition, and another 300,000 escudos in cash — both pending, of course, the success of the revolt.

Throughout the negotiations, however, Philip maintained a strong outward show of legality and legitimacy. He would grant material aid to the League in fighting heresy but not in overthrowing the crown, even though he believed the revolution essential to the Catholic cause and had instigated it himself. Guise soon learned just how religiously Philip adhered to his strange principles when, after the successful revolt in Paris, Philip refused to recognize these so-called Articles of Soissons because Henry's government still stood. After the Day of the Barricades and the establishment of the Paris commune, a new arrangement had to be made between Philip and Guise.

The revolt in Paris was apparently also designed to draw Épernon out of Picardy and permit the Catholic parties there to control enough of the vital coast to provide ports of refuge for the Armada if they were needed. Considered particularly imperative in the Armada venture was the complete control of Boulogne, which was at that time loyal to Épernon and the king.[32] Previous attempts by Aumale to win the city had failed, but it was hoped that with Épernon away from Boulogne it could be dominated by League forces and used to great advantage, both in supporting the Armada and in preventing the embarkation of any possible aid to Elizabeth. On May 9 the Armada was finally ready to sail; at noon of the same day Guise began a triumphal entry into Paris.

THE DAY OF THE BARRICADES

The events of 9–12 May 1588, which Mendoza and others had been carefully planning for many weeks, were carried out so awkwardly and hesitatingly that most historians have been led to consider the entire affair a spontaneous revolt without direction or goals.[33] It is questionable how much the Paris masses knew about the project — probably little, if anything — but the higher echelons of the League were undoubtedly in very close contact with Guise. Mendoza's own reporting of the events throws some additional light on the meaning of the revolt, but on the whole his accounts are very impersonal.[34]

Accompanied by eight or nine of his closest followers, Guise entered the city at the Porte Saint-Martin and proceeded directly to the residence of the queen mother at Hôtel de Soissons. Soon he was recognized by people along the way who then burst into shouts of "Vive Guise! vive le pilier de l'Église!"[35] Before he was half way across the city, says the Florentine ambassador, a crowd of 30,000 had gathered around him until he could hardly proceed further.[36] Catherine de' Medici was astonished and frightened when she heard of his approach, even though the duke entered the palace, we are told by Enrico Davila (whose brother was one of Catherine's pages), "full of respective humility and profound submission."[37] When questioned about his purpose in coming to Paris, Guise replied that it was to defend himself against those who were blackening his character and slandering his name, and to justify his conduct to the king in person. Catherine did not question him further, but sent Luigi Davila to the Louvre to inform the king of Guise's arrival.

At the Louvre, Henry was in council with Villequier, Bellièvre, La Guiche, the Abbé del Bene, a Savoyard adviser to the king, and the fiery Corsican captain, Alphonse d'Ornano. Henry was thrown into a state of frustration and anger by the news of Guise's coming, and had he been endowed with more courage he might have taken the determined advice of Ornano to do away with Guise immediately. But a glance at the growing crowd in the streets below and the reasoned appeal of his mother to exercise moderation convinced Henry of the folly of such a move. The interview between the two men was short and curt, and its very occurrence, in defiance of the king's orders, was a strategic victory for Guise. As the duke returned to his headquarters at the Hôtel de Guise, exhausted by the ordeal of the audacious meeting, Henry feverishly began adding to the strength of his palace guard.

The following day, May 10, Guise and the king met again in the Louvre palace, but this time the duke was accompanied by a suite of 400 followers, carefully armed. Their conversations were cordial on matters of war with the Huguenots, the activities of Épernon, and the allegiance of the citizenry of Paris, but throughout the day both sides cautiously mobilized their military strength. By nightfall the Louvre and the Hôtel de Guise gave the appearance of two great arsenals.[38]

On Wednesday, May 11, Henry's reception of Guise was notably colder for he had received word that the 4000 Swiss infantry and 2000 French guards he had summoned from Lagny were now approaching the gates of Paris. Henry sent Marshal Biron to bring them into the city and ordered his Parisian forces — archers of the Scottish guard, the Swiss royal guards, and the French guard — to stand by at the Louvre.[39] Before dawn on the morning of May 12, the distant roll of drums and sound of the fifes announced Biron's entry at the head of the regiment of seasoned Swiss professionals. Quickly and in perfect order the marshal divided the companies and posted them at the Pont Saint-Michel, the Petit Châtelet, la Place de Saint-Jacques, at the bridges to the Ile-de-la-Cité, and at other strategic squares and intersections.[40]

Guise, in the meantime, fortified his own position and sent the papal nuncio, Morosini, to the king to beg him not to bring troops into the city, for it would certainly lead to a great and useless slaughter. The threat of the king's new force stunned the populace at first, and for more than an hour the city lay in hushed abeyance; but stupefaction soon gave way to indignation as barricades began springing up throughout the city. Chains were stretched across the streets and furniture, stones, and debris were heaped into fortifications, as rumors spread that the troops had been summoned to massacre the Catholic leaders in Paris and all who supported them. The loyalist captains awaited the order to attack and destroy the barricades before they became too strong. But the order did not come. Henry, in another of his moments of stupor, did nothing.

Suddenly, from the Latin Quarter across the river poured a flood of students, clerks, priests, and shopkeepers who had breached the loyalist weak spot at the Place Maubert. For some unknown reason, Davila notes, Biron had failed to secure this key square adequately. Mendoza infers that it was more than oversight that caused Biron to neglect Maubert, and further declares that Marshal Brissac was sent to the Latin Quarter by Guise to organize the students at the university. The flare-up at Place Maubert was the signal for a general uprising throughout Paris as the cathedral bells called the city to arms.[41] By noon the soldiers were helplessly cut off and at the mercy of the frenzied populace. Barricades were within fifty yards of the Louvre. The people now charged the soldiers from all sides and with every weapon at their grasp — stones, tiles, bricks, and arquebuses. Still the king gave no order for the troops to attack. Finally the Swiss, exhausted by fatigue and hunger and exasperated by the king's torpidity, abandoned their officers and surrendered to the cheering barricaders. Mendoza reported that 300 of the Swiss had been killed in the short but furious encounter. As their more famous successors were to repeat two centuries later, the Paris populace had defied and defeated the king of France.

Henry's attempt to overawe Paris by a parade of force had backfired ominously and now by mid-afternoon he knew he must negotiate or lose everything. Within the hour Catherine de' Medici was escorted into the Hôtel de Guise to learn the duke's terms for surrender. His demands were stern and definite: (1) Guise should be made lieutenant-governor of the kingdom; (2) his appointment must be confirmed by an assembled Estates General in Paris; (3) Navarre and any other prince of the house of Condé to be irrevocably excluded from succession to the throne; (4) the duke of Épernon, and any other enemies of the League in Henry's councils, should be deprived of office and permanently banished from court; (5) the king's private guard, the *Taillagambi*, was to be disbanded; (6) principal governmental posts were to be given to the heads of the League and faithful Catholics; and (7) administrative regulations were to be established which the king should have no power to change.[42]

Henry's counselors were divided. Some wanted him to refuse the impertinent demands and wage war on Guise, others counseled appeasement, while Catherine believed further negotiation could bring easier terms.[43] The next morning, Friday the thirteenth, it was decided between Henry and his most intimate advisors that escape was the only alternative remaining. Most sources affirm that Catherine took part in the decision for Henry's flight, but Mendoza suggests that she was as much in the dark about the king's plans as anyone was. Whatever the case, that night as Catherine occupied Guise with several hours of verbal patter, Henry and fifteen or sixteen of his courtiers rode out of Paris through the unguarded Porte Neuve adjoining the Tuilleries, vowing never to set foot in the city again until it was at the head of a victorious army. Guise did not become aware of the king's escape until the latter was well on his way to Chartres.

The impact of the Day of the Barricades on the European courts was immediate and varied. Philip II, as might be anticipated, expressed no surprise and very little concern, except over the escape of Henry III. This he felt was unfortunate and, of course, altered his responsibility to Guise, since the duke had not carried out his "operation" with complete success.[44] The duke of Parma was even more distressed over the king's escape, believing that Guise's blunder could eventually prove costly.[45] The reaction of the pope was one of incredulous disgust at the cowardly performance of the French king. From a personal interview with the pope, Giovanni Gritti, the Venetian envoy, reported to the doge the following pontifical remarks about Henry's conduct:

> Why did he call the Swiss? Either he suspected the Duke, or he did not. If he did, why did he not retain him, and if he had found that by retaining him a disturbance ensued (which would not have proved the Duke's culpability) why not cut his head off, and throw it into the street? People would have been appeased. . . . It is said that, if the Duke were killed, the "Lorraine," who was armed, would have created a disturbance, and revenged himself. Nothing of the kind would have occurred. Not a soul would have moved. Now the King has left Paris. What had he to fear? and if he had anything to fear, how can he seek his salvation in a flight from his capital? If, in the riots which have taken place at Venice, your forefathers had fled, would they have left you that liberty (the independence of the Republic) which you enjoy? Why fly from Paris? From fear of being killed? If he had been killed, he would at least have died as a king.[46]

The repercussions in France were also varied. Navarre was surprised at the audacity of Guise, but quickly perceived the advantage it had given him in the probable severing of the Nemours alliance. As a result of the Barricades, Politique opposition to the League became stronger and more outspoken. This flagrant humiliation of the king brought many of the moderates to a realization of their danger, and to a commitment in favor of the crown and against the League. The Parlement de Paris, in spite of quick retaliation by Guise, also declared its loyalty to the king.[47]

The apprehension disclosed by Philip and Parma and the amazement expressed by Sixtus V were not shared by Mendoza, who was satisfied that his immediate project in France had been a success. The ambassador's attitude has been described in this manner by Garrett Mattingly in his recent study on the Armada:

> If Bernardino de Mendoza was worried about the king's escape from Paris, he did not show it. Between the lines of his severely factual account of the Day of the Barricades, one can read the pride of the craftsman in a difficult, complicated piece of work punctually and successfully accomplished. Whether Henry III knuckled under

to Guise now or tried to oppose him scarcely mattered. Epernon could not hold Normandy now, and there was no longer the slightest danger that the French would molest the Low Countries in Parma's absence. Parma's flank was secured and so was Medina Sidonia's. As far as danger from France was concerned, the Armada had sailed in perfect safety, just as Mendoza had promised that it should.[48]

Guise had probably blundered in letting the king escape at the very moment of his triumph, just as Henry had in not taking more forceful action against the duke on May 9 when Guise was almost completely in his power, and again in his confused handling of the Swiss and French troops. But now that it was over Guise felt somewhat relieved that he did not have to hold the king a precarious and dangerous prisoner in Paris. With the Sixteen and other League officials of the city, he now began to reorganize the municipal government.

On May 14, the Arsenal and the Bastille surrendered to Guise without a shot, the Château de Vincennes was seized, and the barricades quickly disappeared. Loyalist officials were removed from office, and opponents of the Catholic cause were arrested. Guise was the hero of the day and his appearance anywhere in the city brought cheers of praise and wild shouts of "À Reims!" [49] (where the kings of France were crowned). On Sunday, May 15, the fanatical preachers of Paris, for the first time in months, exhorted their congregations to obedience and quiescence.[50]

The next step, which was greatly facilitated by the existing League organization, was to form a provisional government for the city. The completed commune, instituted at the Hôtel de Ville between May 17-20, was a truly revolutionary organization.[51] The municipal charter under which Paris had been governed since 1380 was overthrown in favor of a usurped regency ruling in the name of the cardinal of Bourbon. Selected members of the lower classes replaced many of the old municipal families in important positions, while the League obtained a constitutional status by identifying itself with the municipality.[52] The city militia was absorbed by the

League and its royalist captains replaced by "elected" Guisard officers.[53] Bussi Le-Clerc became governor of the Bastille, and the jurisdiction of the Châtelet was given over to the League.[54] La Chapelle-Marteau became *prévôt des marchands* (mayor), and Nicolas Roland, Jean de Compans, François de Costeblanche, and Robert des Prés were named as *échevins* (magistrates in the governing council, the *Bureau de la Ville*).[55] Pierre d'Épinac, archbishop of Lyon, was Guise's closest personal and political advisor.[56] The only stumbling block in the municipal reorganization was the Parlement de Paris, with its devoutly royalist president, Achille de Harlay, who refused to recognize the new government.[57] This situation was not immediately solved by Guise, and during the succeeding months the Parlement de Paris continued to increase the scope and effectiveness of its resistance to the League.

As soon as the Day of the Barricades was over, Guise began a propaganda campaign to present the events of the preceding days in favorable light to the other cities and people of France. His letters urged the other "good cities of the realm" to unite with the Leaguers of Paris in throwing off the oppressive Valois yoke.[58] Many League cities, like Amiens and Orléans, responded immediately by electing new magistrates and officers and by associating themselves more closely with the Paris League.

PERSONA NON GRATA

Mendoza does not reveal in his letters the extent nor the type of assistance he gave to the Paris revolt during the "Barricades." Perhaps he preferred to remain in the background, after having participated and led in its planning, but it is more likely that he also took an active part in its execution. At least the French king was convinced that he had, for on May 20 he wrote to Philip II, complaining about the actions of the Spanish ambassador and accusing

Mendoza of having taken sides in the domestic affairs of France and given valuable assistance to the League in its rebellion against the crown.[59] At the same time, Henry ordered his ambassador in Madrid, Longleé, to present formal charges against Mendoza to the Spanish king.[60]

This was an extremely delicate situation. Henry III was still king of France, if not of Paris, and as such could refuse to acknowledge the credentials of any foreign ambassador. Philip knew this, but he also knew that Mendoza was indispensable in France at the present crucial moment. For almost a year Mendoza's movements had been under close surveillance by agents of the crown, but until the Day of the Barricades he had covered himself well enough to remain free from incrimination, if not from suspicion. In July 1587, Philip had warned Mendoza that he was being watched in Paris and that Longlée suspected him of being intermediary in negotiations between Guise and Parma over military assistance to the League. Philip instructed his ambassador on how to answer these charges, should they be made against him by the French king, and admonished him to proceed with caution in his vital work.

On the first point, reply in general and elusive terms that no one should be astonished at the amity I show for the duke of Parma, my cousin, and that I cannot believe he would plan anything that might be harmful to France. Besides, the news of the German levies could not but cause the taking of extra precautions for the security of my estates which the duke will do without the slightest deviation from the path of peace and loyalty . . .

In response to the denunciations against the duke of Guise, say that the same considerations prompt me never to interfere in questions foreign to me. As for you, guard with the greatest secrecy the intelligences which you might have with Mucio, or with the others, concerning both the duke of Parma as well as yourself. And in summary, assure the king of France always that I have no other purpose than the good of his kingdom, which results in the glory of our Lord Jesus Christ, and the success of the Catholic cause.[61]

During the invasion in the fall of 1587, everyone in Paris was too concerned about saving his own life and property to keep a close eye on the Spanish ambassador, but by the beginning of 1588 Mendoza was again being carefully watched by Henry's agents. Early in February, Longlée sent a dispatch to Henry recommending that he ask for Mendoza's recall,[62] and a week later, he reminded the French king that Mendoza should be recognized "as an insolent man, with evil intentions and very pernicious." [63] But at that point Henry could not risk making another enemy; he already had more than he could manage. He was still on friendly terms with the king of Spain and hoped to stay that way, at least until he found himself in a stronger position at home. For the time being he decided to say nothing to Philip about Longlée's suspicions and ordered his ambassador to do the same.[64]

By June the situation had radically changed. Away from Paris, Henry felt much more daring. He was aware of the part Mendoza had taken in the revolt, and knew that Spain not only favored the League but had a formal alliance with it. He also knew that, because of the Armada, Philip had as much need for his friendship as he had for Philip's, so he could afford to be somewhat more demanding. Besides, by publicizing Mendoza's activities Henry might win valuable sympathy in some of the other courts of Europe. On July 10, therefore, in response to Henry's orders, Longlée presented to the king of Spain a formal written protest against Mendoza's participation in the recent Paris affair and against the supposed threat of armed intervention from Parma's troops in Flanders.[65]

After careful deliberation, Philip issued a written reply to Longlée on July 18; on July 26 he sent a copy of it to Henry, along with a short note of explanation.[66] Philip's reply was a surprise and shock to Henry. Far from condemning Mendoza, it praised him highly for his fidelity and energy in performing his duties. If it appeared at times that the ambassador was acting outside the range of his commission, Philip explained, it was only because his zeal in the Catholic cause made it difficult for him to remain idle during such an affair as the recent Paris turmoil. His Most Christian Majesty could rest assured, said Philip, that Mendoza's intentions were always for the maintenance of friendship between their two kingdoms and the promotion of the Catholic cause, "in which Your Majesty, too, has always made such a show of assisting." [67] Philip concluded his message with a sharp reprimand for the French king himself to show more diligence in the future in defending the principles he proclaimed and stop interfering with those who were trying to promote the "service and glory of God, the good of the Catholic cause, and obedience to the Roman Church."

On July 28, the Spanish Council of State reviewed Philip's note to Longlée and granted a full approval of its contents. They also recommended that a copy of the reply be sent to Mendoza and to Guise.[68] Three days later, Philip sent a copy of the document to Mendoza, which he was to show to Catherine de' Medici and to Guise, and included a note commending Mendoza on his faithful service during the Paris difficulties.

> With this I am remitting to you what I set forth in a letter of the 18th of the present in response to the note of Longlée, which you are to give to the queen mother. You will see by the other copy I have sent . . . that you are not committed to deliver it to the king, since no one is sure where he is, and because of the jealousy and ill will he shows toward you, although I am very satisfied with the way you have served me. I send you this other copy for your own information; you do not have to do anything with the king about it.[69]

The effect of this affair, as might be expected, was an outward surrender by Henry III to Philip's will, but a justifiable intensification of his sullen hatred of Mendoza, and of Guise.

THE EDICT OF UNION

Catherine de' Medici soon began her efforts to make some reconciliation between the king and Paris, and once more became the chief agent in negotiations between her son and the duke of Guise. A week after Henry fled from Paris, the League presented a memo to Catherine stating its terms for an agreement with Henry. It was primarily a charge against

Épernon and his brother as the principal causes of the financial and religious evils of the realm. The League memorandum also requested that two armies be raised and sent against the heretics — one to be commanded by the duke of Mayenne and the other by the king, with Catherine remaining in Paris as regent of the crown. Catherine rejected the proposals with the counterdemand that first the city of Paris must "lay proper submission at the foot of the king." [70]

In the meantime, negotiations with Henry were opened on another level through the mediation of Jean de la Barrière, abbé de Feuillants.[71] Tentatively, Henry agreed to abandon his mignons, and when Épernon arrived at Chartres on May 22, the king told him he would have to resign the governorships of Normandy, Metz, Saintonge, and Angoumois. Épernon agreed to give up Normandy, provided it was not given to his enemies, but he refused categorically to release the others. In a rage he left for Angoulême where he opened negotiations with the Politiques and Huguenots of the south.[72] On May 24 a delegation from Paris arrived at Chartres and received from the king a promise of forgiveness to all Parisians who had aided Guise on the Day of the Barricades if they would now return to their duty of loyalty to the crown. Henry also announced his willingness to convoke the Estates General at the end of the year and submit to that body's selection of a Catholic successor to Henry.[73] In June, Henry moved to Rouen where he continued treating with the League through the mediation of his mother and the abbé de Feuillants.[74]

The negotiations continued throughout the month of June. Every facet was considered, every possibility exploited by both sides to gain their ends. In an emotional interview with Mendoza on June 28, Catherine tried desperately to get the Spanish ambassador to guarantee that no Spanish army in the Netherlands would give aid to the enemies of the French crown — meaning Guise and the League, of course. Mendoza replied curtly that Henry had helped the late duke of Anjou in support of the Dutch rebels, and further reminded her that at least the Leaguer princes were good Catholics.[75] Mendoza for his part tried to get Catherine to agree to a union of their two kingdoms with all the other Catholic states of Europe in a holy crusade against heresy.[76]

Day by day Henry became more weary of negotiations and more confused about his political and religious allegiances. Soon he began granting more and more of the League demands until by early July he had conceded almost everything. The thirty-two articles of the *Edict d'Union* were drawn up and signed at Paris on July 15, then sent to the king in Rouen and incorporated into the larger Treaty of Rouen. The edict was then signed by the king and sent to the Parlement de Paris for registration.[77] According to this Edict of Union, the kingdom was now to submit to the church, Protestant succession was renounced, and Épernon was disgraced. Guise was created commander-in-chief of the army and lieutenant-general of the kingdom. Aumale was given the governorship of Picardy, Montpensier that of Normandy, the duke of Nemours that of Lyonnais, and the cardinal of Guise was appointed legate of Avignon. The king also agreed, in conformity with the League demands, that the decrees of the Council of Trent would be published and observed in France, political interests of the king would be subordinated to religion, the alliance with England would be repudiated, and the Estates General would be convened at Blois in September.[78]

The edict was duly registered by the Parlement on July 21, and on August 3, Guise and the king met at Chartres for their first encounter since the Day of the Barricades. The meeting was neither cordial nor hostile. Henry, without fear, since he had almost nothing left to lose, proposed a toast, "To our good friends the Huguenots," then added with a disturbing smile, "and to our good barricaders of Paris, we must not forget to pledge them also." [79] Guise returned the smile as he drank, but the king's jest carried sinister overtones.

Chapter VIII

TRIUMPH OF THE LEAGUE

✤ ✤ ✤ ✤

THE spectacle of the humiliation of the French king by an ambitious noble supported by the unruly masses of Paris and a rather sinister organization of fanatical propagandists and revolutionaries left a deep impression on the minds of thoughtful Europeans. Even those who did not yet comprehend the meaning of the revolution which was taking place in France nor the extent of Spanish involvement in French affairs understood that the event was not only unique but highly charged with implications and dangers and that a landmark had in some ways been passed. The League had reached its pinnacle but in doing so had planted the seeds of its own destruction.

MENDOZA AND THE ARMADA

Throughout the summer of 1588, Mendoza's chief concern was the vital Armada venture. His instructions were explicit and he fulfilled them well, considering the improbity of the monarchy with which he had to deal and the complete chaos of political and religious loyalties in France. He had been instructed in April to secure from Henry III the guarantee of friendly treatment to any ships of the Armada which might make port at a French harbor,[1] and a promise to issue no decrees which would make it difficult for merchants of these towns to sell supplies for the Spanish vessels. He was also charged with obtaining the complete loyalty of one or two ports near the Flanders coast, preferably Boulogne and Calais, to prevent any possible French aid from reaching Elizabeth, and to insure the safety of the Armada while it was loading Parma's *tercios*.[2]

Allusive promises of a similar sort had already been granted by Henry on numerous occasions, but Philip wanted to make it a matter of formal treaty. He was unable to postpone the sailing of the Armada again so had to rely solely upon Mendoza's assurances of a successful agreement being reached. An audience was duly arranged by Villeroy between Henry and Mendoza for May 12, at which time these agreements were to be concluded. This meeting was never held. As Henry fled from the capital, he left word for all ambassadors to deal henceforth with the queen mother as his regent in Paris. On May 23, Mendoza was granted an audience with Catherine and his complete proposals were laid before her. On nearly every point she acquiesced to his demands, and formal agreements were reached for free entry and exit for ships of the Armada at all French ports.[3]

Mendoza knew Henry well enough not to consider the contract reached with Catherine a positive guarantee of open ports. Consequently, he decided to go to Chartres in person and demand not only Henry's guarantee of no aid to Elizabeth and free ports to Spanish vessels, but even to suggest Henry's active support of the Armada enterprise. The ambassador's stirring address to the king on that occasion was shortly published in a small brochure, a few copies of which are still in existence.[4] Mendoza boldly declared that the title held by the king of France and the examples and heritage left by his predecessors obliged him to render faithful obedience to the Roman Church at all times. Especially now, when Christendom was in such grave danger from heresies fostered and supported by the queen of England, it was his sacred duty to assist the king of Spain in his holy enterprise. Furthermore, he reminded Henry, Elizabeth had committed a shocking crime against the church, against royalty, and even against the French people, by her execution of Mary Queen of Scots, who was also a queen of France, and for this crime Elizabeth would have to pay. He called on Henry to forbid his subjects from impeding the success of Philip's plans by placing obstacles in its path and to offer whatever positive assistance he could toward the righteous venture.

Henry's answer to the trenchant ambassador was agreeable and submissive. There remained but two kinds of subjects in his realm, the king replied, just as in that of the Most Catholic King: the one was obedient to his commands, and the other was not. As to the former, he could assure the ambassador that they would neither help nor favor the queen of England, and the latter he would hamper as best he could.

Mendoza knowingly took Henry's docile reply suspiciously, and proceeded to promote his sovereign's cause by additional means. First he made every effort to secure several ports in Picardy by encouragement and increased subsidies to the duke d'Aumale, who had been in the province for several months consolidating the League positions there. In July he obtained from Philip an extra 25,000 escudos to be used for securing the necessary French ports.[5] Mendoza and Guise also employed the 300,000 escudos promised by Philip in raising an army from the League towns of northern France. This force was to be mobilized along the frontier and as soon as Parma embarked with his army for England it was to move into Flanders and maintain Parma's lines.[6] Mendoza's purpose in advocating this maneuver seems to have been not so much to keep the Netherlands from advancing into the territories held by Parma as to prevent Henry from taking advantage of Parma's absence and marching a force of his own into Flanders.[7]

During June and July, Mendoza carefully gathered every scrap of information gleaned by his agents concerning the Armada's sailing and the preparations being made in England to oppose it, and rushed these by courier to Philip.[8] Mendoza knew of the Armada's first encounter with the Atlantic gales and its unfortunate delays at Coruña almost as soon as Philip did, and reports of the first engagement of the two fleets off Plymouth were received and confirmed by Mendoza less than a week after the event.[9]

Then came news of the August 2 encounter off Portland Bill, which reported that Medina Sidonia had successfully cut the English fleet in two and had won a decisive victory for the Armada. Agents in Le Havre, Dieppe, and Calais rushed this news to the Italian merchant Issoardo Capello, in Rouen, who in turn brought it to Mendoza on August 8. Mendoza's brief report of the victory, sent to Philip on the 9th, reached Madrid on August 18, and was the king's first notice of the encounter.[10] In his dispatches of August 10, the ambassador reported in greater detail on the Armada's success, and included in the pouch Capelo's own letter and a five-page account sent by Mendoza's agent in Rouen, which had now been put into cipher.[11]

In triumph Mendoza rode off to Chartres, without waiting for the confirmation of his report, to announce the victory in person to Henry III, and to secure further the Spanish-League domination of the French king. As he neared the imposing spires of the Chartres cathedral, Mendoza must have felt mounting pride in the momentous success of "The Enterprise" in which he had played such a significant part. Forneron records that "Mendoza arrived at Chartres, dismounted from his horse in front of the great doors of the Cathedral, and announced that he had received news of a grand victory for the Spanish forces, demanding therefore that a *Te Deum* be sung in their honor." Then, says Forneron, in the midst of this triumphant procession, Henry coldly remarked that he had received more recent news from Calais which announced a complete victory for the English fleet. Mendoza, shocked by this sudden turn of events, returned to Paris, "couvert de confusion." [12]

Philip received word of the great victory "that God has given my Armada, after its giving battle to that of the enemy on the 2nd," with great rejoicing. It was the first news of the engagement received by the king, and in a very cheerful reply to his ambassador, on August 18, Philip thanked Mendoza for his alert reporting of this and other happenings, and encouraged him to keep up the good work, expressing the hope that all his letters might bring equally good news. [13]

But they did not. The next reports received by Mendoza told of less favorable skirmishes between the two great armadas, and the following days brought more news of indecisive encounters, of fire ships, canonnades, and mishaps, but no word of a rendezvous with Parma's troops nor of a landing in England. [14] The invasion which was intended to bring England back to the Catholic fold and end its exasperating aid to the Dutch was not to be. Unable to achieve its primary purpose, the Armada also failed to accomplish its secondary — the breaking of the English naval power. Mendoza's four years of longing for a triumphant return to London to fulfill his oath to the despised queen had come to a disastrous end.

Throughout August and September, a few remnants of the scattered fleet limped into French ports where their reception varied from open arms and willing aid to a barrage of canon fire from the coastal guns. [15] When Mendoza learned of the hostile reception at some of the ports he stormed to the palace to demand an explanation from the queen mother for this violation of their agreement. In a dispatch to Philip late in August, he described his efforts to correct this situation, and explained that, in spite of Catherine's insistence that Henry had notified every coastal town of his friendship toward the king of Spain (though many of them, she said, had refused to accept the king's orders), the real reason for the action of the ports was that Henry had failed to apprise them of the agreement and they were therefore uninformed as to the intentions of the Spanish vessels.[16]

A matter which caused considerable excitement for a while was the escape of some sixty Turkish galley slaves from two ships stranded at Calais and Dieppe. Many of his associates, Mendoza remarked, thought he should take immediate action to have the slaves returned to their ships or, if that were impossible, to send them to Spain. The ambassador, however, refused to petition the French king for their return, for reasons which he outlined in a terse note to Philip on September 24. First of all, he explained, there still existed an ancient law in France (ignored, of course, but still useful for propaganda purposes) which said there were no slaves within the kingdom. Secondly, the cost of rounding up and transporting them back, plus the bad will it would cause, was more than the slaves were worth. Besides, Mendoza reflected, such a great concern and fretting over sixty or eighty galley slaves would hardly be commensurate with the size and might of His Majesty's Armada. Mendoza made no protest, therefore, when the Turks petitioned the Most Christian King, by right of his treaty with the Sultan, to return them to their own land. Henry III, with a great show of magnanimity, gave them two écus apiece and transported them to Marseilles where they were set free.[17]

Still Mendoza held as tenaciously to his faith in the Armada as he possibly could, and grasped at the occasional bits of evidence of its safety to assure Philip that the reports of its destruction were mere rumors spread by the English. On September 24 he announced the arrival of a ship from Lübeck, which reportedly had met the Armada in the North Sea. The seamen assured Mendoza that it was composed of 115 to 120 sails, and proceeding rapidly and in good order.[18] Mendoza also reported the arrival in Paris of a Danish diplomat who (as he rounded Scotland enroute from Lisbon) had seen the Armada passing between the Orkneys and Shetlands, and affirmed that there were 120 large ships plus many smaller ones. Furthermore, he declared, the men of the Armada had caught great quantities of fish while passing the Great Banks and had sold them to the Scots for goodly sums. In addition, he continued, the Armada had captured a large Dutch and English fishing fleet and was now returning to Spain with almost 300 ships! Eventually, however, even Mendoza had to admit that the Armada as such had been destroyed.

AFTERMATH OF THE ARMADA

The failure of the Armada to achieve its goals had a great effect upon the situation in France. Navarre had actually taken part on the side of England by sending a squadron of fourteen ships from La Rochelle to join Drake's fleet in July; thus he felt that the defeat of the Armada was, in part at least, a personal victory over the League and Spain. In the fall of 1588 he started to make positive plans for a more vigorous campaign against the League, since the danger from Spain had lessened. Épernon's allegiance and intentions were still uncertain, but from his headquarters at Angoulême he seemed at the moment to be increasingly friendly toward Navarre.

Guise found himself in an anomalous position after the Armada fiasco. The Catholic cause in general and his own paymaster in particular had suffered a great setback, yet his own and the League position in France had never been more favorable. The king had been reduced almost to impotence by the signing of the Edict of Union and by the royal *lettres patentes*, published on August 4 and 17, making Guise commander-in-chief of the French armies[19] and declaring the cardinal of Bourbon first prince of the blood and next in succession to the throne.[20] But Guise was not sure just how strong he might be without the backing of Spanish money and the assurance of Parma's *tercios* in an emergency. The strong support he had just received from the Paris League and the near unanimous acclaim of the French populace had given him additional courage and self-assurance which at times bordered on rashness.

The Armada disaster was a deep personal blow to Mendoza who, no less than Philip himself, had had unfaltering faith in its success. Nevertheless, he was a realist, and, although it seemed incomprehensible that the tragedy could have occurred, it had, and that meant only that he must now put forth even greater efforts to improve their position in France, which now became more vital than ever before. His first step was to reaffirm Spanish support and assistance to Guise and the League; the second would be determined by the degree of Catholic success in the forthcoming Estates General at Blois.

Mendoza was also more realistic about Henry's schemes than was Guise. On August 9, he sent a long communication to Philip giving his favorable opinion of the recent *rapprochement* between Henry and the League, but expressing his doubts about its permanency and his suspicion of the means to which the Valois king might resort in order to re-establish his power.[21] He warned Guise to beware of the king's unreliability, but Guise confidently reminded him of his many friends around the court and assured Mendoza that they would advise him if he were in danger. Villeroy himself, Guise remarked, would keep him informed on all of Henry's schemes.

As for Henry III, the defeat of the Spanish Armada had given him a new confidence and outlook. His fear of Spanish power and of Philip's resolute ambassador was reduced considerably, and his hatred of Guise and the League was now uncompromised. He had lost none of his duplicity, however, while regaining his nerve, and continued, after the news of the Armada fiasco, to play the role of sycophant of Guise and the League. On August 17 he followed up the honors bestowed upon Guise by granting almost unlimited powers to the cardinal of Bourbon.[22]

Just when it seemed that Henry had completely resigned his crown to the League, he suddenly dropped a political bomb. On September 8, without the slightest forewarning, Henry carried out an abrupt palace coup. With a curt note, written in his own hand, he dismissed eight of his closest advisors and secretaries: Chancellor Chéverney, first counselor of state Bellièvre, secretaries of state Villeroy, Brulart, and Pinart, the royal steward Combault, and the royal treasurers Grand-le-Roy and Molant.[23] They were immediately replaced by relatively unknown men who had shown persistent loyalty to the king and who had no dealings with the queen mother. François de Montholon, a former advocate of the Parlement de Paris, became the new keeper of the seals; Martin Ruzé de Baulieu, Louis Revol, and M. de Fizes became secretaries of state.[24] The new secretaries were also forbidden to hire subordinates who had previously served under the dismissed ministers.

Mendoza disclosed no particular reaction to the dismissals, but in a dispatch of September 24, he reported that Henry justified his actions to his mother on the grounds that "the chancellor was a grafter, Bellièvre a Huguenot, Villeroy an ambitious braggart who wanted to keep all business in his own hands, Brulart was worthless, and Pinart an avaricious scoundrel who would sell his own father and mother." [25] Villeroy maintained that Henry had accused him of having too much credit and authority, of opening letters and pouches without the king being present, and writing letters and instructions to many on his own responsibility, revealing state secrets to the League.[26] Mendoza believed, however, that the real reason for the palace coup was Henry's plan for recapturing his power, and he needed men close to him whom he could trust and who had no other commitments.[27]

The king had suspected (with reason) that his former ministers really considered Catherine the king of France and reported directly to her rather than to him. Now, with his fear of Spanish power reduced, Henry intended to make his word supreme in France. He was now ready to make his first bid for power since the humiliating Day of the Barricades. If he could control the Estates General, which was to convene in the Château de Blois beginning on September 15, he would soon control the refractory provinces of France (except those under Huguenot rule). "You would hardly believe," reported Guise to Mendoza on September 21, "all the artifices resorted to here [by Henry] for hindering the affairs of the king of Spain." [28]

THE ESTATES GENERAL OF BLOIS

While the king was occupied with his council changes and with dreams of the future, Guise and other members of the League were busy soliciting support for the show of force in the Estates General. Into every province and district, except those controlled by the Huguenots, Guise sent men to preach the importance of sending responsible Catholics to the assembly to insure its success. By early September he confided to Mendoza that he was certain a majority of the delegates would support the League in all of its efforts at Blois.

> Throughout all France they are trying to arrange the election of deputies who favor the princes of the blood, and want, under pretext of lessening taxes, peace with the Huguenots. I have left nothing undone on my side, but have sent into all the provinces and *baillages* men whom I can trust to work against their efforts. I believe that I have so far succeeded that the majority of the deputies will be for us.[29]

Guise further informed Mendoza that he was prepared for any tricks the king might try. "The marquis of Conti, the count of Soissons, and the duke of Montpensier [princes of the blood who had been vacillating between loyalty to the king or to the Huguenots] will come here within a few days with a train of nobles, mostly Huguenots. I have sent word to my friends in all directions and I shall not be the weaker." [30]

A number of factors favored Guise on the eve of the convocation of the Estates General. His ambitious leadership had endeared him to all of the League partisans and the ardent Catholics of France, as well as to many others who admired his animation and verve. His zealous Catholicism had finally won him the confidence and esteem of Philip II. In spite of the duke's apparent strength, however, Mendoza sensed a situation of impending danger and warned Guise not to attend the Estates General in person, lest he meet the same fate as his father.[31] But Guise, now more certain of himself and of his position than he had ever been, reassured Mendoza and Philip of his personal safety.

The results of the elections tended to verify Guise's confidence. Of the 191 deputies elected by the third estate, 150 belonged to the Parisian or provincial leagues. The nobility was more divided: 96 were Leaguers and 84 were not. The 134 members of the clergy, however, were Leaguers almost to the last man, giving the League an over-all strength of 380 out of a total of 505 deputies.[32] At the organization of the three estates, La Chapelle-Marteau was elected president of the third estate, the count of Brissac became spokesman for the nobles, and the cardinal of Guise represented the first estate. The Huguenots were unrepresented at the Estates General but called an assembly of their own among the Protestant provinces of France, which convened at La Rochelle in November.[33]

The assembly was scheduled to open on September 15, but, as preparations could not be completed in time, the opening session was postponed until October 16. In the meantime, a sudden shift in the international situation almost upset Guise's carefully made plans. At this ill-chosen moment, Charles Emmanuel, duke of Savoy, decided to invade the tiny French-held marquisate of Saluzzo in northwestern Italy. Saluzzo, with its chief town of Carmagnola, was the last remnant of French possessions in Italy, acquired during the Italian wars of the first half of the century. The marquisate was geographically associated with Piedmont and had long been coveted by Charles Emmanuel and his father. The immediate pretext for occupation was to protect it from the Huguenots.[34] Henry III was furious, and was easily convinced that this encroachment against French territory had been instigated by Guise. The king's council, the Politiques, and especially the Huguenots were certain that this was another attempt by Guise to betray the interests of France for his own evil designs. The insult so aroused the deputies at Blois that they accused Guise of treasonable conduct, and for a moment the entire second estate was willing to set everything else aside and prove to the world that the French could not yet be totally ignored in international affairs.

Contrary to the accusations, Guise was not guilty this time. News of the action of the duke of Savoy was as much a surprise to him as it was to the rest of Europe. His concern over the affair is attested by his first letter to Mendoza after the arrival of this news at Blois.

This accident of Carmagnola I fear will upset all my intentions and plans, and I am afraid the king may seize the opportunity for an agreement with the heretics in order to make war on the duke of Savoy. This could kindle a fire which would not be easy to extinguish and which would undoubtedly bring the ruin of Christendom and the loss of our religion. I beg you to consider this matter and find out if there is some means of pacifying the duke of Savoy, in order that we may continue our objectives here [at Blois].[35]

Four days later he complained further to the Spanish ambassador:

Concerning the news of Saluzzo, I hasten to send you word testifying to the apprehension I have over this dangerous accident which has occurred. If it had not been for this I was certain that, with the help of God and my friends, we would have obtained from the Estates a confirmation of the Edict of Union, along with an oath of the king and of the three estates for an express declaration of open war against the heretics to their final extermination, without his Majesty's being able to leave or enter into any treaty with them. . . . Soon even the Protestants and heretics of England and Germany would have been ruined. But now our plans are so upset by this new affair that already a good number of the deputies are ready to consent to a general peace with the Huguenots for the purpose of uniting with them, and if this is accomplished it will lead to the total desolation of our holy religion and the inevitable ruin of Christianity. Before matters become even worse, if there is something the king, your master, can do to intervene and, with his wisdom and authority, bring about a settlement, all good people will be infinitely obliged to him — and I believe it would be to the benefit and service of his own affairs.[36]

On this note of tension and discord the Estates General formally opened on 16 October 1588. The pageantry and ceremony of the auspicious gathering, which has been vividly portrayed by numerous contemporary writers, formed a bizarre backdrop for the critical events which were about to take place.[37] Guise, as grand master of the household, sat at the foot of the throne, facing the assembly, as Henry III rose to open the proceedings and address the august council. His speech was delivered with dignity, and at times approached eloquence, as he petitioned the estates to assist him in remedying the miseries of the country and in maintaining its monarchical and Catholic foundations. He paid a rich tribute to his mother's services and declared his intention of maintaining the church and appointing a Catholic successor. "Lend favor to my upright motives," he exhorted, "which are only to cause the glory of God and of our holy Catholic faith to shine forth more brightly, to extirpate heresy from the provinces of this kingdom, to re-establish good order, to relieve the poor people who are so greatly oppressed, and to raise up my own authority which is now so unjustly abased."[38]

But Henry's words began to fall on less receptive ears as he proclaimed, "The evidence is sufficiently well known . . . as to the zeal and steadfastness with which I have ever proceeded to the extirpation of heresy," and as he further declared, "God is my witness how freely I have convoked this assembly, and I have not intrigued against the liberty of the deputies nor corrupted the electors. Had I done so I would blush for my conduct, as those should blush who have resorted to such unworthy means." Finally, he turned to condemn the League and its leaders in a frontal attack. "Do not imagine that I alone am responsible for the afflictions of the country. . . . I am about to order matters so that those who have been blind enough to depart from their duty and their obedience will be constrained to recognize their error. By my Edict of Union," he continued, "I have expressly forbidden every association formed without my authority; all raising of troops and of money, both within and without my kingdom; and I now declare that those who persist in such criminal intelligence in spite of my prohibition shall be counted guilty of high treason." He concluded by declaring that he had been prevented from making the reforms he had intended, and from prosecuting the war against the heretics, by the "inordinate ambition" of some of his subjects, and charged the Estates General with the responsibility of supporting his "good intentions."

These were indeed bold words for Henry III, and they did not go unchallenged, although the succeeding speeches by Montholon, the archbishop of Bourges, and La Chapelle-Marteau, were complimentary to his words.[39] Enough pressure was exerted by Guise in the next two days to force Henry once more to swear to the Edict of Union (on October 18) and to have it publicly read and declared as a fundamental and irrevocable law of the land.[40]

On October 24, Guise was able to tell Mendoza, "At last, in full assembly of the Estates, our Edict of Union has been solemnly sworn to and established as a fundamental law of the kingdom, having surmounted all of the hindrances and difficulties made by the king."[41] He admitted that it had been a hard struggle and that the enterprise launched by the duke of Savoy had almost upset his chances of uniting enough of the deputies behind him to accomplish it. "It caused so strange an embarrassment," he confessed, "that it almost ruined the sequence of our plans, and alienated the good will of many of the Catholics." Mendoza took up the problem of Saluzzo, writing numerous dispatches to Philip about it and keeping Guise closely informed. Philip tried to remain aloof, though his sympathies were with his son-in-law. He refrained from open support of Savoy for fear of hurting his position in France.[42]

Guise was finally able to regain enough support from the first and second estates not only to have the Edict of Union proclaimed, but also to eliminate the Saluzzo affair from the agenda entirely and concentrate on heresy, finances, administration, and succession.[43] Week after week the estates made greater and greater demands of the king, and step by step he was forced to accede to their will. They won a slashing tax reduction, concessions against the sale of offices, and consideration of a proposal to declare Navarre guilty of *lèse-majesté*, thus making it impossible for him ever to succeed the throne.

With each concession made by the king, Guise and the Leaguers grew more sure of themselves and more careless in their actions. At every session of the first and third estates, insults were boldly poured out upon the king, and on every Sunday he was viciously assailed from the pulpit, until he hardly dared venture into the streets.[44] Henry's hatred of Guise deepened into loathing and malevolence as the gloom of winter descended on the stately château at Blois and turned its cold stone walls into a gray and silent mausoleum.

"THE KING OF PARIS IS DEAD"

The tragic termination of the Estates General at Blois has been vividly told many times and need not be recounted here except in its barest outlines.[45] Guise was not without warnings of the growing peril of his position; Mendoza remained in constant touch with him from Saint-Dié (a village a few miles east of Blois where the ambassador had retired at the end of October to be near the king and the Estates General) and cautioned him to be wary of the king, who was most dangerous when cornered.[46] He also passed on to Guise the frequent admonitions from Philip for his safety and moderation. A conference was even held by some of the heads of the League to decide whether he ought to leave Blois entirely until after the estates had adjourned, but it was finally decided that for the good of their cause he should remain at Blois.[47]

Guise refused to become alarmed in spite of the frequent warnings. "He who gives up the game," he is reported to have replied, "has lost it." He reminded Mendoza again that he had plenty of friends and "If an enterprise is begun against me, I shall end it more roughly than I did at Paris." "Moreover," he insisted, "had I a hundred lives, I would freely sacrifice them to be the means of giving some rest to the poor people of France, who are so grievously afflicted." [48]

As Christmas drew near, the king was seen to increase his devotions daily. He had arranged to go on December 23 to the famous shrine of Notre Dame de Cléry, but on the evening before he announced that he had decided to go instead to La Noue, a hermitage some six miles from the château.[49] A meeting of the royal council was called for 8 o'clock in the morning, giving him time to reach La Noue by noon, and Guise was summoned to be in attendance. In the meantime, Henry had instructed the members of his guard to be in his chamber at 5:00.

Contemporaries report that the weather on that day was the dreariest that had ever been known.[50] When Guise entered the council chamber where his brother the cardinal, the archbishop of Lyon, and a few others were gathered, he asked to have a fire kindled, and when its warm glow began to lift the gloom of the damp forboding chamber he joined the others at the table. Shortly after the council began its business, Révol, one of Henry's secretaries of state, appeared and announced that the king wished to see the duke of Guise in his *vieux cabinet*. As Guise entered the royal antechamber, through which he had to pass, the door was quickly shut behind him and he realized he had walked into a trap. But escape was impossible now. He had taken no more than two steps beyond the door when Géraud de Montserrier, who was standing by the mantel, advanced swiftly and stabbed him in the breast. Guise struck back with the only weapon in his hand, his sweet-box, just as three more of Henry's assassins, who were concealed behind the tapestry, fell upon him, followed only moments later by a dozen more of the *Taillagambi*, stationed in the king's bedchamber, who completed the bloody orgy.[51]

In a final tour de force, Guise dragged himself and his assailants the full length of the room before he finally fell dead at the very foot of the king's bed. Moments later, Henry mustered up enough courage to emerge from the cabinet and cautiously ask, "Is it done?" He then looked at the corpse of his rival and was heard to exclaim, "I did not know he was so tall, he seems larger dead than alive"; and then with a flourish of his hand and a kick at the dead body he proclaimed, "Now I am the only king." [52] He was soon to learn that his first observation was more correct than his last. Henry ordered the body searched, and in addition to the duke's jewelry found a crumpled piece of paper bearing the words, written in Guise's own hand, "To maintain the war in France 700,000 livres per month are necessary." [53]

In the council chamber the cardinal of Guise heard the muffled cries of his brother and with the archbishop of Lyon tried to rush to his aid, but they were stopped by marshals d'Aumont and Retz and on the orders of the king were imprisoned in a lower cell of the castle. For a day Henry hesitated, not sure whether he should take the next fateful step or not. He dared not let the cardinal go, but was scarcely less afraid to murder a prelate. But the pleasure of his new-found power was too much to be supressed at this point, as he reasoned clearly that the job was only half complete as long as the cardinal remained alive. On Christmas Eve he ordered the cardinal of Guise removed from his cell, and as he was led through the narrow corridor he was murdered by the guards. The archbishop of Lyon, along with most of the League heads who were at Blois — Brissac, La Chapelle-Marteau, Compans, and others — were imprisoned in the nearby Château d'Amboise.[54] Early the next morning Henry triumphantly announced at the bedside of his ailing mother that he was now king of France, "The king of Paris is dead!"

Chapter IX

MENDOZA LEADS THE PARIS LEAGUE

✤   ✤   ✤   ✤

O<small>N</small> the day Guise was killed, Mendoza sent one of his trusted personal servants to Blois with two letters from Parma for the duke. The servant returned to Saint-Dié with the disturbing news that the whole city was in arms and that Guise and his brother the cardinal had been arrested and thrown into prison.[1] This was the first rumor of the tragedy to reach Mendoza and was soon followed by more detailed and accurate accounts of the fatal drama at Blois.

SALVAGE OF THE *Sainte Union*

Mendoza was stunned by the news of Henry's action and began to fear that everything he had built up during the last four years in France was about to collapse. In a very despondent letter to Philip, dated December 27, he expressed his deep concern over the turn of events and disclosed for the first time a feeling of defeat and despair.[2] He feared that the heads of the League who had been arrested and sent to Amboise would shortly meet the same fate as Guise, and that Mayenne too would probably be assassinated before he could be put on the alert. That would leave only the duke d'Aumale to lead the Catholic forces of France, and he was considered too young and inexperienced to be very effective. If all this should happen, the union of the cities would probably be broken and the League overthrown.

Shaken and confused as he was, Mendoza could only plead

with his master to send more money to help maintain the Paris League and to prevent the murder of Mayenne. In another letter of the same day, Mendoza continued in his mournful mood to declare his sorrows and fears to the king. One of his chief worries was that Pericart, Guise's personal servant and secretary, who had been arrested by Henry after the murder, might disclose to his captor the complete projects of the League and the full extent of Mendoza's involvement in it. If this should happen, he warned Philip, it would mean not only a complete rupture between France and Spain but possibly an alliance between Henry III and the Protestants of France and of England.[3]

In view of this situation, Mendoza sought to be released from his post and allowed to return to Spain. "It is only my zeal for the interests of my master, not fear," he commented, "which prompts me to make this humble request at the foot of the throne. I know that God has given me life only that I might consecrate it entirely, and even lose it, in the service of Your Majesty." But under the present conditions, he felt that his remaining in France would be more of a liability to the interests of the king than a service.

Since Mendoza supposed that Henry III would immediately consolidate his power in Paris, he also felt grave concern over his personal belongings and the official papers and documents of the embassy, which were still in Paris. He expressed particular anxiety over three documents: an original of the July 1588 Edict of Union; a receipt from the duke of Guise for the 300,000 escudos sent by Parma to Guise and delivered by Juan Iñiguez just before the Day of the Barricades; and the last letter of the Queen of Scots before her execution, bidding Mendoza farewell and containing information on her final will and testament. Of equal concern to Mendoza was the safety of an almost priceless diamond which Mary had sent him along with the letter. As he closed this long communication, Mendoza reported that he had just received word that

Pericart had given Henry a written statement of the League activities in France against the crown, and that the king and queen mother would probably summon him shortly to explain his connections with it.

News of the assassinations came as an unexpected shock to Philip; at least he reportedly mourned the loss of these two "princes of the church" more than he had the lost of his Armada. But Philip had met many tragedies in his life and was not one to be deterred from his goals by temporary reverses. On 15 January 1589, he wrote a long letter of encouragement to Mendoza, calling on the ambassador to continue the struggle for the faith and ideals of Catholicism and not become disheartened by the "unfortunate happenings of recent weeks." [4] He urged Mendoza to remain at his post, since it might appear to others that he was returning to Spain because of fear of Henry III. He advised Mendoza to go to Paris as soon as Henry returned there and wait a few weeks to see what might develop. He was not to seek an audience with the king until after Philip had received from Henry's ambassador in Madrid an explanation of the king's actions and a declaration of his intentions, but was to go directly to the queen mother and procure a guarantee of safety for the Catholics of France and the release of the cardinal of Bourbon, the archbishop of Lyon, and the other prisoners. When this was done, Philip promised to consider Mendoza's request to be recalled.

As for the embassy papers, Philip advised that for the present they would probably be safer left in Paris until Mendoza could return there. If it transpired that he was unable to go to Paris, then Philip suggested they be removed by some trusted servant and taken to Flanders where they would be safe, and could be transferred from there to Spain at any time. Three days later he also sent Mendoza 10,000 escudos credit to enable him to proceed as instructed. [5]

Long before he had received this letter, Mendoza had regained his composure and was once again formulating a plan of action. On January 5, three weeks before he received his orders from Philip, Mendoza arrived at Blois to get a closer view of the situation and confer with the queen mother. For this purpose he arrived too late. Catherine de' Medici had only a few more hours to live. The events of the preceding two weeks had been too much for her aging body, and before the day had ended she breathed her last. Her passing marked the end of an epoch, but, though she was one of the most influential women in history during her fifty-five-year reign as queen, regent, and queen mother of France, she died unmourned and almost unnoticed. Her passing created no greater sensation, said one of her contemporaries, than would the death of a goat.[6]

Mendoza went immediately to visit the cardinal of Bourbon, who was imprisoned at Blois, and to confer with others of the Catholic party there. The Estates General had not yet formally ended and he was able to learn a good deal about the prevailing climate of opinion.[7] He also wrote three letters to Philip and one to Martín de Idiáquez reporting his observations. Mendoza found that the king's position was not so favorable as he had presumed, and that the League cities were taking much more vigorous action against Henry than he had dared hope. He further reported that Mayenne had received word of the murder of his brothers before Henry's hired assassin, Alphonse d'Ornano, could reach Lyon, and was able to gain safety at Dijon in Burgundy. There Mayenne would undoubtedly raise an army against the king.

Mendoza refused to have any dealings with the king at Blois and on January 20 he withdrew from the court and took up residence in the Château Arnault at Saint-Victor, where he could be close enough to observe Henry's movements, yet far enough removed for safety.[8] The subsequent activity of Mendoza and the League and the accompanying sluggishness of the king caused in three short months a complete reversal of the situation presented on 24 December 1588.

CATHOLIC REACTION TO BLOIS

Henry III, after a short outburst of resolution and energy, soon returned to his somnolence and vacillation, and let the initiative he had gained slip from his grasp. Instead of arming himself and advancing on Paris or Orléans before the League had time to recover from the blow he had just delivered, he trifled away his time at Blois writing declarations of the motives for his assassination of the duke and cardinal.[9] It soon became apparent to Leaguer and Huguenot alike that he was neither to be admired nor feared.

The king held the Estates General to its sessions and tried to give the appearance that nothing out of the ordinary had happened. The archbishop of Bourges was appointed to head the first estate and Etienne Bernard, deputy from Dijon,[10] took the place of La Chapelle-Marteau, and the proceedings continued until January 16, when the Estates General was formally closed.[11]

In the meantime, Henry concerned himself primarily with justifying his actions to the papal legate, Morosini, who in turn communicated the case to the pope.[12] But Sixtus V, infuriated by the murder of a cardinal of the church, severely reprimanded Henry through his ambassador in Rome, the marquis de Pisany, and the cardinal of Joyeuse, protector of France.[13] The pope issued a brief against the French king demanding his appearance in Rome, or that of a representative, to seek absolution for his crime. A few months later the pope issued a bull of excommunication.[14] Henry's elated exclamation after his murder of Guise, that "Now I am king of France," was never less true than during those last seven months of his reign.

The revolution that had begun in Paris with the Day of the Barricades spread rapidly through northern and eastern France after the death of Guise. The assassination of the leader and idol of the Catholic party kindled a fanatic and spontaneous demonstration throughout France which fed on hatred of the ignoble "Vilain Herodes" (Anagram composed from "Henri de Valois") and could only be appeased by ultimately devouring the king. News of the events at Blois reached the stunned populace of Paris on Christmas Eve.[15] Shops and markets were closed as the anguished people rushed to the Hôtel de Guise, to the public squares and parks, and to their parish churches to learn more details. Starting with midnight mass at Notre Dame, the Paris preachers bewailed the catastrophe and called down the vengeance of God upon the "wicked Valois race." These fanatical preachers and pamphleteers soon aroused the hatreds and resentment of the Parisian masses and lashed the people to a frenzy. They not only stirred up the emotional sensitivity of the populace and gave the League movement its greatest drive but also provided the intellectual framework which shaped League theory and policy for the next three years.[16] The agitation increased when it was learned that Guise's brother had also been killed. The fury of the Parisians knew no bounds. The royal arms were torn from the churches and all public places, the king was denounced at every pulpit in Paris, and his image was burned in effigy in great all-night processions. On January 31, the emotions of the Parisians were again aroused when the widowed duchesse de Guise was carried to the Hôtel de Soissons with her infant son, born on January 20. The city assumed sponsorship of the child who was christened François-Paris de Lorraine.[17]

More than mass hysteria had gripped the city; there were also organized and quasi-legal measures taken to denounce the Valois king. On January 8, the theological faculty of the Sorbonne formally and solemnly declared Henry guilty of *lèse-majesté* and thenceforth deposed as king of France. The people were freed from their allegiance to him and were authorized to take up arms against him.[18] The Council of the

Sixteen, minus La Chapelle-Marteau, Compans, and others who were prisoners of the king, recovered from their shock and promptly seized the full control of government in Paris. They mobilized the armed strength of the city and proceeded to secure the bridges, squares, and other strong places, and to post guards around the houses of the suspicious Politiques. Charenton and Saint-Cloud were garrisoned, artillery was moved into place to reduce the castle of Le Bois de Vincennes to obedience, and the defenses of the Hôtel de Guise were strengthened. With military control of the city insured, they next held an open assembly where they elected the duke d'Aumale governor of Paris.[19]

In other cities of the realm similar demonstrations took place. The inhabitants of Orléans barricaded the streets and fortified the town with an entire army against a possible attempt of Henry to subdue it by force.[20] The city of Amiens also fortified itself and issued a public declaration against Henry of Valois.[21] In Chartres, Troyes, Bourges, Lyon, Rouen, and many other cities the League openly declared against the king. The executive system of the Paris League was copied in the provincial towns. In Toulouse the Council of the Eighteen controlled all municipal institutions, including the powerful Parlement de Toulouse, and governed the city through its eighteen classes and professions represented in the council.[22] Even the smallest of League towns had its executive committee of eight, or twelve.

League political theory also became more radical in 1589 under the active pens of Boucher, Rose, Launoy, and others. The divine and contractual basis of monarchy were knitted together in a manner giving the people ultimate sanction over kings. The original political contract, Boucher affirmed, was between God, people, and monarch; and, if the king violated the compact with either of the others, the people were absolved from their allegiance to him. Henry III, by his activities of the preceding year-and-a-half culminating in the betrayal at Blois, had severed his pact with both people and God and forfeited his right to rule in France.[23]

THE LEAGUE GOVERNS FRANCE

On February 15, Mayenne entered Paris amid the wild acclamation of the populace and began to reorganize the League government of France. It was agreed that a central council of government was needed, with powers not only to coordinate the decisions of the various league cities but to serve as a provisional government of France until a new king could be instituted.[24] The great council which emerged on February 17 was chosen from among the Leaguers of Paris and surrounding cities. Four bishops (of Senlis, Meaux, Agen, and Rennes) were among the first members, along with the violent Paris priests of Saint-Benoist (Boucher), Saint-Séverin (Prévost), Saint-André des Arts (Aubry), Saint-Jacques la Boucherie (Pelletier), and Saint-Nicolas des Champs (Pigenat). Some twenty-one lawyers were also represented on the council and the remainder was composed of military officers loyal to Mayenne.[25] This new ruling body of Catholic France, officially titled the *Conseil général de l'Union* but popularly known as the Council of Forty, claimed all the prerogatives and authority of the crown. It assumed the appointment to all state offices and crown benefices, maintained the right of pardon, claimed the power of sending and receiving diplomatic representatives (two envoys were immediately dispatched, one to Philip and one to the pope, to solicit their protection and support with money and men),[26] and demanded the receipt of all royal revenues.[27] The council won immediate popularity in much of France by reducing the amount of taxation and by abolishing the sale and purchase of administrative offices.[28]

One of the first acts of this Council of Forty was to name the duke of Mayenne as lieutenant-general of France, to act as head of the state until a new king was installed. This was to be done by an Estates General which was called to meet in Paris on July 15, to create "a new king and to establish a definitive government." [29] To make the break with the past complete, the new government had a new state seal engraved, obtained a formal declaration from the Sorbonne, and had the edict of sovereignty registered by the Parlement de Paris.[30] With the Paris success, even the Politique Jean Bodin joined the League at Laon and in March took the oath of allegiance to the new union.[31]

The League apparently now governed France, yet Mendoza maintained a cautious attitude in his reporting to Philip. He favored the declaration of the Union, but he was doubtful about the efficiency of such a large governing body and uncertain of Mayenne's intentions. He was also convinced, as early as February, that Henry of Valois would now attempt a *rapprochement* with Navarre, which could be very damaging to the Catholic cause.[32]

But proclaiming a new government and having it recognized and accepted can be very different things. The new League council, with Mayenne at its head, did not win immediate national and international support. Henry III, just as Mendoza had predicted, began to awake to the peril of his situation and to look around for friends and allies. His first and clumsiest steps were toward a reconciliation with Mayenne and the League nobility.[33] These overtures were rebuffed, however, and Henry angrily issued a declaration against the League.[34] The king turned next to his brother-in-law, Henry of Navarre, and proposed an alliance of the two against the League-dominated north. Navarre was now in a much better bargaining position than he had been in 1586, and was able to win favorable concessions from the French king. Among other things, the Protestants would be permitted to retain all of their previous possessions and conquests; as Navarre advanced northward across the Loire he would be granted a city or fortress in every district (*sénéchaussée*) conquered by him (the rest were to be turned over to Henry); and in all of the cities Navarre should take, even those returned to the French king, the free exercise of the Protestant religion was guaranteed.[35] On 3 April 1589, the alliance, negotiated in behalf of Navarre by Du Plessis-Mornay, was completed.

Mendoza was aroused by the agreement which he considered to be another example of the king's complete unscrupulousness. In letters to Spain the ambassador vigorously denounced Henry, and even wrote to the French king himself, censuring him for joining the heretics in their ignoble campaign against the Christian world.[36] In his informative dispatch of April 26, Mendoza attributed a large share of the responsibility for reconciling the two kings to the activities of the Politiques, who, he felt, were ruining the country and the church by their selfish personal interests and their lack of religious principles.

On April 30, the alliance was consummated by the meeting of the two kings at Plessis-lès-Tours, where they drew up their plans for the forthcoming campaign.[37] This new alignment was of utmost importance, for it marked a major shift in the tenuous power balance in France. Had it not come about there is a strong likelihood that the League would have gained complete control of the country. It also reveals the increasing political orientation of the opponents to the League. It was really the position and philosophy of the Politiques, not that of the Huguenots, that prevailed at Plessis-lès-Tours and provided the bond between the two kings. The war was rapidly becoming one of religious fanaticism and theocracy versus political reason of state rather than Catholicism versus Protestantism.

MENDOZA AND MAYENNE

Philip II, like the other monarchs of Europe, was not yet ready to recognize the new revolutionary government in

Paris as long as the legal ruler, Henry III, was alive and still maintaining himself with a certain amount of power. Philip left no doubt that he would continue to support Mayenne and the League, but officially he still acknowledged Henry as king and refused to sever relations with him. Mendoza remained as Philip's resident ambassador to the French crown and official spokesman at the court of the Most Christian King. Nevertheless, Mendoza's status had been altered considerably since the assassination of Guise. Philip had ordered his ambassador to reject any audience with the king[38] and that order had not been countermanded. For his own part, Henry, who had no love for Mendoza anyway, rebuffed the ambassador with words forceful enough to let him know he was no longer welcome at court.[39] Philip's instructions to Mendoza were to remain close to the king and find out all he could about Henry's intentions, moves, and negotiations, without direct intercourse with the court itself.[40]

In March, when Henry moved from Blois to Tours, Mendoza once more resumed his residence in Paris where he would be in a more favorable position to follow the activities of both Henry and Navarre.[41] But an equally compelling reason for the move was the fast-changing events in Paris itself. The widespread manifestations of the League against Henry III were welcomed by Philip and Mendoza, but they could also become dangerous to the Catholic cause if not properly oriented and led. The new revolutionary Council of the Union, with Mayenne at its head, was as much a question mark to the Spanish king and ambassador as it was to the king of France.

In Mendoza's mind, the most uncertain link in the new union was Mayenne himself, who was a very different person from his brother. Guise had been a strong defender of the universal Catholic ideology in France, and by his death Spain had lost one of the greatest supporters of its crusade to reestablish the *res publica Christiana*. In many ways his death was an irreparable loss to the cause he represented. His ability to lead both the nobility and the masses, his reckless energy and quick decision, and his self-confidence and unscrupulousness were not reproduced in his younger brother. Even the Huguenots — though they could not tolerate the cause he represented — never depreciated Guise's personal courage nor his capacity as a shrewd tactician and a vigorous and skillful military leader. Some who knew him intimately even saw an element of patience and mildness mixed in with Guise's fanaticism.[42]

Mayenne, on the other hand, was no demagogue. He had little feeling for the lower classes and disliked the violence of the mob as well as the "democratic" leanings of the Paris League. He was an honest aristocrat who preferred the company of other aristocrats and refined gentlemen. Where Guise was rash, lavish, and ambitious, Mayenne was cautious, thrifty, and conservative. Even their causes were not the same. Guise saw the Holy League as an institution for promoting his personal ambitions; but it was also a means of restoring the religious unity of Europe, and, although he was undoubtedly less idealistic about Christendom than was Philip, he saw no great contradiction nor disloyalty in supporting and being supported by the king of Spain. Outwardly at least, they were both working toward a common goal. Mayenne was not moved by such ideals. His loyalties were confined to France; his enemies were the enemies of France. Mayenne distrusted the more fanatical manifestations of the League as he distrusted the interference of Spain. His only goal was the continued religious orthodoxy of France and the seating of a Catholic prince on the vacant Valois throne.[43] In a very real sense, Mayenne was a Politique himself. The contradiction of this position was his almost complete dependence upon Philip for financial aid. From February on, the League began to move in two different directions.

Mendoza was not slow to perceive the change of climate in

Paris. He set to work immediately to re-establish the proper course for the League. He emphasized in meetings with the Council of Sixteen the assistance his master had given them in all of their endeavors and assured them that aid would continue as long as heretics remained in France and as long as the League continued to crusade for the religious unity of Christendom.[44] The treachery of Henry III, Mendoza affirmed, was further witnessed by his present alliance with the archenemy of France and Christianity, and made it even more vital for the League to continue cooperating with the policies of Spain.[45]

Mendoza's campaign was partially successful and many elements of the League were willing to follow his leadership. But many others, like Mayenne, who dreaded becoming too dependent upon Spain, held back and began looking to other sources for help. By April and May the split in the League had become pronounced. The League nobility, the high judicial and municipal families, and many members of the Council of Forty were mostly behind Mayenne; while the Council of the Sixteen, the clergy, the friars, and a large part of the citizenry of Paris supported Mendoza.[46] It was now the ambassador's delicate task to support and strengthen the Holy League while preventing the Mayenne wing of it from growing too strong or independent.

Mayenne's envoy to Philip II was instructed to request a continuation of the financial subsidies agreed upon in the Treaty of Joinville. He was further directed to seek military assistance from the Catholic King and diplomatic recognition through an accredited ambassador.[47] Philip was not quite ready to make such a final break with the French crown, and preferred to negotiate within the legal framework of the established monarchy, but he could see merit in having someone in closer contact with Mayenne (who was seldom in Paris) to assist Mendoza in coordinating the activities of the League. Philip therefore selected Juan de Moreo (who had fulfilled

several special assignments for him in France and the Netherlands since his participation in drawing up the Treaty of Joinville) for this mission. Moreo was well known and liked by
Mayenne and the house of Lorraine, and promised to be a valuable addition to Philip's diplomatic staff in France.

Moreo arrived in Paris early in May with instructions to
remain as close to Mayenne as possible, to advise Parma and
Tassis in Flanders on matters of financial subsidies to the
League, and to inform Mendoza of the duke's movements and
intentions.[48] This would enable Mendoza to keep a closer
watch on Henry and still be apprised of Mayenne's activities.[49]
Mendoza was given clearance by Philip not only to dispatch
information on the situation in France but also to counsel
Mayenne and the League on how they should proceed in all
matters and to keep them faithful to the Catholic cause. But,
he cautioned, this must be done "with such skill that nobody
can rightfully have a complaint against anything you are
doing." [50]

MENDOZA'S RECALL

Philip's admonition was well-timed, but Henry knew that
Mendoza not only was playing a double role as ambassador to
France and liaison to the League, but was now the chief advisor and leader of the Paris Sixteen itself. With his new-found
security and courage, as ally of Navarre, Henry insisted once
more on the dismissal of the obstreperous ambassador. On
April 28, Henry wrote to the Spanish king, declaring his own
forthright and Catholic intentions and desires for peace in his
kingdom, and complaining that Philip's ambassador persisted
in fomenting disorder and rebellion against the crown to
which he was accredited.[51] This note was followed in May by
a lengthier communication formally asking for Mendoza's
dismissal. This *mise en demeure* was delivered to Philip in
person by Pierre de Fresne Forget, one of Henry's secretaries
of state.[52] Henry declared in these articles that he refused to

negotiate with Mendoza on any matter, and that the ambassador would no longer be admitted near the person of the king nor at court.

Philip was now faced with a very perplexing decision. He knew of Mendoza's immense service to the Catholic cause and to his own, and needed his presence in Paris now more than ever before. Yet Philip was strongly motivated by the external conformity to diplomatic protocol. If Henry insisted on Mendoza's removal, Philip had no further recourse than to accede to the demand. Still, the effect of such a move might be disastrous to his policy in France and detrimental to his entire international position. Public opinion was not as prominent a factor in foreign policy then as it is now, but it did have a part, and the opinion of other sovereigns was extremely important — especially that of the pope. On June 18, Philip replied to the articles of Fresne Forget in a six-page letter to Henry. He argued that the king's charges were exaggerated and sometimes untrue, but agreed to consider seriously the matter of his ambassador's recall.[53]

In the meantime a short and heated exchange of letters between Henry and Mendoza made it apparent that this time the king was not likely to change his mind.[54] For his own part, Mendoza was not against returning to Spain — twice previously he had requested to be relieved of his duties and allowed to go home — but he disliked being ordered from his post by someone he considered not really to be king of France at all. He shared Philip's anxiety over the effects of a forced dismissal upon the attitude of the pope and other sovereigns, and he refused categorically to recognize Henry's ultimatum until his own servant and aide, Hans Oberholtzer (who had been seized by the count of Rochefoucauld and turned over to Henry III, while en route to Madrid with some important letters from Mendoza) was released. The illegal detention of a royal courier bearing official dispatches to the king of Spain, Mendoza insisted, was an open breach of diplomatic immunity and left the "so-called king of France" in no position to accuse him of felonies against the state.[55]

On June 23, therefore, Mendoza sought to avoid the stigma of again being declared *persona non grata* by once more requesting to be relieved of his duties. The justification given for his petition was poor health and failing eyesight. Mendoza's physical condition had deteriorated markedly during his five years in France. He had suffered from occasional attacks of dysentery, and two years before he was the victim of a very serious intestinal disorder which, with the frequent bloodletting prescribed by the doctors, had left him weakened.[56]

But Mendoza's real burden was with his eyes. He had returned from England with sore and inflamed eyes which continued to grow worse after he came to Paris. In June 1585 they caused him such intense pain, he reported to Idiáquez, that he could scarcely move them, and they drained liquid continuously.[57] A year later a cataract made him totally blind in the left eye. Several physicians recommended an operation, and, due partly to the recent success of a similar surgery performed in Paris, Mendoza decided to submit to it.[58] On June 26 the cataract was excised, but when the bandages were removed he was still unable to see out of the eye. Four months later he confided to Idiáquez that he was happy just to be able to see the sun by day and the light of his lamp at four paces by night.[59] Nevertheless, in the succeeding two years the vision in his right eye improved slightly, and occasionally he could pick up glimpses of bright objects with his left. But the doctors cautioned him against overoptimism, and assured him that it would be a long time before he regained even the poor vision he possessed before the operation. The warnings were well-founded, for in the same spring of 1589 he started to have trouble with the right eye, which soon appeared to be following the pattern of the left.

Informed of his ambassador's ill health, Philip sent a note to Henry III on July 14, notifying him that, because of his failing eyesight, Mendoza was being relieved of his ambassadorial duties. Philip courteously requested that he be issued a passport to leave the country and granted safe conduct to the border. Accompanying this letter, and bearing the same date, were several others addressed to Mendoza and granting him his requested permission to retire.[60] Philip congratulated Mendoza on his handling of the Paris embassy and thanked him for his service to Spain and the Catholic cause. He included some recommendations on securing the embassy papers and other documents in Paris until his successor arrived, sent instructions for completing the pending business with agents in England and elsewhere, and enclosed 10,000 escudos for terminating his affairs in France and traveling to Madrid.[61]

But Mendoza's illustrious career was not destined to end so abruptly. He was to spend two more years in France before finally returning to his home, and another thirteen years in Spain, rising gradually to moderate prominence as a writer, poet, and scholar before his death in 1604. The violent events of August 1–2, 1589, opened a new phase of Mendoza's embassy, which ended with the blind ambassador's last futile attempts to prevent the coronation of Henry IV.

FROM TOURS TO SAINT-CLOUD

When Mayenne learned of Henry's presence in the city of Tours he elected to attack the vital stronghold in force before Navarre's reinforcements had time to arrive. The prospects of taking this key point, and also the king, would perhaps never be better. Early in May, the duke advanced southward from Vendôme and began laying siege to the outskirts of Tours.[62] After a few hours, Saint-Symphorien, the northern suburb of the city, was in his hands and only the single bridge crossing the Loire stood between him and victory. But the key span was never crossed by Mayenne. Barely in time to turn the tide, Châtillon arrived at the head of 500 arquebusiers (the advanced guard of Navarre's main army) and Mayenne was forced to withdraw. A few days later, Aumale, defending the northern approaches to Paris, was defeated at Senlis by a loyalist and Huguenot army under Longueville and La Noue. In this encounter, Mayneville, Guise's loyal officer and agent, was killed.[63] The Catholic position suddenly became critical.

Late in May, news of the papal bull of excommunication pronounced against Henry III reached the embattled country and brought varied effects. The duke of Nevers and some of the other dubious Leaguers seized this chance to renounce their League affiliation and declare themselves in support of the king. Most of the League cities, however, saw in this endorsement from the pope a further justification of their cause and redoubled their efforts against the Valois and Bourbon heretics. To the camp of the two kings at Étampes it brought disappointment and then renewed vigor in their attack.

Late in June the decision was made to lay siege to Paris. Navarre reanimated Henry with the assurance that it was sometimes success or failure which distinguishes right from wrong. "And for that reason," he declared, "Your Majesty should strive to be conqueror, for then your absolution will follow as a matter of course, but if we are overcome we shall all die condemned heretics."[64] The mission of Schomberg and De Thou to recruit mercenaries from Germany had met with success, and Sancy joined the king in July with 10,000 men from Switzerland. The royal army now numbered some 40,000 and was ready to engulf the capital. On July 25, Pontoise was taken,[65] and four days later Henry was in possession of the bridge at Saint-Cloud, where he fixed his headquarters for the final assault on Paris. Navarre's troops were deployed along the south as far as Charenton. The attack was planned for August 2.

Everything was in readiness for the decisive action when, early in the morning of August 1, a young Jacobin friar named Jacques Clément secured admission to the royal lodging and sought an audience with the king. His alleged purpose was to bring plans of the royalists in Paris to assist in the forth-coming assault. As Henry took the friar aside to hear his confidential report, Clément struck him a fatal blow with the knife he carried in his robe. Clément was quickly dispatched by soldiers of the king, but he had completed his maleficent mission. In a few hours the last of the Valois was dead.[66]

Chapter X

THE STRUGGLE FOR A THRONE

✦ ✦ ✦ ✦

T HE assassination of Henry III once more caused a decisive change in the situation in France and sharply altered Mendoza's position there. Henry's death created the situation which the League had been organized to prevent — the accession of a Protestant heretic to the throne of France. But the League had been preparing for several years to meet the problem when it arose, and quickly took an active position against Navarre. There is ample evidence that the League was aware of Clément's intentions some days before the actual murder. It is certain, at least, that he talked to many people about it, including the theological faculty at the Sorbonne, to inquire about the future status of his soul if he were to kill a tyrant. Most of those he talked to, however, thought he was only joking. Some nicknamed him "Capitaine Clément" for his frequent boasting about killing the king. Some authors affirm that he planned the deed along with Mayenne and Madame de Montpensier.[1] Mendoza makes no mention of such a relationship. After it was accomplished there was great rejoicing in Paris and among Catholics throughout France. Some, including Mendoza, even believed he had been inspired by God to perform the deed.[2]

NAVARRE AND THE CATHOLIC NOBLES

Henry of Navarre found himself in a precarious and ambiguous position after the murder of the Valois king. Henry

III's final testament to those gathered around him at Saint-Cloud was a declaration that Navarre should be his legitimate and immediate successor as Henry IV. Navarre accepted the honor without hesitation, but soon found that the obstacles to his becoming *de facto* king of France were considerable, and even his *de jure* right was denied by almost half of the realm.

Navarre was confident of the support of the Huguenots, but the Catholic nobles under Henry III were divided in their allegiance. The Politiques would sustain the new king, but some of the staunch Catholics, fearing the destruction of their religion, declared against him. Navarre's first move was to make certain the loyalty of the Swiss mercenaries previously recruited by Henry III.[3] This task was skillfully accomplished by Sancy, who induced the Swiss captains, whether Catholic or Protestant, to transfer their service from the Valois to the Bourbon. The Swiss were not really so concerned over the religious convictions of their employer, nor of his legal rights to the throne, as they were over his ability to pay for their services. According to the somewhat doubtful authority of the *Mémoire de Nevers*, however, Sancy persuaded them to take an oath to serve Navarre for three months without pay.[4] Some of the royalist nobility also threw their support to Navarre, as Givry, Humières, and Aumont declared their forces ready to follow his already famous white plume.

But many of the royalist nobles of Henry III hesitated to join Navarre. Among these were the dukes of Montpensier, Angoulême, Espeises, d'O, marquis de Vitry, and marshal Biron, who refused to recognize Navarre as long as he persisted in the heretical faith. Navarre, however, not a whit behind the politics of his day, made them tempting offers of money, rank, and territory in exchange for their service and loyalty. He realized that to become king of France he would have to buy as well as fight his way to the throne. Even then, the road to Paris was less muddy than it might have been had the new king not possessed such abundant qualities of leadership and personal magnanimity. Biron was easily secured by a gift of the county of Perigord, but Henry soon found that with each succeeding concession the price of loyalty went up, and with it the problems of financing his regime. When the dispositions and realignments were completed, Navarre was able to hold about half of Henry's army — not as many as he had hoped for, but nevertheless a considerable addition to his own forces.[5]

On August 4, Navarre issued a formal statement, known as the Declaration of Saint-Cloud, in which he proclaimed himself, as king of France, defender of the rights of the subjects and nobles of the realm. He agreed to continue, under the provisions of the joint declaration issued in April, the war against the League and all other enemies of France.[6] As a further effort to win the support of the Catholics, he agreed to retain the Catholic religion throughout the kingdom and to introduce no changes in its worship or government. Beyond that he refused to commit himself for fear of alienating the core of his support and of his army, the staunch and militant Protestants.[7]

MENDOZA RESUMES DIRECTION OF THE PARIS LEAGUE

In Paris, equally decisive steps were being taken by Mendoza and the League to prevent the accession of Henry IV. On the day after the assassination, Mendoza rushed a dispatch to Philip telling him of the events at Saint-Cloud and assuring him that the Catholic cause would most certainly go more smoothly with Henry III out of the way.[8] But to Mayenne and the other leaders the position of the League in relation to Spain was no longer certain. Would Philip continue to grant them financial aid? Would he still support the cardinal of Bourbon as king of France in view of his recent refusal to sever diplomatic relations with Henry III after the murder of Guise? These questions were uppermost in the League councils of early August.

Knowing that the delay involved in getting word to Philip and receiving his reply might be very detrimental to their cause, Mendoza once more assumed the responsibility to pronounce a vital decision in the name of the king. He assured Mayenne that the candidacy of the cardinal of Bourbon was unequivocally supported by the king of Spain, and suggested that he be declared king of France without further delay. Mendoza further promised Mayenne and the League that the financial assistance would continue as long as they were actively engaged in promoting the good of Christendom and the preservation of the Catholic faith.[9] With these guarantees from Mendoza, Mayenne proclaimed the cardinal king of France, as Charles X. But, since the cardinal-king was still a prisoner of Navarre, at Fontenay-le-Comte, Mayenne retained his title and functions as lieutenant-general of the state and crown of France, and continued, as chief of the army, to campaign against the Huguenot forces.

In a reply from Madrid of September 7, Philip fully accepted Mendoza's *démarche* and congratulated the ambassador heartily on his quick and wise decision. Philip expressed regret that a legitimate monarch had been murdered, and especially by a friar of the Catholic Church; but, since it had happened and could not be undone, he felt that Mendoza had taken the correct steps to avert the greater catastrophe — the accession of a heretic to the throne. His letter of appreciation to Mendoza and assurance to the League was clear and precise:

The offer you made to the duke of Mayenne in my name, after the death of the king, for help in maintaining the Catholic religion in that kingdom, was very well done, and at the right time. No less opportune was your declaration to the same duke of Mayenne in favor of the cardinal of Bourbon at a time when they were confused and doubtful as to which way to turn. The cardinal of Bourbon has such a good legal right to the throne, is as Catholic as can be desired, and has proven his integrity by many trials and sufferings for the cause of religion, that they should in no wise neglect to accept him as their king. Therefore, and because it is of greatest importance to Catholics, I am infinitely pleased with what you have counseled in my name, and I hold your service in particular esteem and ask that you continue in the future to advise and help the Catholics of France as much as possible, that their cause may prosper. What you have already pointed out in this connection seems very sensible to me.

In regard to the other matters which you showed them, they can be assured that when they have need for assistance, for whatever matter concerning religion, I will gladly help with whatever is agreed upon. For their cause is such that I am honored to befriend and protect them.[10]

Mendoza was asked to ignore the letters of recall, and to suspend his return to Spain until further notification. Enclosed with Philip's letters of September 7, was a paper of specific instructions which were to be followed jointly by Mendoza and Moreo in dealing with the League and with other matters of France. These instructions are so enlightening on the purposes and methods of Spanish diplomacy in Paris that I have considered them of sufficient value to reproduce in their entirety.[11]

What His Majesty [Philip II] orders Don Bernardino de Mendoza and Comendador Moreo to observe and effect in order to carry out this assignment.

Since it is desirable that the cardinal of Bourbon be king, you should therefore promote and assist this cause, as Don Bernardino has already done up until this time, that His Majesty may be well-satisfied, and also endeavor, by all available means, to secure the cardinal's release from prison.

In the name of His Majesty, remind and exhort the city of Paris and all of the nobles and Catholic villages of France to be united in resolution and in furthering the common good of the Catholic cause, in electing the said Bourbon to the throne — to the exclusion of Béarn [Navarre] — and in the extirpation of heresy, without deviating from these goals. Counsel them each to attend to those particular matters which divide them, to bury their differences, and to put all other things aside than those which will promote this goal.

When the said cardinal of Bourbon gains the crown, remind him of, and see that he complies fully with, the conditions of the League agreement [Treaty of Joinville] between himself and His Majesty, jointly with the others of the Catholic League, and ratified anew; and see that it is put into execution in all of its points and articles.

Also affirm the matter of who will succeed the said cardinal of Bourbon to the throne. This should be done by means of some marriage, which might be agreeable both to His Majesty and to the said new king, and to the benefit of that kingdom and this.

In whichever of these matters you are dealing, the duke of Mayenne is to retain the title and charge of lieutenant-general, affirmed and secured, as one so deserving should have, with many favors and thanks for the great part he has taken in resolving these negotiations.

Take careful note also to honor and advance the person of the young duke of Guise as is fully merited by the memory, the blood, and the death of his father and grandfather, both for the Catholic cause.

In particular, see that the matter of Cambrai is soon complied with, as agreed to in the treaty.

Also see to it that upon coming to the throne the said cardinal of Bourbon begins to satisfy and pay back to His Majesty all the expenses and benefits I have given to the League. Have him do this immediately, as the expenses have been so great and continue to increase more every day, that not having sufficient money now to be able to pay them immediately, I shall have to give them pledges [notes] instead, and also some fortified cities. (But he should be advised, when that time comes, to say nothing that would prevent His Majesty from negotiating in the future if it seems advisable. There is no reason for mentioning this now, however, so just omit it for the time being).

When he comes to the throne, try to gain whatever advantage possible along the English Channel, for this could be a very important factor against that kingdom [England].

If you should be unable to secure the liberty of the cardinal of Bourbon and his purpose, or, if after obtaining it the Catholics still find themselves hard-pressed on the defensive by Béarn and his heretics, they should ask, as they have done before, to be commended into the hands of His Majesty, make certain that they abandon any suspicion that His Majesty wants to appropriate the kingdom for himself. But do not deny them the protection and refuge they seek, in order that heresy may be destroyed and that His Majesty may have their Catholic king as a friend and associate. For this reason I will try to be a good protector to them and will expect them to not accept any offers of a third party without first negotiating with His Majesty.

And next, inform me as to who would be the most likely, and would have the strongest support of the Catholics, as a successor of Bourbon to the throne. Advise me also of the rights, background, military strength, patrons, and friends of each one of those who might be a possible choice.

Do not neglect skillfully to drop a few hints to certain people concerning the rights of the Señora Infanta to those states acquired by their kings through force and by marriages and also those usurped from His Majesty. But do not say this all at one time; rather mention a little here and a little there, with whatever diplomacy the occasion might demand, in order to feel out their opinions and spirit and take note of how the idea is received, without giving the wrong impression.

Whatever you are successful in accomplishing on any of these points be sure to inform me immediately, especially on the matters of a successor to Bourbon and the marriages which would obligate them to His Majesty and make them dependent upon his arbitration.

If, by the time you receive this paper, which is to serve as a guide and instruction, you have already made some agreements with the French Catholics in the name of His Majesty and the conditions you reached are inferior to those contained herein, try to improve them to conform to these points. On the other hand, if you have gained greater advantages than those asked for here, I commend you and request that you maintain them thus without paying any attention to this note, but inform me immediately so that having it understood I can order whatever needs to be done in this case.

This set of instructions to Mendoza and Moreo was followed by a short postscript which shows Philip's suspicions of Navarre's future moves, and advises Mendoza on how to counter them:

In the event that Béarn proclaims his intention and desire to be reconverted, there is little I can prescribe to persons as familiar with his motives as you are, and the deceit in which he envelops himself. But endeavor to see to it that all the Catholics are on the alert and advised to this truth, so that such talk from him will not be listened to. Inform His Holiness also that the wolf will try to wear sheep's clothing in order to cause greater trouble to the Catholics, who would all do well to be wary of this fraud.

This communication from the king, along with the accompanying letters of September 7, constitutes the principal ambassadorial credentials possessed by Mendoza during the remaining two years of his ministry in France. Philip did not recognize the pretentions of Navarre to the throne and consequently did not accredit his ambassador to that court. Had the Cardinal Bourbon been free to assume the title, as bestowed upon him by the League, Mendoza would probably have been accredited to him, but as long as the cardinal-king remained a captive of the Huguenot king, Mendoza remained an ambassador without portfolio, assigned to negotiate with, and also counsel and advise, Mayenne and the League, as well as the other Catholics of France.

CRUCIAL NEGOTIATIONS

From Philip's point of view the situation was decisive. Navarre had lost the allegiance of many of the royalist nobles and even some of his former Huguenot followers,[12] yet in some respects he might even have gained strength because of the greater integration now achieved under a single head. He immediately launched a swift campaign into Normandy, designed to intercept any aid from Parma to the League and to facilitate the landing of English reinforcements to his own army.[13]

Two additional difficulties beset Philip in the fall of 1589: the split within the League itself, and the doubtful position of the Roman pontiff. Clarification of these issues was Philip's immediate goal in September and October. If the Spanish, League, and papal policies and forces could be integrated and directed toward a common goal, a victory for the Catholic cause could be assured. But with the influence and strength of the Politiques everywhere on the increase, with the Mayenne faction of the League growing ever more national in its objectives and sentiments and more suspicious of Philip's intentions, and the pope continuing in his recalcitrance and occasional opposition to Spanish policy, the issue was far from decided.

In order to strengthen his position within the League, Philip granted Mendoza even greater powers as his personal representative to that body, with instructions to advise, counsel, and direct it.[14] An interesting letter from Mendoza, dated 30 October 1589, reveals something of his method of dealing with the League. He declared that he never made direct proposals to the council because "the French are very suspicious of anything that does not come from themselves." He therefore found it helpful to talk informally with some member of the Sixteen and include in the conversation the suggestions he wished to impart to them as though it were something he had heard from someone else. The proposals would always find their way to the central committee of the League and from there would usually emerge as formal resolutions. In some cases, however, Mendoza explained, it was necessary for him to give direct advice to the council on matters of vital importance.[15]

To attempt a reconciliation and closer cooperation between the Paris League and the followers of Mayenne, Philip sent one more agent to represent him in France. Jean Baptiste de Tassis was recalled from Flanders to serve with Mendoza and Moreo as representatives to the League.[16] This "Triumvirat Espagnol" became the symbol of Philip's intense concern over the French situation and, although it was more symbolic than effective, it did for a short time give greater influence and penetration to Spanish policy than might have been done by a single envoy.

Winning the support of Pope Sixtus V was in some ways an even more difficult task than holding the League together. According to the 1585 papal excommunication, Henry of Navarre could not become the legal ruler of France, but since that date Sixtus V had made numerous statements, both private and public, of admiration for Navarre, and it was not at all certain that he would still endorse his earlier decree. Philip was determined, therefore, to get a republication of the ban and, if possible, the issuance of a new papal pronouncement against him.[17]

Mendoza, in the meantime, had opened a new line of negotiation with Henry III's former secretary of state, Villeroy, in an attempt to prevent a *détente* between Navarre and Mayenne.[18] Villeroy, as an active Politique, had been engaged in just such a project for some time and had ingratiated himself with Mayenne to such an extent that he had become one of Mayenne's closest advisors.[19] Mendoza now attempted to use this new alignment to bring Mayenne into closer cooperation with Spain.[20] Villeroy could not be won, however, and he continued to counsel Mayenne to separate himself even more from the entangling chains of Spanish policy. Mayenne was in as difficult a position as anyone. Although he distrusted and feared Spanish influence in France, he was in dire need of the assistance and support that only Spain could offer.[21]

THE SPANISH TRIUMVIRATE AND THE PAPAL LEGATE

Late in the fall of 1589, the attention of Philip and his representatives in France was centered on the arrival of the new papal legate to France, Cardinal Cajetan. Sixtus V had withheld pronouncement on the situation there for the report of this special envoy. Cajetan was sent to Paris to meet with the League, determine the rights and suitability of the cardinal of Bourbon to become king of France, establish a favorable relationship between the new monarchy and Rome, and look into the League request for financial aid.[22] Cajetan was accompanied on this mission by a large retinue of prelates, preachers, and Jesuits, including the archbishop of Avignon, the archbishop of Florence, Patriarch Pietro Cajetan (the cardinal's brother), and the renowned Jesuit theologian and political theorist, Bellarmine.

Early in November, Mendoza, Tassis, and Moreo were together in Paris awaiting the arrival of the papal legate. On November 16 they received their detailed instructions for his reception. This eleven-page document describes in detail their aims and purposes in regard to the papacy, and the precise steps which each of the three was to follow in bringing about

a favorable report to Rome and in procuring Cajetan's influential support for Spanish and League policies in France.[23]

Mendoza was instructed to meet the legate personally as
soon as he reached Paris, and present him, on behalf of the
Spanish king, with the letter of introduction and commendation which had been enclosed with the ambassador's instructions. He was at that time to offer Cajetan his services, and
those of Philip's other emissaries in Paris, to assist the legate in
carrying out his mission in France.

"If at this time the legate speaks of his commission there,"
continued Philip, "and even if he doesn't, explain to him, as
soon as the right moment presents itself, the dangerous state
in which the Catholic cause finds itself in France, and suggest that His Holiness immediately declare himself in favor
of the League, and assist them with his authority and with
goodly sums of money."

The worthiness of the cardinal of Bourbon as king of
France was to be declared and his liberation urged, as the
best and quickest way to re-establish Catholic unity there.
"The pretensions of the prince of Béarn should be emphatically disavowed because he is such an obstinate and confirmed heretic, who was suckled on heresy along with milk," [24]
and he has contributed to its evil growth with all his forces
"to the extent of glorifying in the excommunication pronounced by the Apostolic See."

Philip also advised Mendoza to urge the legate to use his
authority to have the League supported also by those cities not
yet belonging to the union, and to have all the parlements
declare in favor of it. At the same time, he suggested that
these proposals be made known to all of the Catholics of
France, that they might also exert pressure on the cardinal
legate for the furtherance of their cause.

The three were then advised that Cajetan was most certainly charged with procuring some additional advantages in
France for the papacy, including the acceptance and publica-

tion of the decrees of the Council of Trent. "It would be well to support the legate with all the means and friends you have, for this will be to the advantage of all." But, he cautioned them, "try to get the many vacant benefices filled with good ecclesiastics of sound doctrine and exemplary lives . . . to discourage the lazy among the Catholics and undermine the glibness of the heretics."

Mendoza was carefully reminded that, should all efforts fail to secure the liberation of the cardinal of Bourbon, and the legate should ask him who his Catholic Majesty favored next, he was to respond with some general statements that the king's principal concern was to establish firmly the Catholic religion in that kingdom and therefore whoever could best accomplish this goal would be the best suited for the crown. For the ambassador's own information, and not as a reply to the legate, Philip reminded Mendoza of his own two claims to the throne by right of his lineage from the house of Valois, and the right of his eldest daughter, the Infanta Isabel Clara Eugenia, as the granddaughter of Henry II.

The Salic Law was only a myth, he asserted, and should in no way interfere with the legal succession to the throne. "Since I am more concerned with the speedy revival of that kingdom than I am with personal interests, however, I am willing to abstrain from asserting the claims which I have to the crown, in spite of their fundamental right." [25] Nevertheless, he continued, if the infanta should marry a Catholic nobleman of France who also had a claim to the throne, their rights could be combined and the best interests of France, Spain, and the Holy Church would be promoted. But this, be cautioned Mendoza, would have to be handled very subtly and skillfully or it might cause suspicions and distrust of the Catholic King. "All this I have intended to tell you clearly that you may make use of it when the proper time or occasion arises, both with relation to the legate and also with the duke of Mayenne, that it may be done for the good and not the prejudice of our cause." Any proposals by the League for a marriage alliance with the infanta were to be immediately forwarded to Philip without making any commitment whatsoever on them, or any indication that they would even be considered by him.

Philip encouraged the calling of an Estates General to ratify the naming of the new king, but cautioned that it should, at all costs, be held in Paris, and as soon as possible, "For an Estates General can not only be very beneficial, it can also be detrimental." He concluded the lengthy instructions with a suggestion for the breakdown of responsibilities among the three in order to make their work more efficient and effective. Mendoza was assigned to carry out all negotiations with the cardinal legate, with the Catholics of Paris and the Council of the Sixteen, and also with the duke of Mayenne when he was in Paris. Moreo was to stay close to Mayenne at all times when he was outside of Paris, keep Philip and Mendoza informed on his movements, and encourage, assist, and advise the duke always. Tassis was to remain in close communication with Parma in Flanders and, through the recommendations of Mendoza and Moreo and the courier services of Juan Iñiguez, provide Mayenne and the League with the financial aid they needed. All correspondence with Rome was to be handled by Mendoza. "Finally, try to see that everything proceeds for the best advantage to the service of our Lord and the good of the Catholic cause, which is my endeavor above all else, and secure the peace and tranquillity of that kingdom." [26]

For a while after the arrival of the papal legate the situation looked increasingly favorable for the Catholic cause. Cajetan turned out to be much more sympathetic to the policies of Philip II than the pope had suspected. On almost every point of negotiation with Mendoza he conformed to the Spanish plans. He declared Henry of Navarre a relapsed heretic and unable to assume the title of king of France. He demanded the release of the cardinal of Bourbon and supported his candidacy for the crown. Furthermore, he forbade the prelates of France to attend the assembly of the estates called by Navarre at Tours.[27] The cardinal claimed the exclusive right to call the prelates together, and strongly urged them all to join and give their support to the Holy League. He even went so far as to grant the League a monthly stipend to help continue the fight against Navarre.[28]

But on one issue, which Mendoza had pushed the hardest, Cajetan refused to agree. Just as Philip had supposed, the League offered (on Mendoza's suggestion) to accept the king of Spain as protector of the Catholic religion and kingdom of France. Mendoza had achieved this victory in November — just before the arrival of Cajetan — through an agreement with Mayenne and both factions of the Catholic League.[29] But the pope, through his legate, refused to recognize this relationship, since he himself claimed the title of protector of the Catholic religion in France, or any place else. Mayenne seized this opportunity to deny that he had recognized the protectorship of Philip II in the treaty of November, and insisted that only the pope (whom Mayenne considered a much less dangerous ally than Philip) could rightfully claim such a title.[30] Thus, by early 1590, France found herself blessed with not only two kings, but also a lieutenant-general of the kingdom, a League executive council, and two royal protectors, each of whom presumed to be the ultimate arbitrator in the affairs of France.

CHARLES X VERSUS HENRY IV: THE LEAGUE SCHISM WIDENS

Shortly after the arrival of the cardinal-legate, the city of Paris made its formal declaration and proclaimed Charles X, king of France. This action was soon followed by Rouen, Dijon, Toulouse, Grenoble, Aix, and other cities.[31] On December 15, the cardinal-king issued letters patent ordering the striking of royal coins bearing his image,[32] and on December

22, he issued a declaration to the people of France calling on them to unite in putting down the threat of destruction at the hands of Navarre and the Huguenots.[33]

At the same time, a campaign was launched by the Sorbonne to strip Navarre of his following and strengthen the pronouncements of Cajetan against him. On 5 March 1590, a second proscription, recognizing Charles X as king of France and again condemning Navarre, was issued by the League and the Parlement de Paris.[34] The publication of the edict was accompanied by a great ceremony in Paris, attended by Mendoza, the papal legate, and all of the city officials.[35]

In spite of this outward evidence of success, matters were not proceeding well for Spain and the League. Part of the difficulty stemmed from the inability of Philip's three envoys to get along with one another. Relations between Mendoza and Moreo were especially strained during the fall of 1589, and by December the two were sharply at odds. Mendoza, who considered himself by age (he was then forty-eight or forty-nine), rank, birth, and seniority to be the leading voice in the "triumvirate," strongly resented Moreo's independent and self-important attitude. Moreo, for his part, considered Mendoza past his prime, and loudly disagreed with the way he managed affairs in Paris.

In a critical letter of October 12, he questioned Mendoza's authority to give him orders, asserting that he had full powers to negotiate and treat with the League, "without need of a teacher or a stepfather." [36] Mendoza answered the note a short time later with a letter of his own in which he carefully set forth his right to act as spokesman for the three, chastising Moreo for acting so impetuously and for being so rebellious to authority.[37] "You are still young," said the ambassador, "and I am old, and I pray that God will grant you a life long enough that you will be permitted to see France without heresy and at peace and rest.[38] But don't believe everything you are told [probably referring to Mayenne], nor suppose that this end can be achieved by other means [than those Mendoza had been pursuing]."

Philip was distressed to hear of this friction; but, convinced that both men were too valuable to lose, he urged them to forget their differences and work together for the cause in which they were all engaged. On 7 January 1590, he wrote to both of them, asking each to disregard the difficulties and minor irritations of the other, which were causing the work to be even harder than it should be, and try to get along. Philip attributed their trouble chiefly to the machinations of the enemy who was trying to come between them and frustrate their plans (referring perhaps to the increased resistance of the "nationalist"-oriented Parlement de Paris which had come to the realization, along with many others, that the League was a tool of Spain). Of prime importance, he insisted, was their reconciliation and working together.[39] On the following day he also wrote to Tassis, who had gone to Flanders, and instructed him to do his best to reconcile the two as soon as he returned to Paris.[40] But even before Philip's commendations arrived, Mendoza and Moreo had settled the grievances between them and were once more working together cooperatively. In December, Mendoza wrote to Don Martin de Idiáquez that he had "passed many pleasant moments with Tassis and Moreo, who have made me forget my melancholy."[41]

The three were now confronted with even graver difficulties. Since Charles X had been officially declared and recognized by the Catholics as king of France, Mayenne saw no further need for the unwieldly Council of Forty, and proceeded to execute a *coup de main* and, under sharp protest by Mendoza and the Paris Leaguers, disband the group. The council, he asserted, expressed a degree of republicanism which was inappropriate and unseemly for a monarchy. In its place he formed a small and controllable ten-man council of state, which was loyal to him and to the concepts of the Gallican Leaguers.[42]

At the same time, Villeroy counseled Mayenne to accept Navarre as king of France immediately, conditioned of course upon his willingness to abjure Protestantism. If he refused to abjure, Villeroy proposed the proclaiming of the count of Soissons, or some other prince of the house of Bourbon, as king.[43] Mayenne, however, was not yet ready to throw in his lot completely with the Politiques, although he was much more amenable to negotiation than his brother had ever been, and more than he himself had been a year before. With each passing day Mayenne, and the segment of Catholic nobility who followed him, moved further away from the ideology of the urban, popularly oriented, and Spanish-dominated section of the League — represented by Mendoza and the Paris Sixteen — and closer to the nationalistic monarchism of the Politiques.[44]

Two things prevented Mayenne from accepting Villeroy's advice in 1590. First, Navarre was not quite ready to forsake his staunchest Protestant followers and return to the Catholic Church, which was a *sine qua non* for even the most conciliatory elements of the League. Secondly, Navarre's victorious march through Normandy during the fall of 1589 and his successful defense of Arques and Dieppe against Mayenne's all-out attack, followed by his decisive defeat of the League forces at Ivry on 14 March 1590, had humiliated Mayenne intensely and made him determined to defeat Navarre first and negotiate afterward.[45]

SIEGE AND FAMINE IN PARIS

The encounter at Ivry, brilliantly led by Henry of Navarre, completely routed Mayenne's army and left the road to Paris open to the swelling Protestant-Politique forces.[46] Reinforced by 5000 troops from England [47] with fresh supplies and money, Navarre, after meticulously taking all of the surrounding towns of any importance, moved his batteries into position for the siege which was to bring Paris to her knees and himself to the throne. By late in April, his preparations were complete and the siege of Paris began. During the next four months the people of Paris were subjected to their greatest hardships and suffering of the religious wars. The agonizing weeks without food or supplies, as the inhabitants of the city doggedly refused to submit under the relentless attack, have been chronicled by several eyewitnesses and participants of varying reliability and insight.[48]

For Mendoza, too, the siege of Paris was the hardest episode of his career, yet in the midst of his deepest physical suffering he rose to his greatest moral stature, at least in the eyes of the Paris masses. Mendoza accepted the challenge of the siege as a personal charge to encourage and lead the population of that city in an uncompromising defense.[49] He was not alone in his determination. The preachers and Jesuits, the Sixteen, the cardinal-legate, and the city officials were almost as one in their fanatical resolve to resist, although the opposition of the Paris Politiques was significant. The ideological conflict had become very real to the people of Paris. Most of them believed they were the last defense against the chaos which must inevitably follow if heresy and Protestantism should prevail.

Mendoza helped promote that belief and liberally expended what money he had left in a series of projects designed to succor the starving people and at the same time strengthen the bonds between them and the king of Spain. He purchased bread and flour and distributed them daily among the sick and starving, with the commendation that this gift was from his master the king of Spain, who would make good his promise of protection and send them food and aid.[50] He established public kitchens in several parts of the city where a porridge was made from the meager ingredients available and distributed free to the people. When his own money was gone, Mendoza melted down what plate he possessed, struck coins bearing the seal of Spain, and distributed them among the poor at the main squares and intersections of the city.[51] The crowd's immediate reply of "Vive Philippe II!" a contemporary tells us, was spontaneous and genuine. The Politiques were equally quick to remind the people that Mendoza's gratuities were for selfish and dangerously anti-French motives. As the supply of food and other provisions in Paris diminished, their price skyrocketed until not even the wealthy possessed enough money to provide for their needs. According to many accounts, it was Mendoza who, after the exhaustion of all other food supplies, proposed making flour by grinding up bones from the cemetery.[52] Throughout the siege Mendoza frequently could be found animating the defenders at the walls and bastions and advising them on how to make their defenses stronger.[53]

Few of Mendoza's urgent messages got through to Philip during those harrowing months, but those that reached him pleaded for prompt intervention to relieve the city.[54] The decision was not an easy one for Philip. He had avoided military intervention in France while Henry III still reigned because of his legalistic aversion to rebellion against constituted authority. That obstacle no longer impeded him but, since the costly destruction of the Armada with its accompanying confusion and disorganization of military units and the near financial bankruptcy of the government, the only effective army which Philip could possibly put into the field in time to relieve the city was that of the duke of Pama in Flanders. He had hesitated to withdraw Farnese from the Netherlands for fear of an advance by the Dutch as soon as he was gone. But the situation was now critical. If Paris were lost, France would fall to the heretics; and if France were lost, the pivot of Philip's foreign policy would be destroyed. In the middle of July he ordered Parma to march south to relieve Paris.

SPANISH ARMS AND AIMS IN FRANCE

Parma receive his orders with serious apprehensions. He had hoped to be given reinforcements to complete the task assigned him in the Netherlands, but he was too good a soldier to disobey commands. Late in August, he crossed the frontier into France with a body of the finest and most experienced troops in Europe. Philip had now committed himself completely and irrevocably to the Catholics of France.[55]

Parma's advance toward Paris was a masterpiece of military maneuvering. He drew Navarre out from Paris by advancing as though he intended to engage the king in battle. But Parma had no intentions of wasting his troops in such a costly foray when his real objective was to relieve Paris. He quickly fortified himself on the Marne, opposite Lagny, then, faking a crossing downstream to draw off Navarre's forces, he threw a boat bridge across at Lagny and with control of both banks poured his troops into that city, then on to Paris.[56] The siege was broken and the capital delivered. Navarre withdrew his army into Normandy where he hoped soon to erase the humiliation of this defeat.

Parma remained in Paris only long enough to insure its safety and deliver the food and provisions brought along for that purpose, then he returned to his job in the Netherlands. But Paris did not revert to tranquillity. During the early weeks of the siege the captive Charles X had died. The Catholic League was now without a king. For the first time Mayenne began to propose seriously his own candidacy and claims to the throne. Pamphlets and genealogies were issued showing his line of descent from Charlemagne, and his firmness in the Catholic cause.[57] But Paris and many of the other League cities opposed this move. With its politics now dominated by the popular preachers and the Sixteen, Paris had many notions of its own about choosing a king.

At this point Philip II openly proposed to the League the

candidacy of his daughter.[58] If the Salic Law were disclaimed, the infanta, as granddaughter of Henry II, would have the strongest legal right of any of the numerous claimants. Mendoza put forth the king's proposals to the people and to the Council of Sixteen. In Paris, the theologians and jurists hotly debated the legalities and technicalities, the merits and objections of each of the many claims.[59] Early in 1591, the debate was even carried by Pierre Jeannin (president of the Parlement de Dijon and advisor to Mayenne) to Spain, where the validity of the Salic Law was being impugned by the Spanish jurists. The result of the Jeannin mission, after much fruitless talk about the creation of a joint Franco-Spanish army, was an agreement that an Estates General should be called in Paris to make a final decision on the succession question.[60]

For the first time in five years the papacy supported the claims and policy of Spain and convinced Philip that the time was ripe for concerted action in France. The reason for this shift in papal preference was the death of Sixtus V and the succession of Hercules Sfrondata as Pope Gregory XIV. The new pope was as convinced as Philip himself that the succession of a heretic to the throne of France would mean the loss of France to the Roman church and the deathblow to hopes for Christian unity. Gregory immediately announced the verification of the previous excommunication of Navarre, and called on the people of France to reject the pretentions of the relapsed heretic.[61] This papal action coincided with Philip's dispatch of a small Spanish force to Brittany to assist the duke of Mercoeur in securing that duchy against Huguenot attack,[62] and the subsequent Spanish raid into Languedoc, where the Leaguer marshal Joyeuse had hopes of wresting some of the Bourbon lands from the tenacious grip of Montmorency.[63]

Chapter X I

COLLAPSE OF THE LEAGUE

✤ ✤ ✤ ✤

THE temporary improvement in the French situation prompted Mendoza to renew his repeated request to be relieved of his duties. The long months of siege had put a great strain on his weakened body, and he was almost totally blind. This time Philip accepted Mendoza's petition, and on November 18 he sent Diego de Ibarra to replace Mendoza as Spanish representative to France and the League.[1] "I have decided to send Don Diego de Ibarra," explained Philip, "who will inform you of the commission he carries, which is the same as that which you have held. But for the best success of the mission do not leave there until he has taken over."[2]

MENDOZA'S RETIREMENT AND LATER LIFE

Mendoza's last dispatch from Paris, dated 31 December 1590, is a nine-page summary report of conditions in France as he left them. In this *relación final* he expressed considerable concern for the particular needs and problems of Paris and for the Catholic League in general.[3] He sharply criticized Parma for returning to the Netherlands without leaving a garrison to defend the city, and reported his own efforts to secure some military force to strengthen the defenses. Mendoza was particularly irritated by the failure of either Parma or Mayenne to provide him with an escort to leave the capital. With Huguenot patrols on all sides of Paris, unescorted travel was impossible. Parma had promised him an escort, but had not complied, and Mayenne refused outright because he could not spare the troops. By the end of the year the ambassador was so tired and discouraged that he threatened to ask safe conduct of the king of Navarre rather than remain longer in Paris.[4]

Finally, on 3 January 1591, he was met by an escort of 200 German soldiers, sent by Mayenne, and conducted to the fortress at Milon, which was commanded by Alexandro del Monte and a regiment of Neapolitans. Del Monte provided the ambassador with an escort to Soissons and from there to Guise. Mendoza's journey was delayed at Guise, however, because his escorting soldiers had pillaged his baggage and taken not only the few valuables he had left, but, even more discouraging, many of his very important papers, including the financial accounts of the embassy.[5] He remained at Guise until the middle of February trying to recover his losses, but with little success.

On February 19, Mendoza wrote a lengthy dispatch from Mons, in Flanders, giving a fuller account of his exit from Paris and his ensuing misfortunes, and a report of the most important financial matters to be taken care of immediately by his successor.[6] It had been decided that he should delay his return to Spain for a few months until his health was better and the passage could be accomplished more safely. Mons proved to be a suitable stopping point, and here Mendoza remained until summer, carrying on frequent correspondence with Philip, Idiáquez, Parma, and others on matters of policy and action in France, and observing the political changes of that year from a more removed vantage point. Late in March he received a gratifying note from Philip — which must have given him deep satisfaction — congratulating him on his performance in France during the preceding six and one-half years under such difficult circumstances.[7]

By summer Mendoza's physical condition had improved, and in June he received permission from Philip to return to

Madrid. He received this news with rejoicing, and immediately took up the slow journey toward his homeland.[8] On
August 23, Mendoza was in Stavelo, where he wrote to Philip
and Martín de Idiáquez about his financial settlement with
Parma. On August 27 he was in Nancy. Here he met a company of German reiters on their way to Italy, and happily
reported to Idiáquez that he would be in Milan within two
weeks.[9] This is the last letter we have from Mendoza, and
there seems to be no further mention of his journey in other
documents, but it can probably be assumed that he reached
Madrid sometime during the late fall or winter of 1591.

The remaining thirteen years of Mendoza's life were devoted primarily to intellectual and literary pursuits, although
he still remained in close touch with international affairs, and
especially with the problems of France.[10] In 1592, he published
the first Spanish edition of his noteworthy *Comentarios*, which
had already appeared the previous year in a French edition.[11]
This vivid military chronicle of the Dutch wars was begun
(and the first part completed) while he was still in Flanders,
and was probably concluded in 1589.

In 1594, as a result of his own long military experience and
active mind, Mendoza completed his ambitious — and in some
ways more valuable — manual of the art of war, entitled
Theorica y practica de guerra (Madrid: Viuda de Pedro
Madrigal, 1595). The *Theorica*, which deals with a great
variety of military tactics and strategy, including naval warfare, was a useful book in its time, and even received a lauda-
tory commendation to Prince Philip by Maestro de Campo
(Field Marshal) Francisco Arias de Bobadilla. It went through
several editions just after its publication, and was translated
more than once. An English edition, translated by Sir Edward
Hoby, appeared as early as 1597. The frequent reflections on
political and moral issues give the book a peculiar interest
today.

In spite of his blindness, Mendoza was remarkably well-read

and very alert to the publications of his day. He was particularly impressed by the writings of the Flemish humanist and stoic, Justus Lipsius,[12] and during the last years of the century he devoted himself to translating Lipsius' *Politicorum sive Civilis Doctrinae libri sex* (which had appeared in 1589) into Spanish for the benefit of "the Spanish nobility who do not read Latin." Mendoza's *Los seis libros de las políticas ó doctrina civil de Justo Lipsio, que sirven para gobierno del reyno ó principado* (Madrid: Juan Flamenco, 1604) was published posthumously just two months after his death.

In addition to these three major works, Mendoza wrote numerous smaller essays, few of which are still in existence, and a considerable amount of poetry.[13] Unfortunately, only scattered fragments of the latter are known to still exist,[14] but we have the testimony of one of his countrymen, that "they are worthy of being better known." [15] The last few years of Mendoza's life were spent in relative seclusion at Madrid, probably in the monastery of San Bernardino, where he died on August 3, 1604.

"PARIS IS WORTH A MASS"

From the standpoint of Spain and the League, the situation in France deteriorated rapidly during the summer and fall of 1591. No matter what methods he used, Ibarra could not control the Paris Sixteen as Mendoza had done,[16] and the influence of the Politiques rose steadily among the royalist followers of Navarre. The split between Paris and the rest of the League became deeper than ever before. In September 1591 a formal document was drawn up by the Sixteen and sent to Philip, recognizing unconditionally the claims of the Spanish infanta to the throne of France and declaring the League, "and all good Catholics of France," under the protection and authority of Philip II.[17] This valuable and controversial document was signed by each of the members of the council, and carried by courier to Spain.

Mayenne soon learned of this action, either through an intercepted dispatch or from his spies in Paris, and demanded a prompt retraction by the Sixteen. But, instead of submission from Paris, he got rebellion. By early November, the Sixteen and the radical preachers had stirred Paris to a new heat against the Politiques (who were also growing in numbers and becoming more outspoken in their resistance to the League), and created a revolutionary tribunal of ten for suppressing the growing movement. Lists were drawn up to expedite the prosecution of individuals suspected of disloyalty to the Paris League or undue sympathy toward Mayenne and his followers.[18]

On November 16, Barnabé Brisson, the moderate Leaguer president of the Parlement de Paris (since the imprisonment of Harlay in 1589) and close friend of Mayenne, was accused by the Sixteen of Politique sympathies. He was arrested, along with two other eminent lawyers, pre-emptorily tried, and promptly executed.[19] When Mayenne heard of this reign of terror in Paris he rushed a regiment into the capital, seized the leaders of the Sixteen, declared the council disbanded, and hanged four of the most troublesome offenders. The violent activities of the Paris Leaguers did not cease as a result of Mayenne's action — during the next two years they were more outspoken and vitriolic in their attacks on Navarre, and especially on the Politiques, than ever before — but the Sixteen was restrained as an organized body and its influence greatly reduced.

Since his attempt to overpower Paris had ended in failure in 1590, Henry of Navarre had undertaken a subtler method of bringing the proud city to its knees. Rouen was the key point in his new plan to cut off the Seine and all other lifelines to Paris. If Rouen could be taken, his line of communication with England would be unbroken and he could exert an unlimited pressure on Paris. In the autumn of 1591, the build-up of supplies and men began; 16,000 German mercenaries, com-

manded by Marshal Turenne, arrived in October to strengthen
Navarre's attack, joined by 6,000 Swiss and a detachment of
4,000 English infantry and cavalry under the earl of Essex.[20]
Mayenne was also reinforced by a motley array of 3,000
Italians, 6,000 Swiss, and 2,000 Neapolitan Spaniards sent by
the pope, under the command of Ercole Sfondrato, duke of
Montemarciano.[21]

In December the siege of Rouen began in force. By March
it seemed certain the citadel would fall. But once again the
veteran *tercios* of the duke of Parma arrived from Flanders,
evaded Navarre's besieging army, and relieved the city. It
became increasingly obvious to Navarre that manpower and
military campaigns alone would not be sufficient to win him
the crown of France. But the relief of Rouen had been more
costly to the Catholics than was first realized. To secure the
best position for relieving Rouen, Parma had taken Caudebec.
His skillful withdrawal from that city and successful return
to Flanders again attested to his pre-eminence as a military
leader — perhaps the greatest of the century. It was his last
campaign, however. On 2 December 1592, he died of a wound
received during the defense of Caudebec.[22]

In January 1593 the long-awaited Estates General finally
met in Paris for the purpose of choosing a king for the tottering realm. Since the assembly was called by Mayenne, and
the Huguenots were not present,[23] it is generally referred to
as the Estates of the League. Philip's claims and intentions
were represented there by his ambassador extraordinary, Lorenzo Suárez de Figueroa, duke of Feria.[24] Diego de Ibarra and
Jean Baptiste Tassis also remained in Paris, close to the meetings of the Estates General, and brought to bear whatever
influence they could on its decisions. Feria's skill in dealing
with the assembly left much to be desired and caused many
of the deputies at Paris, even some of the staunch Leaguers,
to become suspicious of Philip's intentions.[25]

In May, Feria imprudently proposed that the Salic Law be

abrogated and the infanta of Spain be accepted as queen of France. This brought an immediate reaction in the assembly and caused some of the Catholics who were previously hostile to Henry of Navarre to look to him as their only possible choice for king.[26] In the meantime, the Parlement de Paris convened and began discussion of issues introduced by Feria. In June, President Le Maistre issued his famous declaration which affirmed in unequivocal terms that under no conditions could the Salic law be put aside.[27] This declaration won the support of the Politique party and contributed greatly to the failure of the League and Spanish intentions. Finally, with the insistence of the Sixteen and some of the Paris clergy, and following precise orders from Philip, Feria proposed the election of the young Duke Charles of Guise as king of France and his accompanying marriage to the Spanish infanta (in order to give legitimacy to the succession). This proposal for a union of the houses of Hapsburg and Guise in order to gain the crown of France elicited immediate and impassioned controversy in Paris.

But the month was July, and by then it was too late for the Spanish-League forces to prevent Navarre from mounting the throne. Paris itself was becoming more amenable as the people began to see the true nature of Spanish-League relations and the extent and danger of Spanish domination of French policies. They realized finally that their national independence was at stake. Religious traditions were still strong enough to prevent a defiant heretic from becoming king of France, but not to oppose a moderate and popular Politique. Navarre, recognizing the improbability of winning the crown as a Protestant, began in May 1593 to accept instruction by the mother church. It was becoming evident to all but the most ardent Huguenots and Leaguers that his conversion would be the most realistic step toward an acceptable solution of the whole succession problem. Even Henry's closest Protestant advisor admitted the desirability of such a move.[28]

On Sunday, 25 July 1593, in an elaborate and colorful ceremony at Saint-Denis, Henry publicly attended Mass and in a solemn recantation formally adjured the Reformed faith. His fellowship with the church, however, was not so sudden as his apparent conversion. The League and the Jesuits loudly denounced his action as an open affront to religion and an insult to God, and many still refused to recognize him as king; but the act of conversion won him more friends and supporters than it lost. Henry's alleged statement that "Paris is worth a Mass" proved to be just as valid as he might have anticipated. By 27 February 1594, after a final fight between the revived remnant of the Sixteen and the Parlement de Paris over recognition of Henry as king, the way was cleared for his coronation at Chartres (Rheims was still held by the League). A month later he made his triumphal entry into Paris. Finally, on 17 September 1595, after further lengthy negotiations, he was granted full absolution by Pope Clement VIII.[29]

END OF THE LEAGUE AND OF THE RELIGIOUS WARS

France again had a king, and a very capable one, but it also still had the problems of disunity, bankruptcy, and war. The Politiques had won the day, yet the League was still powerful in many of the provinces, and was now receiving continuous open military assistance from Spain. Nevertheless, the deterioration of the League was rapid after Henry undermined its ideological appeal by his reconciliation with the church. The complete submission of the League to Spain brought it the stigma of disloyalty at a time when patriotism was beginning to have a rebirth under the aegis of Henry IV. Support of the League now meant the acceptance and promotion of Spanish interests in France, and was considered by an increasing number of Frenchmen as an open act of treason. "The final rejection of the League," Wilkinson summarizes, "was caused by the growing nationalism of the people: the feeling that Spain and the internationalism of the Jesuits were the common enemy." [30] Anti-Spanish feeling in France was rapidly reaching its zenith.

Early in 1594 one of the most famous and influential of the thousands of polemical pamphlets produced during the religious wars was published in Paris, after circulating for many months in manuscript. The *Satyre Ménippée* was a work of joint Politique authorship intended primarily as a burlesque of the Estates General of 1593 and a denunciation of Spanish intervention in France.[31] The *Satyre* systematically assailed the supporters of the League: the Paris preachers, the Jesuits, the duchess of Montpensier, the papal legate, Mendoza, Parma, Mayenne, and Guise, while proclaiming the legitimacy and strength of Henry IV. In a succession of wit, sarcasm, and invective, in both verse and prose, the authors delivered their pungent strokes through the mouths of deputies to the Estates General. The climax was reached in a summation speech by M. d'Aubray, delegate of the third estate, who, in an eloquent discourse, exposed the fallacies in the League arguments against Henry's succession. The author of this discourse, Pierre Pithou, insisted that the religion of the king is unimportant in comparison with his hereditary right and with his ability to rule, and even maintained that until Spanish influence corrupted France no one there paid any particular attention to the religious beliefs of the monarch. The case for the king was no better stated in the *Satyre Ménippée* than it had been by Bodin in 1576, but it fell on more sympathetic ears. The political situation had changed greatly in twenty years, and France longed for stability and an end to civil war.

Henry IV won further sympathy and support by his announcement that he would not lay down his sword until all Spaniards had been driven from French soil. But the way ahead was still uncertain when he received the jeweled and coveted crown in February 1594. How many of the League commanders like Mayenne, Aumale, and Mercoeur would stay with the Spanish in opposition to the anointed king of

France? If they were not moved by patriotism could they be bought with cash? What effect would Henry's defection have upon his former Huguenot companions? Would they support him in war against Spain, or would they oppose him as a traitor to the faith? What was Elizabeth's reaction to the change of events? Would she continue to give aid to Henry now that he had renounced the Protestant cause, or would she withdraw once more to her island fortress?

The answers to these uncertainties were soon forthcoming. Late in 1593, Henry assured the English queen, through her special agent, Sir Thomas Wilks, that he would "continue the offensive and defensive league with Elizabeth against the king of Spain so long as he continued in war against the queen, and never make peace nor accord with him without first advising her and making satisfactory provision for her inclusion in the settlement." [32] Elizabeth hesitatingly reciprocated this agreement and it became the basis for their joint operations against Spain during the following months, although the queen coyly restricted her military actions on the continent to areas where she hoped to gain permanent advantage: the Dieppe-to-Calais coast and northern Brittany. The Huguenot problem was postponed for future solution with the acceptable promise that the previous edicts of toleration of 1577 and 1591 would be maintained and enforced in their behalf. Most of the Huguenots supported Henry's war against Spain. The isolation of the League commanders and their vulnerability to bribe, coupled with Henry's own personal magnetism, enabled him to win as many by diplomacy as by the sword.

His first, and perhaps greatest, victory came with the occupation of Paris in March 1594. The defense of Paris had been given to Charles de Cossé Brissac who willingly accepted a subsidy from Henry in return for his submission of the League capital to the king. On March 22, Henry rode triumphantly into the city and the small remaining Spanish garrison was allowed to withdraw, with the reported parting salute of the king, "Commend me to your master, but never come back again." [33] The occupation of Paris added immeasurably to the growing prestige of the new king and gave momentum to his operation. The only remaining strongholds of the League were Burgundy and Brittany, with substantial but declining strength in Champagne, Poitiers, Picardy, and Normandy. The cities of Rouen, Le Havre, and others in Normandy soon passed to the king, and shortly afterward the principal cities of Picardy. On 17 January 1595, Henry IV formalized his position toward Spain by an official declaration of war.

With the disclosure of the papal absolution in September, more of the Catholic leaders ended their resistance to the king. The young duke of Guise surrendered Champagne for 3,888,830 livres, and in January 1596 Mayenne himself capitulated. But Henry's military campaigns against the Spanish defenses in Brittany, at Amiens, and at La Fère were not so successful. In fact, while he pounded at these strongholds, Spanish troops took Cambrai and Doullens, and on 26 April 1596 they seized Calais. It was not until September 1597 that Amiens was finally recovered, and Mercoeur held out in Brittany until March 1598.[34]

In the meantime, peace negotiations had begun at Vervins, but for many weeks they were stalemated by Philip's reluctance to give up the conquests he had made in the north. With Mercoeur's surrender in Brittany, however, and his own waning health, Philip became anxious to conclude a separate peace with Henry. On 2 May 1598 the Treaty of Vervins was signed, reaffirming the approximate territorial lines of the 1559 Treaty of Cateau-Cambrésis, and ending the Franco-Spanish war.[35] Four months later Philip II died.

The final step in the termination of the Wars of Religion in France was the issuance of the famous Edict of Nantes which granted the Huguenots liberty of conscience, freedom of worship (except in certain large cities such as Paris), equal civil and political rights with the Catholics, bipartisan judicial bodies, two hundred fortified cities and some three thousand other strongholds, and promised government funds for the support of Protestant schools and the payment of pastors.[36] This magnanimous recognition and protection of a second religious profession alongside the official religion of the state marked the first significant step toward the achievement of religious toleration in France.

CONCLUSIONS

Some summary observations about the general nature of the period covered in this study and the particular place occupied in it by Mendoza and the League seem in order. It is only by recognizing the importance of religious motivation in the minds of many of the policymakers of the time that the international activity between Spain and France comes into a consistent focus. Personal, dynastic, economic, and political factors all contributed heavily to the course of events in France, but it also seems adequately demonstrated that the religious issue played a leading role, at least in the policies of Philip II and of the League between 1584 and 1591. Philip's costly support of an organization which in structure and in political theory was the very antithesis of his own beliefs and traditions and which was led by one of the most serious rivals to the house of Hapsburg makes little sense in political and economic terms. In view of the religious goal and duty envisaged by the Catholic King, his actions are more comprehensible. Yet, it is not always easy to distinguish between Philip's Spanish policy and his Catholic policy; to him they appear to have been synonomous.

The turning point in the direction pursued by the League after its refounding in 1584 was the murder of the duke of Guise at the end of 1588. With Guise removed from the helm, the League swerved recklessly from its course. Some segments of it, gathered in and guided by Mendoza and the Paris Sixteen, continued to follow the path marked out by Philip's conception of the Counter Reformation, but an ever-growing body of Leaguers joined with the more nationalistic aims of Mayenne and veered sharply toward the nationalist Gallicanism of the Politiques. Nothing Philip would do could prevent the split. The more actively he participated in the affairs of that kingdom, the more Catholics he alienated. Mendoza's retirement in 1591, the fanaticism of the Sixteen, Parma's death in 1592, the growing nationalistic and anti-Spanish feeling in France, and the effective work of the Politiques and the Parlement de Paris all prepared the way for Navarre's success in 1593.

What did the defeat of the extremists, both Catholic and Protestant, and the victory of the Politiques, mean to France and to the future religious and political development of Europe? First of all, it meant the revival of personal, and soon almost absolute, monarchy in France. Parties and principles gradually gave way to authority and political expediency. Royalism became more popular and fashionable than it had been for many decades. The freshness and spirit of the new Bourbon dynasty won the loyalty of many segments of French society which had felt nothing but contempt for the declining Valois. But some of the methods used by Henry IV to win the fidelity of his subjects created endless difficulties for the future. Much of the immediate loyalty and support he gained was at the expense of long-range control over the nobility and the bureaucracy. His heirs were to feel the real effects of Henry IV's popularity.

In France the triumph of the Politiques meant a victory for the Gallican Church, but, even more important, it revealed the first flicker of light announcing the dawn of a distant day of religious toleration. The beginning of this new attitude toward religion was a victory for the kind of tolerance represented by Montaigne, as characterized in his criticism of the Religious Wars:

> In my time I have seen marvels in the prodigious ease with which people allow themselves to be led by the nose, and made to believe and hope whatever their leaders please. . . . A man is no member of a movement if he dares to breast the wave, if he does not roll in with the tide. As for me, I should have to hate too many people. . . . We have no need to harden our hearts with steel armor; enough if our shoulders are hardened. It will do to dip our pens in ink, without dipping them in blood. Righteousness must be made to prevail over duty.[37]

As for the rest of Europe, the end of the League also began a decline in the supranational religious ideal represented by Philip of Spain. Religious controversies did not cease in 1598 and religious motives in political affairs were prominent for years to come, but the biggest step toward creating a predominantly secular approach to political affairs, especially in international relations, had been made. No one after Philip II ever seriously attempted to recreate the *res publica Christiana* in Europe. England and Germany were still to struggle through their own religious wars, but the solution found in France to the problems unleashed by the Reformation eventually became recognized as the most practical solution for the rest of Europe.

A concluding word about Mendoza himself. The League was not an isolated French institution. It was intricately involved in the international struggle which engaged all of western Europe in the late sixteenth century. Mendoza's connection with it, even while he was accredited ambassador to France, can hardly be overemphasized. Through the various mediums described, Mendoza was able to influence and guide the strategy of the Council of Sixteen, and with it much of the League, in accordance with the desires and plans of the king of Spain. Even more important was Mendoza's friendship and continual communication with the duke of Guise. As a rule, Paris and the other League towns of France adhered rather closely to Guise's orders and leadership, while he in turn — in spite of strong personal ambitions — did what he was instructed from Spain. Few of the major League decisions or operations between 1584 and December 1588 were undertaken without direct orders from Philip, or at least with complete Spanish knowledge and approval. After the death of Guise, Mendoza's role in the activities of the League, and especially of the Sixteen, was even more intimate. Many times decisions were made and tactics planned under his leadership and advice. When Henry III was removed from the scene in 1589, Mendoza became an official agent to the League, with instructions to advise, influence, and even direct its activity and planning. In the meantime, the split which occurred within the League reduced the extent of Mendoza's influence, although within its smaller orbit he seems to have been stronger than before. On the other hand, the wing of the League led by Mayenne disliked him almost as much as they did Navarre and the Huguenots.

As the ideal ambassador, in the sense understood in our day, Mendoza would probably rank far down the list. His capacity for compromise, for assuasive talk and indulgent debate, was definitely limited. He possessed a strong and aggressive personality which, when energized by the intensity of the religious conflict, became overbearing and dogmatic. He was intelligent and had broad experience, but the fervor of the ideological absolutism which dominated his day also determined his outlook as a diplomat. Diplomacy in the Age of Religious Wars was merely another arm of the military, to be used by the king as he would use his artillery or cavalry for crushing the enemy. In such a framework, Mendoza would perhaps be considered one of the most effective and capable diplomats of his age.

Even his personal traits can be understood and correctly appraised only in the light of this life-or-death conflict in which he believed he was engaged. Mendoza was born into a world split by the impact of ideological warfare, and in a country which had taken the lead on one side of that struggle. It is not surprising that he became a bigot. His deepest personal inclinations were probably toward intellectual pursuits and scholarly achievements, but the fire of religious dogmatism had ignited all of Europe by the 1560's and had penetrated deeply into Mendoza's homeland. Instinctively he plunged headlong into the turbulence and took his place at the battle-front. For the next twenty-five years, whether it was astride a horse in Flanders or leading the diplomatic offensives in London or Paris, Mendoza remained a soldier. He knew that battles and wars were won by audacity and attack, and he applied this rule wherever he was sent or whatever title he bore. His weaknesses and limitations were also the weaknesses and limitations of the Religious Wars and of the narrow ideological concepts which inspired them.

The real criterion for evaluating a diplomat in this or any other period is whether he accomplished honorably and successfully the mission to which he was assigned, not whether his contemporaries thought he was a nice fellow. Mendoza was sent to France with important instructions to keep his government informed continuously on the political and religious situation there, give advice and support to the Catholics who were fighting heresy, and use his influence and skill to keep France within the Catholic camp. There were, of course, many other objectives of his ministry, and innumerable exigencies which required his attention. Whether these policies were sound or ephemeral is of no concern at the moment, but how he went about accomplishing them, and with what success, is.

As a high-level political observer and commentator, Mendoza was perhaps not above the average of his contemporaries. Through his friends, pensioners, and coreligionists, he was able to remain in touch with a wide range of activity in Europe and keep his government adequately informed. The very extensiveness of his intelligence system, however, reduced its accuracy and effectiveness. Too much reliance was placed on the purchase of information, which many times turned out to be not only inaccurate but even purposely falsified. Mendoza tended at times to be uncritical, even gullible, in accepting favorable reports without question, while remaining highly skeptical of those which were not so propitious. His reporting of the Battle of Coutras, and the defeat of the Armada are two outstanding examples of this. His excessive faith in the right and inevitable triumph of the Catholic cause blinded him to a great many conditions and situations which he otherwise had the ability and opportunity to appraise more judiciously. He was particularly unable to cope with the opposition of the Politiques who, after the death of Henry III, were his principal adversaries. Their recognition of his motives and activities was costly to him, and he was never able to comprehend, let alone appreciate, their form of secular patriotism.

Yet, as a personal observer of the political machinations in France and as a subtle judge of character, Mendoza demonstrated remarkable skill and insight. He usually anticipated the actions of the French king in sufficient time to advise his government and to alert the duke of Guise, and he generally had a fair grasp of the intentions and allegiance of the various Paris factions. He knew the people with whom he had to deal, and used this to an advantage in his negotiations, especially with the League. But again his religious zeal caused him to believe in a propensity of European populations — in France, England, Scotland, and elsewhere — toward Catholicism. He felt certain that the people of England were strongly Catholic at heart and would welcome a return to Rome as soon as they were liberated from the Elizabethan tyranny. Similarly, he believed the Huguenot heresy in France would crumble with the defeat of Navarre, who, with the other Calvinist leaders, had blinded their followers with sophistry and flattery.

As a negotiator, while not possessing those qualities of compromise and moderation considered essential in a diplomat, Mendoza did achieve a certain degree of success. What he lacked in amiability he compensated for in a judicious blending of firmness and finesse. In negotiations with Henry III and his mother, the Spanish ambassador usually attained his objectives, although the cost in personal disfavor was sometimes high. In dealing with the League, Mendoza was even more successful. Here his ability to negotiate is revealed at its best. Undoubtedly one of the chief factors in the degree of cooperation achieved between the League and Spain was the liaison work of Don Bernardino.

The extent of the ambassador's influence upon the shaping of Spanish policy during the 1580's would be very difficult to determine, but Mendoza was unique among functionaries of the Catholic King in the confidence and esteem with which he was held by Philip II throughout the period of his embassy. Philip seems to have trusted Mendoza almost completely, and placed great responsibility upon his shoulders. This rapport which existed between king and ambassador was certainly strengthened, if not created, by their similar politico-religious views. Mendoza's correspondence, as well as Philip's letters and instructions to him, give ample evidence of their general agreement. Outwardly at least, they both equated their personal ambitions with their religious goals and, as with most dogmatists, really believed their political actions were for religious or other equally idealistic reasons.

APPENDIX

APPENDIX

✦ ✦ ✦ ✦

Spanish diplomatic ciphers of the late sixteenth century took many forms but the most frequently used was the simple substitution cipher, such as the one illustrated here:

A B C D E F G H I K L M N O P Q R S T U X Y Z

It was customary to substitute some single sign or combination of signs, numbers, or letters for many of the more commonly used words. In this way, "ambassador" might be written *G* , "France" *99* , "until" *by*, "that" *eç* , and "Your Excellency" *for*. These symbols never followed any set pattern, and presented one of the greatest headaches for the cryptanalyst.

One of the ciphers used in France by Jean Baptiste de Tassis showed a notable deviation from the pattern shown above. It followed a very old and simple procedure but also foreshadowed the versatility and systematization of many post-sixteenth-century ciphers. By writing the numbers from one to zero in two rows, one vertical and the other horizontal, then blocking in the square with the letters of the alphabet, giving a greater number of spaces to vowels and high-frequency consonants, a wide variety of two-digit numbers can then be substituted for any letter of the alphabet. Tassis's table was constructed in this manner:

	1	2	3	4	5	6	7	8	9	0
1	A	A	A	A	A	A	B	B	C	C
2	C	D	D	D	E	E	E	E	E	E
3	E	F	F	G	G	H	H	I	I	I
4	I	I	I	I	I	L	L	L	L	M
5	M	M	M	N	N	N	N	N	O	O
6	O	O	O	O	P	P	P	P	Q	Q
7	Q	R	R	R	R	R	R	S	S	S
8	S	S	S	T	T	T	T	U	U	U
9	U	U	U	X	X	Y	Y	Y	Z	Z

In this system, the letter "E", for example, can be represented in one message by any of seven number combinations, 20, 25, 26, 27, 28, 29, and 31, by reading from vertical to horizontal. The versatility of the system is further emphasized when we observe that another complete set of coordinates can be created simply by reading from horizontal to vertical, or by beginning the alphabet not at position 11, as above, but, say, at 71, 31, or at 58, etc. The appearance of such an endless succession of numbers as would be used in a multi-page ciphered dispatch might well have been baffling enough to cause many a would-be interceptor to give up even before putting the cryptogram to a careful analysis. The disadvantage of this cipher was that once a letter or two in the message had been identified the entire cipher was broken.

The basic structure of Mendoza's syllabic cipher of 1584–1586 was a substitutional alphabet of numbers, signs, and letters with suppressed frequencies of the most used letters:

A B C D E F G H I L M N O P Q R S T U X Y Z

△ ℓ 9 2 7 3 6 4 5 10 22 11 ε 12 ✗ 13 19 14 18 15 17 16

ᵹ c d e f ᵹh ᴣ 17mn o p q r s t v x y ᴢ a

b   ꝗ   ᴢ

Also represented in this cipher (generally by a two-digit number) were the commonly used digraphs:

BL	BR	DR	CH	CL	CR	FR	GU	PR	QU	TR
23	24	ꝓ	25	26	27	29	6+	33	20 (ᶻ)	34

In addition to these substitutions there was also a set of five signs representing the vowels once more and used as *syllable* endings when attached to their accompanying consonant symbols. This is the most characteristic feature of Mendoza's cipher. These syllable endings were:

A   E   I   O   U

The language itself provided the key to this interesting feature of the cipher. Most Spanish words are made up of combinations of two-letter syllables with a consonant as the first letter and a

Ciphered dispatch from Mendoza to Philip

vowel as the last. This succession of consonant-vowel combinations is occasionally interrupted by the presence of an additional consonant, in which case the cryptographer merely inserts the accompanying sign for that letter and proceeds to the next syllable. Many Spanish words also end with one of the three busy consonants N, R, or S (called cognates to the vowels), for which the cipher provided the following signs: $\prime$, $)$, $\wedge$. Occasionally L or M (also considered cognates) stand at the end of a word, in which case they were represented by a dot ($\cdot$) above the preceding sign for an L, and a dot (.) below the preceding sign for an M. Double letters, such as ll, rr, and ss were provided simply by placing a $+$ over the letter to be doubled, and a null was created by inserting a small ($\circ$) above any legitimate symbol or letter, which thereby cancelled out its meaning.

Many proper nouns, titles, names of individuals, and a long list of frequently used words were ciphered by the separate use of arbitrary symbols, generally composed of short meaningless letter combinations or else two-digit numbers (sometimes underlined), which had no relation to the foregoing system. "Cardinal," for example, was ciphered 77 , "kingdom" became xil , a "dispatch" was 33, and "so that" gal . An incomplete but indicative list of these symbols shows the type of words and phrases substituted in this manner:

num	vassal	6̲0̲	army
pem	Venetian	*nul*	prince
2̲l̲	mail	*zel*	fortification
3̲3̲	dispatch	*Xu*	number
dal	office	*co*	people
bel	nuncio	*lo*	England
hem	His Holiness	*gi* ^	heretics
9̲9̲	France	*yu*	negotiation

va	much	*L3*	council
49	God	*re*	manner
66	empress	*xel*	queen
*La^*	infantry	*xal*	king
be	force	*53*	duke
77	cardinal	*tul*	religion
fo	place	*gel*	part
rum	Your Majesty	*lim*	time
*pum^*	Huguenots	*75*	captain
GL.,	ambassador	*40*	after
gil	particular	*85*	horse
86.	cause	*fa*	war

The following sentence from one of Mendoza's ciphered dispatches of 16 July 1585 will illustrate more clearly just how the cipher worked.

74 △ 19+6+ 7 14p 19+ 72. 7 xalf '19+'22., 12., 4112p,16714. SL
El dia siguiente siendo el Rey en Sanmor por haver buelto aqui
The next day at Sanmor, where the king had returned the previous night

△ xₑi◦10. ₂ₑ 41 7l41, d!lo1 xel 296226 hₑ, 19613. 13 40
aquella noche ha estar con la Reyna su muger tuvo consejo despues
to be with the queen his wife, he met after dinner for more than six

2ₑd. 22ₑ, sa 2ₚl 9ₚ l7ε. 13 7 dₑ1312. d!19ₒ 2227ₑf' 77 2ₑ
de comer mas de seys horas encerrado con su madre el cardinal de
hours behind closed doors in council with his mother, the cardinal of

l., l.!f· 5̲3̲ 2ρ ιο.ι3ℓ ιΗf'2ρ h₊ι9̅₊j j 2ρ 5. ι7. ι9̅₊f· 2ρ ι2ρ,ο! Z

Borbon, el duque de Lorena, el de Guissa, el de Joyossa, el de Pernon, y

Bourbon, the dukes of Lorraine, Guise, Joyeuse, and Epernon, and Secre-

Zul H ιο̅₊ι3. 7ι72ρ ιο̂₊î ₊ι23₊ι3! Δgℓ(ρ̧ xα(ι9ꜱ2₂ι27ℓ Zf·

Secretario Villaroe y dellas hablaron aparte el Rey, su madre y el

tary Villeroy. And out of this group the king spoke in private with his

5̲3̲2ρ h₊ι9̅₊ιg. ιο.^ Sa 2ρ(ο̂₊î34ℓ̂ 3 Η ι3₊9₊ Δ'2. ιοℓ j xα(2ρ

duque de Guissa solos mas de las tres acariciandole el Rey de

mother and the duke of Guise for more than half the time, showing such

rℓ xℓ Δ ιο.^2ρ Sa ιο̂ℓ 4ι2ιe. 9ꜱ ι72ιe. jι9ℓ'2ρ, xℓ yuι2. H Δ́

manera que a los demas les ha dado cuydado entender que negocio podian

affection for him [Guise] that the others were anxious to know what

3 4₊ι4ι,9.!ι4₊'2. ι4ρ2 6ℓ ι4.

tratar con tanto secreto.

affair they might be planning in such secret.

Mendoza's 1587 cipher was one of the most unusual and decep-
tive to be used by the diplomats of the late sixteenth century.
The first letter (or consonant) of each syllable was represented
by a single-digit number and the vowel was represented by another. The most interesting feature of this new cipher was its use
of the *same* number for two or more consonants (a necessity,
since there are more letters than single digit numbers), and *two
different* numbers for each single vowel, with the letter value of
the first being determined by the second. A diagram of the letter
and number equivalents would look something like this:

B,C	D,F	G,H	L,M	N,P	Q,R	S,T	X,V	Y,Z
1	2	3	4	5	6	7	8	9

	A	E	I	O	U	
	0,5	1,6	2,7	3,8	4,9	

One short example should illustrate the method of its use. In a
cryptogram, the numbers 74 and 79, if it were known that they
represented syllables, would be expected to signify syllables having the same first letter and different second letters. With Mendoza's system, however, the opposite was true. Since the 7 repre-
sents two different consonants (S and T), the 4 and 9 the same

vowel (U), and the selection of the first is determined by the value of the last, the 74 becomes "su" and 79 is "tu." The system also provided for a full selection of digraphs by simply adding another number and showing its connection with the first two by a small semi-circle above them. The most common of these consonant combinations were:

Bl,Br	Ch,Cl	Cr,Dr	Fl,Fr	Gl,Gr	Pl,Pr	Tr,Vr
60	61	62	63	64	65	66

To these would be added the number signifying the appropriate vowel in order to form the desired syllables, just as shown above. The complete set of vowel cognates (L, M, N, R, S) were indicated by various accent marks, also placed above the syllable numbers. This is the key to this cipher, which Mendoza devised and sent to Idiáquez on 9 April 1587.

Key to Mendoza's numerical cipher

The main features of Mendoza's fourth cipher resembled those of his first (1584–1586) syllabic cipher, with a different set of substitutes. In this case, all of the letters of the alphabet were represented by numbers (with an occasional set of garbled letters used for vowels); and the vowel cognates, used as syllable endings, were grammatical symbols (·· ⁄ : ＼ .) representing L, M, N, R, and S respectively. Final "r"s of a word were represented by a ＋ above the last letter; double letters were indicated by a ⌒; and ⊖ signified a null.

Pseudonyms were frequently used in both ciphered and unciphered correspondence to prevent the quick idenification of obvious persons. The following appear most often in the Mendoza papers.

Philip II	Fabio
Henry III	Camilo
Catherine de' Medici	Hortensio
The duke of Savoy	Julio
The duke of Montmorency	Furio
The duchess of Montmorency	Lepido
The duke of Guise	Mucio (occasionally Curio)
The Duchess of Montpensier	Silvio
Henry of Navarre	Iulio

Deciphered letter from Mendoza to Philip

As far as I have been able to determine, there is no authentic portrait of Bernardino de Mendoza extant. The alleged sketch of Mendoza printed in the Espasa-Calpe *Enciclopedia universal ilustrada* (XXXIV, 623), is from an anonymous engraving in the Junta de Iconografía Nacional in Madrid, but is of another Bernardino de Mendoza (1501-1557) — brother of the statesman and author, Diego Hurtado de Mendoza, and of Antonio de Mendoza, first viceroy of New Spain — who was captain general of the Spanish Galleys and for six months in 1555 was lieutenant general of Naples. This sketch, printed in Antonio Parrino, *Teatro eroico e politico de governi de viceré del regno di Napoli* ([Naples, 1692], I, 209), is catalogued in Angel M. de Barcia's *Catalogo de los retratos de personajes españoles* ([Madrid, 1901], p. 515), with the incorrect and misleading date 1595 instead of 1555. The same picture exists in the Biblioteca Nacional in Madrid, in the Bibliothèque Nationale in Paris and, with the correct date, in the British Museum. A similar sketch, taken from the Bibliothèque Nationale print, is published in Francisco Barado's *Historia del Ejército Español* ([Barcelona, 1883-1887], II, 177).

BIBLIOGRAPHY

✦ ✦ ✦ ✦

PRIMARY SOURCES

MANUSCRIPTS

Archivo General de Simancas. Sección de Estado. Legajos: K. 1448, 1449, 1450, 1495, 1496, 1497, 1498, 1499, 1563, 1564, 1565, 1566, 1567, 1568, 1569, 1570, 1571, 1572, 1573, 1574, 1575, 1576, 1578, 1579, 1581, 1582, 1584, 1585, 1586, 1592, 1594, 1674. Registros de Decretos de Oficio.

Archivo Histórico Nacional, Madrid. Sección de Estado. Despachos Reales, 1587–1598.

Biblioteca Nacional, Madrid. MS V. 1629, fol. 295. MS 12948. Gayangos papers on France, 1598–1616. Venetian Reports, 1574–1610.

Archives Nationales, Paris. MSS X. 8639, 8633, 241, no. 3. K. 674, and museum piece 745.

Bibliothèque de l'Institute de France, Paris. MS Godefroy, 283, fol. 69.

Bibliothèque Nationale, Paris. Fonds français, MSS 3301, 3975, 3997, 15892, 15909, 16093, 16109, 16110, 17294. Nouveau acquisitions latins, 1634, pièces relatives à l'ordre des Jésuites, LB 34.472. Collection Brienne, nos. 207, 214.

British Museum. MS C. 33. b.25, T. 1716(4).

PUBLISHED DOCUMENTS AND CORRESPONDENCE

Abord, Hippolyte. *Histoire de la Réforme et de la Ligue dans la ville d'Autun.* Vol. III, Pièces justificatives. Paris: Durand et Pedone-Lauriel, 1886.

Albèri, Eugenio, ed. *Relazioni degli ambasciatori veneti al Senato durante il secolo decimosesto.* 1st ser., 6 vols., Florence: Clio, 1830–1862.

Auvray, L., and B. de Lacombe, eds. *Documents sur les guerres de religion dans l'Orléanais.* Orléans, 1902.

Bernard, Auguste, ed. *Procès-verbaux des États généraux de 1593.* Paris: Imprimerie Royale, 1842.

Biron, Baron de. *The Letters and Documents of Armand de Gontaut, Baron de Biron, Marshal of France,* coll. S. H. Ehrman; ed. J. W. Thompson. 2 vols., Berkeley: University of California Press, 1936.

Bodin, Jean. *Lettre de Monsieur Bodin*. Paris: Chaudière, 1590.

Bureau de la Ville. *Registres des délibérations du Bureau de la ville de Paris*, ed. Paul Guérin and François Bonnardot, vols. VIII-X. Paris: Imprimerie Nationale, 1896–1902.

Cecil Papers. *See* Historical Manuscripts Commission.

Charles IX. *Lettres de Charles IX à M. de Fourquevaux, ambassadeur en Espagne (1565–1572)*, ed. Célestin Douais. Paris: Alphonse Picard, 1897.

Cimber et Danjou [Louis Lafaist], ed. *Archives curieuses de l'histoire de France*. Paris: Beauvais, 1834–50. 1st ser., vols. X, XI, XII, XIII.

Colección de documentos inéditos para la historia de España, ed. the marqués de la Fuensanta del Valle, et al. 112 vols., Madrid: Miguel Ginestra, 1842–95; esp. vols. LXXXIV, XC, XCI, XCII.

Collection de documents inédits sur l'histoire de France. Paris: Imprimerie Nationale, 1835 et seq.; esp. vols. VIII, XIII, XVIII, XXII.

Condé, Louis de Bourbon, prince of. *Mémoires de Condé, ou recueil pour servir à l'histoire de France, contenant cequi s'est passé du plus mémorable*. 6 vols., London: C. du Bosse, J. Nillor, 1740; and Paris, 1743.

Croze, Joseph de. *Les Guises, les Valois et Philippe II*. Paris: Amyot, 1866, I, 329–417 II, 277–419 (Letters of the duke of Guise).

Desjardins, Abel, ed. *Négociations diplomatiques de la France avec la Toscane*, coll. Guiseppi Canestrini. 6 vols., Paris: Imprimerie Imperiale, 1859–86.

Du Bois, Alexis-Auguste. *La Ligue: documents relatifs à la Picardie d'après les registres de l'échevinage d'Amiens*. Amiens: E. Yvert, 1859.

Dumont, Jean, ed. *Corps universel diplomatique du droit des gens; contenant un recueil des traites d'alliance, de paix, de treve, de neutralité, de commerce, d'échenge, etc.* 8 vols., Amsterdam: P. Brunel, 1726–31; esp. vol. V.

Fourquevaux, Raymond de Rouer, sieur de. *Dépêches de M. de Fourquevaux, ambassadeur du roi Charles IX en Espagne (1565–1572)*. 3 vols., Paris: Ernest Leroux, 1896–1904.

Gachard, Louis P., ed. *Relations des ambassadeurs vénitiens sur Charles-Quint et Philippe II*. Brussels: M. Hayez, 1855.

Goulart, Simon, *Mémoires de l'estat de France sous Charles IX*. 3 vols. in 6, Meidelbourg: Henry Wolf, 1578.

——— *Mémoires de la Ligue. Contenant les évenements les plus remarquables depuis 1576, jusqu' à la paix accordée entre le Roi de France et le Roi d'Espagne, en 1598*. 6 vols., Amsterdam: Arkstée and Merkus, 1758.

Granvelle, Antoine Perrenot, cardinal de. *Papiers d'état du cardinal de Granvelle, d'après les manuscrits de la bibliothèque de*

Besançon, ed. Charles Weiss. 9 vols., Paris: Imprimerie Royale, 1841–52.

——— *Correspondance du cardinal de Granvelle (1565–1586)*, ed. Charles Piot and Edmond Poullet. 12 vols., Brussels: Hayez, 1877–1896; (continuation of Weiss).

Great Britain, Public Records Office. *Calendar of Letters and State Papers, Relating to English Affairs, of the Reign of Elizabeth, Preserved Principally in the Archives of Simancas*, ed. Martin A. S. Hume. London: H.M.S.O., 1895; esp. vol. III.

——— *Calendar of Letters, Despatches and State Papers Relating to the Negotiations between England and Spain, preserved in the Archives at Vienna, Simancas, Besançon, Brussels, Madrid, and Lille*. Vol. XIII, *Philip and Mary (July 1554-November 1558)*, ed. Royall Tyler. London: H.M.S.O., 1954.

——— *Calendar of State Papers, Foreign Series, of the Reign of Elizabeth, Preserved in the Public Record Office*, ed. Sophie Crawford Lomas. London: H.M.S.O., 1927; esp. vols. XIX–XXI.

——— *Calendar of State Papers and Manuscripts, relating to English Affairs, Existing in the Archives and Collections of Venice, and in other Libraries of Northern Italy*, ed. R. F. Brown. London: H.M.S.O., 1894; esp. vols. VII–IX.

Henry III. *Lettres de Henri III, roi de France*, ed. Michel François. Vol. I, 1557–août 1574. Paris: C. Klincksieck, 1959.

——— *Articles accordees au nom du Roy, entre la Royne sa mere d'une part, et M. le Cardinal de Bourbon, le Duc de Guyse, etc.* Paris, 1588.

Henry IV. *Recueil des lettres missives de Henri IV*, ed. Berger de Xivrey and Joseph Gaudet. 9 vols., Paris: Imprimerie Nationale, 1843–1876.

——— *Lettres intimes de Henri IV*, ed. L. Dussieux. Paris: J. Baudry, 1876.

——— *Lettres inédites au Chancelier de Bellièvre du 8 février 1581 au 23 sept. 1601*. Paris: Bibliothèque Nationale by E. Halphen, 1872.

——— "Lettres inédites de Henri IV à M. de Pailhès, gouverneur du Comté de Foix, et aux consuls de la ville de Foix, 1576–1602," pub. Charles de la Hitte, *Archives Historiques de la Gascogne* (Paris: Honoré Champion), ser. I, 10:5–98 (1886).

Hérelle, Georges, ed., *La réforme et la Ligue en Champagne: Documents*. 2 vols., Paris: Champion, n.d.

Historical Manuscripts Commission. *Calendar of the Manuscripts of the Most Hon. the Marquis of Salisbury, K.G., preserved at Hatfield House*, parts III and IV. London: H.M.S.O., 1889, 1892.

Isambert, François André, and others. *Recueil général des anciennes lois françaises depuis l'an 420 jusqu'à la révolution de 1789.* Paris, 1821–1833.

La Noue, François de. "François de la Noue et le conversion du roi. Lettre de Monsieur de la Noue (Bradefer) sur le changement de religion," intro. Henri Hauser, *Revue Historique*, 36:311–323 (1888).

L'Aubespine, Sébastien de. "Dépêches de Sébastien de l'Aubespine, ambassadeur de France en Espagne sous Philippe II," *Revue d'histoire diplomatique*, 13:583–607 (1899), and 14:289–302 (1900).

Lettenhove, Kervyn de [Joseph Marie Bruno Constantin], ed. *Relations politiques des Pays-Bas et de l'Angleterre sous le regne de Philippe II.* 9 vols., Brussels: Hayez, 1882–1900.

L'Hôpital, Michel de. *Oeuvres complètes de Michel de l'Hospital, chancelier de France,* ed. P. J. S. Dufey. 5 vols., Paris: A. Boulland, 1824–1825.

Longlée, P. S. de. *Dépêches diplomatiques de M. de Longlée, résident de France en Espagne (1581–1590),* ed. Albert Mousset. Paris: Société d'Histoire Diplomatique, 1912.

Loutchitzki, Jean, ed. *Documents inédits pour servir à l'histoire de la réforme et de la Ligue;* materiaux pour "L'histoire de la réaction féodale en France au 16 et 17 siècles," tome 2, vol. XIV of *Universitetskiya Izvestiya,* August-December, Kiev, 1874, pp. 1–297.

Marguerite de Valois. "Lettres inédits de Marguerite de Valois, 1579–1606," pub. Philippe Lauzun. *Archives historiques de la Gascogne,* 1st ser., 11:1–53 (1886).

Mayenne, Charles de Lorraine, duke of. *Correspondance du duc de Mayenne,* ed. E. Henry and C. Loriquet, 2 vols. Reims: P. Dubois for the Academie Imperiale, 1860–1862.

Mayer, Charles Joseph, ed. *Des États généraux et autres assemblées nationales.* 18 vols., Paris: Buisson, 1788–89; vols. XIV, XV.

Medici, Catherine de'. *Lettres de Catherine de Médicis,* pub. Gustave Baguenault de Puchesse. 9 vols., Paris: Imprimerie Nationale, 1901.

Mendoza, Bernardino de. *La harangue au Roi Très-Chrétien faite à Chartres par monseigneur l'ambassadeur pour le Roi d'Espagne vers sa Majesté.* Lyon: B. Rigaud, 1588.

Montluc, Blaise de. *Commentaires et lettres,* ed. Alphonse de Ruble. Paris: Jules Renouard, 1864–72.

Parma, Prince of. *Correspondance d'Alexandre Farnèse, prince de Parme, gouverneur général de Pays-Bas, avec Philippe II dans les années 1578, 1579, 1580 et 1581,* ed. Louis P. Gachard. Brussels: C. Muquardt, 1853.

Philip II. *Correspondance de Philippe II sur les affaires des Pays-Bas*

(*1558–1577*), ed. Louis P. Gachard. 5 vols., Brussels: Librairie Ancienne et Moderne, 1848–79.

—— *Correspondance de Philippe II sur les affaires des Pays-Bas* (*2ᵉ partie, 1577–1598*), ed. Joseph Lefèvre. 4 vols., Brussels: Palais des Académies, 1940–60; (continuation of Gachard).

Pollen, John H., ed. *Mary Queen of Scots and the Babington Plot.* Edinburgh: Scottish Historical Society, 1922.

Read, Conyers, ed. *The Bardon Papers: Documents Relating to the Imprisonment and Trial of Mary Queen of Scots.* 3rd ser., vol. XVII, London: Camden Society, 1909.

Real Academia de la Historia. *Archivo documental español.* Vol. VII, *Negociaciones con Francia* (*1565*). Madrid: R.A.H., 1953.

Saint-Sulpice, seigneur de. *Ambassade en Espagne de Jean Ebrard, seigneur de Saint-Sulpice, de 1562 à 1565, et mission de ce diplomate dans le même pays en 1566.* Albi: Imprimerie Nougiès, 1903.

Serrano, Luciano, ed. *Correspondencia diplomática entre España y la Santa Sede durante el pontificado de Pio V.* 4 vols., Madrid: n.d., 1914.

Teulet, Alexandre, ed. *Relations politiques de la France et de l'Espagne avec l'Ecosse au XVIᵉ siècle: Papiers d'état, pièces et documents inédits.* Paris: Jules Renouard, 1862; vols. IV, V.

Tommaseo, M. N., ed. *Relations des ambassadeurs vénitiens sur les affaires de France au XVIᵉ siècle.* 2 vols., Paris: Imprimerie Royale, 1838.

Voisin, Charles Joseph, ed. *Lettres inédites de Philippe II, du prince de Parme, du cardinal de Granvelle, etc. adressées à Messire Oudart de Bournonville, l'un des chefs des malcontents* (*1578–1585*). Vol. IV of *Mémoires de la Société Historique et Littéraire de Tournai* (Tournai, 1856), pp. 155–295.

Wilkinson, Maurice. "The Wars of Religion in the Périgord; Documents." *English Historical Review,* 23:292–317 (1908), and 26:127–138 (1911).

MEMOIRS AND OTHER CONTEMPORARY WRITINGS

Angoulême, Charles de Valois, duc d'. *Mémoires, pour servir à l'histoire de Henri III et de Henri IV* (*1589–93*). Vol. XI of Michaud and Poujoulat. Paris: Didier, 1854.

Annales de la Société des soi-disans Jésuites, ou Recueil historique chronologique de tous les actes, ecrits, etc. Paris, 1764.

Bassompierre, Maréchal de. *Mémoires de maréchal de Bassompierre.* Vols. XIX–XXI of Petitot. 2nd ser., Paris: Faucault, 1823.

Bèze, Théodore. *Du droit des magistrats sur leurs sujets.* Lyon, 1574.

—— *Histoire ecclésiastique des églises réformées au royaume de*

France, ed. G. Baum and B. Guintz. 3 vols., Paris: Fischbacher, 1888–89.

Bodin, Jean. *Les six livres de la République.* Paris: J. Du Puys, 1576.

Boucher, Jean. *De justa abdicatione Henrici tertii.* Paris: N. Niuellium, 1589.

Bouillon, Henri de la Tour d'Auvergne duc de. *Mémoires du vicomte de Turenne, depuis duc de Bouillon, 1565–1586, suivis de 33 lettres du roi de Navarre et d'autres documents inédits,* ed. Baguenault de Puchesse. Paris: Renouard, H. Laurens, 1901.

Brantôme, Pierre de. *Oeuvres complètes de Pierre de Bourdeilles, seigneur de Brantôme,* ed. Ludovic Lalanne. 11 vols., Paris: Jules Renouard, 1864–1882.

Brutus, Stephanus Junius (pseud.). *A Defence of Liberty Against Tyrants [Vindiciae contra Tyrannos],* ed. Harold J. Laski. London, 1924.

Buchon, J. A. C., ed. *Choix de chroniques et mémoires sur l'histoire de France (XVIe siècle).* Paris: A. Desrez, 1836.

Cabrera de Córdoba, Luis. *Felipe II, rey de España.* 4 vols., Madrid: Ariban, 1876–1877.

Camden Society. *Embajada Española* (anon.), ed. H. J. Chayter. *Camden Miscellany,* vol. XIV. London: Camden Society, 1926.

Cheverny, Phillipe de. *Mémoires de M. Philippe Hurault, comte de Cheverny, Chancelier de France.* Vol. X of Michaud and Poujoulat. Paris: Didier, 1854.

Coningsby, Thomas. *Journal of the Siege of Rouen, 1591,* ed. J. G. Nichols. *Camden Miscellany,* vol. I, no. 4. London: Camden Society, 1847.

Cornejo, Pedro. *Compendio y breve relación de la Liga y confederación Francesa: con las cosas en aquel Reyno acontecidas desde el año de ochenta y cinco hasta el presente de nouenta.* Brussels: R. Velpio, 1591.

D'Aubigné, Théodore Agrippa. *Histoire universelle,* ed. Alphonse de Ruble. 10 vols., Paris: Société de l'Histoire de France, 1886–1909.

———— *Mémoires,* ed. Buchon in *Choix de chroniques.* Paris: Desrez, 1836.

Davila, Arrigo Caterino. *Dell' istoria delle guerre civili di Francia.* 6 vols., Milan: Società Tipografica de' Classici Italiani, 1807.

De Thou, Jacques-Auguste. *Histoire universelle, depuis 1543 jusqu'en 1607.* 16 vols., London, 1734; and Basle: Jean Louis Brandmuller, 1742.

———— *Mémoires.* Vol. XI of Michaud and Poujoulat. Paris: Didier, 1854.

D'Orléans, Louis. *Apologie ou défense des catholiques unis les uns avec les autres, contre les impostures des catholiques associés à ceux de la prétendue religion.* N.p., 1586.

Du Plessis-Mornay, Philippe. *Mémoires et correspondance; pour servir à l'histoire de la réformation et des guerres civiles et religieuses en France.* 12 vols., Paris: Treuttel et Würtz, 1824–25.

Gentillet, Innocent. *Discours d'estat sur les moyens de bien gouverner et maintenir en bonne paix un Royaume ou autre Principauté; Contre Nicolas Machiavel, Florentin.* Lausanne: n.d., 1576.

———— *Remonstrance au roy tres chrestien Henry III.* Francfort, 1574.

———— *Apologie ou défense pour les chrestiens de France qui sont de la religion évangelique ou réformée . . . à ceux qui ne veulent vivre en paix et concorde avec eux.* Geneva, 1578.

Goulart, Simon. *Recueil des Choses Memorables Avenues en France sous le Regne de . . . et Henri III, etc.* Geneva, 1595.

Groulart, Claude. *Mémoires de Messire Claude Groulart, premier President du Parlement de Normandie, ou voyages par lui faits en cour.* Vol. XI of Michaud and Poujoulat. Paris: Didier, 1854.

Haton, Claude. *Mémoires de Claude Haton, contenent le récit des evénéments accomplis de 1553 à 1582,* pub. F. Bourquelot. Paris: Imprimerie Imperiale, 1862.

Herrera, Antonio de. *Historia de los sucessos de Francia, desde el año de 1585 que començo la Liga Catolica, hasta el fin del año 1594.* Madrid: Lorenço de Avala, 1598.

Hotman, François. *La Gaule françoise,* Fr. trans. of *Franco-Gallia* by Simon Goulart. Cologne: H. Bertulphe, 1574.

La Fosse, J. B. de. *Journal d'un curé ligueur de Paris sous les trois derniers Valois, suivi du journal du secrétaire de Philippe du Bec.* Paris: Didier, 1866.

La Huguerye, Michel de. *Ephéméride de l'expedition des Allemands en France, août-décembre 1587.* Paris: Jules Renouard, 1892.

La Place, Pierre de. *Commentaires de l'estat de la religion et république sous les rois Henry et François II et Charles IX* [1565], in Buchon, *Choix de chroniques.*

La Planche, Louis Regnier de. *Histoire de l'estat de France, tant de la république que de la religion . . .* [1576], in Buchon, *Choix de chroniques.*

L'Estoile, Pierre de. *Mémoires-Journaux de Pierre de l'Estoile,* ed. Brunet et al. 12 vols., Paris: Alphonse Lemerre, 1875–96; vols. I–III, *Journal de Henri III;* vol. IV, *Les belles figures et drolleries de la Ligue;* vols. V–XI, *Journal de Henri IV.*

———— *The Paris of Henry of Navarre as seen by Pierre de l'Estoile.* Selections from his *Mémoires-Journaux,* tr. and ed. Nancy Lyman Roelker. Cambridge, Mass.: Harvard University Press, 1958.

Lucinge, René de *Dialogue du François et du Savoysien (1593),* ed. Alain Dufour. Paris: Minard; Geneva: E. Droz, 1961.

Marguerite de Valois. *Mémoires de Marguerite de Valois, reine de France et de Navarre*. Vol. XXXVII of Petitot. Paris: Foucault, 1823.

Matthieu, Pierre. *Histoire des derniers troubles de France (1585–1589)*. Lyon: E. Bonaventure, 1596.

—— *Histoire veritable des gverres entre les devx maisons de France et d'Espagne*. . . . N.p., 1603 (bound with *Histoire des derniers troubles*).

Mayenne, Charles de Lorraine, duke of. *Discours de la bataille de Garenne (Ivry) en mars 1590*. Paris: Eugène Halphen, 1875.

Mendoza, Bernardino de. *Comentarios de lo sucedido en las guerras de los Paises-Bajos, desde el año de 1567 hasta el de 1577*. In *Biblioteca de autores españoles, desde la formación del lenguaje hasta nuestros dias*, vol. XXVIII, *Historiadores de sucesos particulares*. Madrid: M. Rivadeneyrs, 1884; Atlas, 1948, part 2, pp. 389–570.

—— *Theorique and Practise of Warre*, trans. Sir Edwarde Hoby. London, 1597.

Merle, Mathieu. *Mémoires sur les guerres de religion, 1572–1587*. Vol. XI of Michaud and Poujoulat. Paris: Didier, 1854.

Michaud, Joseph-François, and Jean-Joseph-François Poujoulat, eds. *Nouvelle collection des mémoires sur l'histoire de France depuis le XIIIᵉ siècle jusqu'à la fin du XVIIIᵉ siècle*. 32 vols., Paris: Didier, 1836–1854.

Moreau, Jean. *Mémoires du Chanoine Jean Moreau sur les guerres de la Ligue en Bretagne*, ed. Henri Waquet. Quimper: Archives Départementales. 1960.

Nevers, Louis Gonzaga, duc de. *Mémoires, 1574–1610*. 2 vols., Paris, 1625.

—— *Discours de la légation de M. le duc de Nevers envoyé par le Roy de France et de Navarre Henri IIII vers le Pape Clément VIII*. Paris: J. Mettayer, 1594.

—— *Traité des causes et des raisons de la prise d'armes faite en janvier 1589 et des moyens pour appaiser nos présentes afflictions*. In *Archives curieuses*, ser. I, vol. XIII. Paris: Beauvais, 1837.

Palma Cayet, Pierre Victor. *Chronologie novennaire*. Vol. XII of Michaud and Poujoulat. Paris: Didier, 1854.

Pasquier, Etienne. *Oeuvres choisies d'Etienne Pasquier*, ed. Léon Feugère. 2 vols., Paris: Firmin Didot, 1849.

—— *Le catéchisme des Jésuites*. 2nd ed., 2 vols., Ville Franche: Guillaume Grenier, 1677.

Petitot, Claude-Bernard, ed. *Collection complète des mémoires relatifs à l'histoire de France*. 130 vols., Paris: Foucault, 1818–29.

Poulain, Nicolas. *Le procez verbal du nommé Nicolas Poulain qui contient l'histoire de la Ligue depuis . . . 1585 jusques au . . .*

12 may 1588. Vol. XI of *Archives curieuses*. Paris: Beauvais, 1836, pp. 289–323; and in L'Estoile, *Mémoires-Journaux*, III, 345–371.

Rossaeus (pseud.). *De justa reipublicae in reges impios authoritate, justissimaque catholicorum ad Henricum Navarreum et quemcunque haereticum a regno Galliae repellendum confederatione*. Paris, 1590.

Saint-Auban, Jacques Pape, seigneur de. *Mémoires de Saint-Auban*. Vol. XI of Michaud and Poujoulat. Paris: Didier, 1854.

Satyre Ménippée, de la vertu du Catholicon d'Espagne, et de la tenue des Estats de Paris. 3 vols., Ratisbone: Mathias Kerner, 1711, 1752.

Saulnier, Eugéne, ed. *Journal de François, bourgeois de Paris, 23 décembre 1588–30 avril 1589*. Paris: Ernest Leroux, 1913.

Tassis, Jean Baptiste de. *Commentariorum de tumultibus Belgicis sui temporis*. In Hoynck van Papendrecht, C. P. *Analecta Belgica*. Brussels, 1743.

Tavannes, Guillaume de Saulx, seigneur de. *Mémoires des choses advenues en France des guerres civiles depuis l'an 1560 jusques en l'an 1596*. Vol. XXV of Petitot, ser. I. Paris: Foucault, 1823.

Valois, Charles, ed. *Histoire de la Ligue*. Vol. I, *Oeuvre inédite d'un contemporain*. Paris: Renouard, 1914.

Velázquez de Velasco, Diego Alfonso. *Odas a imitación de los Siete Salmos Penitenciales del Real Profeta David*. Antwerp, 1593.

Villeroy, Nicolas de Neufville. *Mémoires d'Etat, 1574–1594*. Vol. XI of Michaud and Poujoulat. Paris: Didier, 1854.

SECONDARY WORKS

BOOKS

Abord, Hippolyte. *Histoire de la réforme et de la Ligue dans la ville d'Autun*. 3 vols., Paris: Dumoulin, 1855–87.

Aguado Bleye, Pedro. *Manual de Historia de España*. 3 vols., Madrid: Espasa-Calpe, 1954–56.

Allen, John W. *A History of Political Thought in the Sixteenth Century*. New York: Barnes and Noble, 1928.

Anquetil, Louis Pierre. *L'esprit de la Ligue, ou histoire politique des troubles de France, pendant les XVIᵉ et XVIIᵉ siècles*. 2 vols., Paris: Janet et Cotelle, 1818.

Anquez, Léonce, *Histoire des assemblées politiques des Réformés de France (1573–1622)*. Paris: Auguste Durand, 1859.

Armstrong, Edward. *The French Wars of Religion: their Political Aspects*. Oxford: Blackwell, 1904.

Astrain, Antonio. *Historia de la Campañia de Jesús en la asistencia de España*. 7 vols., Madrid: Sucesores de Rivadeneyra, 1902–25.

Aumale, Henri d'Orléans, duc d'. *Histoire des princes de Condé pen-*

dant les 16ᵐᵉ et 17ᵐᵉ siècles. 7 vols., Paris: Calmann Lévy, 1863–96.

Bailly, Auguste. *Henri le balafré, duc de Guise.* Paris: Hachette, 1953.

Baird, Henry M. *The Huguenots and Henry of Navarre.* 2 vols., New York: Charles Scribners, 1886.

Ballesteros y Beretta, Antonio. *Historia de España y su influencia en la historia universal.* 9 vols., Barcelona: Salvat, 1918–41.

Baschet, Armand. *La diplomatie vénitienne. Les princes de l'Europe au XVIᵉ siècle: François Iᵉʳ, Philippe II, Catherine de Médicis, les papes, les sultans, etc. . . . d'après les rapports des ambassadeurs vénitiens.* Paris: H. Plon, 1862.

Bazeries, Etienne. *Les chiffres secrets dévoilés. Etude historique sur les chiffres, appuyée de documents inédits tirés des différentes dépôts d'archives.* Paris: E. Fasquelle, 1901.

Beame, Edmond Morton. "The Development of Politique Thought during the French Religious Wars (1560–1595)," unpub. dissertation, University of Illinois, 1958.

Benoist, Elie. *Histoire de l'Edit de Nantes, contenant les choses les plus remarquables qui se sont passées en France avant et après sa publication, à l'occasion de la diversité des religions . . . jusques à l'édit de révocation en octobre 1685.* 5 vols., Delft: A. Beman, 1693–1695.

Bitton, R. Davis. "The French Nobility as Seen by Contemporaries, 1560–1630," unpub. dissertation, Princeton University, 1961.

Black, John R. *Elizabeth and Henry IV: Being a Short Study in Anglo-French Relations, 1589–1603.* Oxford: Blackwell, 1914.

—— *The Reign of Elizabeth.* Vol. VIII of the Oxford History of England. Oxford: Clarendon Press, 1936 and 1959.

Blond (Abbé), Louis. *Les Jésuites à Paris. La maison professe Saint-Louis de la rue Saint-Antoine (1580–1763).* N.p., 1955.

Bouille, René de. *Histoire des ducs de Guise.* 4 vols., Paris: Amyot, 1850.

Boullée, M. A. *Histoire complète des États-généraux et autres assemblées representatives de la France, depuis 1302 jusqu'en 1626.* 2 vols., Paris: Langlois et Leclercq, 1845.

Buisson, Albert. *Michel de l'Hospital, 1503–1573.* Paris: Hachette, 1950.

Capefigue, Jean Baptiste H. R. *Histoire de la réforme, de la Ligue, et du règne de Henri IV.* 8 vols., Paris: Duféy, 1834–35.

Caprariis, Vittorio de. *Propaganda e pensiero politico in Francia durant le guerre di religione.* Vol. I, 1559–1572. Naples: Edizioni Scientifiche Italiane, 1959.

Catalina García, Juan. *Biblioteca de escritores de la provincia de Guadalajara y bibliografía de la misma hasta el siglo XIX.* Madrid, 1899.

Chalambert, Victor de, *Histoire de la Ligue sur les règnes de Henri III et Henri IV*. Paris: Firmin Didot, 1898.

Champion, Pierre Honoré J. B. *Charles IX, la France et le contrôle de l'Espagne*. 2 vols., Paris: Bernard Grasset, 1939.

Charleville, Edmond. *Les États généraux de 1576. Le fonctionnement d'une tenue d'états*. Paris: A. Pedone, 1901.

Chéruel, Pierre Adolphe. *Marie Stuart et Catherine de Médicis: Étude historique sur les relations de la France et de l'Écosse dans la seconde moité du XVIᵉ siècle*. Paris: Hachette, 1858.

Church, William F. *Constitutional Thought in Sixteenth Century France*. Cambridge, Mass.: Harvard University Press, 1941.

Corbett, Julian S. *Drake and the Tudor Navy*. 2 vols., London & New York: Longmans, Green, 1898.

Crétineau-Joly, Jacques. *Histoire religieuses, politique et littéraire de la Compagnie de Jésus, composée sur les documents inédits et authentiques*. 6 vols., Paris: J. Lecoffre, 1845–46.

Combes, M. F. *L'entrevue de Bayone de 1565 et la question de la Saint-Barthélemy, d'après les archives de Simancas*. Paris, 1882.

Croze, Joseph de. *Les Guises, les Valois et Philippe II*. 2 vols., Paris: Amyot, 1866.

D'Agapayeff, Alexander. *Codes and Ciphers*. London: Oxford University Press, 1939.

De Crue, Francis. *La cour de France et la société au seizième siècle*. Paris: Firmin Didot, 1888.

——— *Anne, duc de Montmorency, connétable et pair de France, sous les rois Henri II, François II et Charles IX*. Paris: E. Plon, 1889.

——— *Le parti des Politiques au lendemain de la Saint-Barthélemy. La Molle et Coconat*. Paris: E. Plon, 1892.

Delaborde, Jules. *Gaspard de Coligny, amiral de France*. 3 vols., Paris: G. Fischbacher, 1879–82.

Desormeaux, Joseph L. R. *Histoire de la maison de Montmorenci*. 5 vols., Paris: Desaint & Saillant, 1764; vol. III.

Devic, Claude; & Vaissete, Jean Joseph. *Histoire générale de Languedoc*. 15 vols., Toulouse: E. Privat, 1872–92; vols. XI, XII.

Devos, J. P. *Les chiffres de Philippe II (1555–1598), et du despache universel durant le XVIIᵉ siècle*. Brussels: Palais des Académies, 1950.

Diges Antón, Juan. *Biografías de hijos ilustres de la provincia de Guadalajara*. Guadalajara: Provincial, 1889.

Doucet, Roger. *Les institutions de la France au XVIᵉ siècle*. 2 vols., Paris: A. and J. Picard, 1948.

Drouet, Henri. *Mayenne et la Bourgogne: Étude sur la Ligue en Bourgogne, 1587–1596*. 2 vols., Paris: Auguste Picard, 1937.

Dupré-Lasale, Émile. *Michel de l'Hospital avant son élévation au poste de chancelier de France.* 2 vols., Paris: Ernest Thorin, 1875–1899.

Ehrenberg, Richard. *Capital & Finance in the Age of the Renaissance. A Study of the Fuggers and their Connections,* trans. H. M. Lucas. London: Jonathan Cape, 1928.

Elkan, Albert. *Die Publizistik der Bartholomäusnacht und Mornays "Vindiciae contra Tyrannos."* Heidelberg: Winters, 1905.

Erlanger, Philippe. *Henri III.* 9th ed., Paris: Gallimard, 1948.

―――― *Le massacre de la Saint-Barthélemy.* Paris: Gallimard, 1960.

Evennett, Henry C. *The Cardinal of Lorraine and the Council of Trent: a Study in the Counter-Reformation.* New York: Cambridge University Press, 1930.

Feist, Elisabeth. *Weltbild und Staatsidee bei Jean Bodin.* Halle.: M. Niemeyer, 1930.

Fernández de Retana, Luis. *España en tiempo de Felipe II (1556–1598).* Vol. XIX, parts 1 & 2 of Ramón Menéndez Pidal's *Historia de España.* Madrid: Espasa-Calpe, 1958.

Figgis, John N. *Studies of Political Thought from Gerson to Grotius, 1414–1625.* New York: Harper, 1960.

Fleissner von Wostrowitz, Eduard B. *Handbuch der Kryptographie. Anleitung zum chiffriren und dechiffriren von Geheimschriften.* Vienna: L. W. Seidel and son, 1881.

Fleming, David H. *Mary, Queen of Scots from Her Birth to Her Flight into England: with Critical Notes, a few Documents hitherto Unpublished, and an Itinerary.* London: Hodder and Stoughton, 1897.

Forneron, Henri. *Les ducs de Guise et leur époque: Étude historique sur le seizième siècle.* 2 vols., Paris: E. Plon, 1877.

―――― *Histoire de Philippe II.* 4 vols., Paris: E. Plon, 1881–87.

Fouqueray, Henri. *Histoire de la Compagnie de Jésus en France, des origines à la supression (1528–1762).* 4 vols., Paris: A. Picard, 1910–13.

Franklin, Alfred Louis Auguste. *Paris et les parisiens au seizième siècle.* Paris: Émile Paul, 1921.

Franklin, Julian H. *Jean Bodin and the Sixteenth Century Revolution in the Methodology of Law and History.* New York: Columbia University Press, 1963.

Freer, Martha W. *Henry III, King of France and Poland: His Court and Times. From Numerous Unpublished Sources, Including MS. Documents in the Bibliothèque Imperiale, and the Archives of France and Italy.* 3 vols., London: Hurst and Blackett, 1858.

Frémy, Edouard. *Essai sur les diplomates du temps de la Ligue, d'après des documents nouveaux et inédits.* Paris: Librairie de la Société des Gens de Lettres, 1873.

Gambier, Paul. *Au temps des guerres de religion. Le président Barnabé Brisson, ligueur (1531–1591)*. Paris: Perrin, 1957.

Guilday, Peter Keenan. *The English Catholic Refugees on the Continent, 1558–1795*, vol. I. London and New York: Longmans, Green, 1914.

Hauser, Henri. *François de la Noue (1531–1591)*. Paris: Hachette, 1892.

—— *Le préponderance espagnole (1559–1660)*. Vol. IX of Halphin and Sagnac, *Peuples et Civilisations*. Paris: Presses Universitaires de France, 1948.

Héritier, Jean. *Catherine de Médicis*. Paris: Arthème Fayard, 1959.

—— *Michel de l'Hôpital*. Paris: E. Flammarion, 1943.

Herre, Paul. *Papsttum und Papstwahl in Zeitalter Philips II*. Leipzig: B. G. Teubner, 1907.

Hübner, Alexander von. *The Life and Times of Sixtus Fifth*. 2 vols., Paris, 1870–82.

Imbart de la Tour, Pierre. *Les origines de la Réforme*. 4 vols., Paris: Librairie d'Argences, 1914–48.

Kervyn de Lettenhove [Joseph Marie Bruno Constantin]. *Les Huguenots et les Gueux. Étude historique sur vingt-cinq années du XVIe siècle*. 6 vols., Bruges: Beyaert, 1883–85.

—— *La conférence de Bayonne en 1565*. Brussels: F. Hayez, 1883.

Kingdon, Robert M. *Geneva and the Coming of the Wars of Religion in France, 1555–1563*. Geneva: E. Droz, 1956.

Klipffel, H. *Le Colloque de Poissy. Étude sur la crise religieuse et politique de 1561*. Paris: Librairie Internationale, 1867.

Labitte, Charles. *De la démocratie chez les prédicateurs de la Ligue*. Paris: Durand, 1865.

Lacombe, Bernard de. *Les débuts des guerres de religion, 1559–1564: Catherine de Médicis entre Guise et Condé*. Paris: Perrin, 1899.

Lacretelle, Charles. *L'histoire de France pendant les guerres de religion*. 2nd ed., 4 vols., Paris: Delaunay, 1822.

Lagarde, Georges de. *Recherches sur l'esprit politique de la Réforme*. Douai and Paris, 1926.

Lange, André. *Traité de cryptographie*. Paris: Félix Alcan, 1925.

Lavin, Michael O. H. "Franco-Spanish Rivalry from the Treaty of Cateau-Cambrésis to the Death of Charles IX," unpub. dissertation, Stanford University, 1956.

Lechat, Robert. *Les refugiés anglais dans les Pays-Bas espagnols durant le règne d'Élisabeth, 1558–1603*. Louvain: J. de Meester, 1914.

Lecler, Joseph. *Histoire de la tolérance au siècle de la Réforme*. 2 vols., Aubier: Editions Montaigne, 1955.

Lefèvre, Louis-Raymond. *Le Tumulte d'Amboise*. Paris: Gallimard, 1949.

Leger, François. *La fin de la Ligue (1589–1593)*. Paris: Editions de la Nouvelle France, 1944.

Lenient, Charles Félix. *La satire en France; ou, la littérature militante au XVIᵉ siècle*. Paris: Hachette, 1866.

Léonard, Émile G. *Histoire générale du protestantisme*. Vol. II, *L'établissement*. Paris: Presses Universitaires de France, 1961.

L'Epinois, Henri de. *La Ligue et les papes*. Paris: Société Générale de Librairie Catholique, 1886.

Lorédan, Jean. *La Fontenelle, seigneur de la Ligue (1572–1602)*. Paris: Perrin, 1926.

MacDowall, Henry C. *Henry of Guise and Other Portraits*. London: Macmillan, 1898.

Maimbourg, Louis. *The History of the League*, tr. Dryden. London: M. Flesher, 1684; Paris: Mabre-Cramolsy, 1683.

Major, J. Russell. *The Estates General of 1560*. Princeton: Princeton University Press, 1951.

―――― *The Deputies to the Estates General in Renaissance France*. Madison: University of Wisconsin Press, 1960.

―――― *Representative Institutions in Renaissance France, 1421–1550*. Madison: University of Wisconsin Press, 1960.

Mariéjol, Jean Hippolyte. *La Réforme et la Ligue, l'Edit de Nantes (1559–1598)*. Vol. VI, pt. 1 of Ernest Lavisse, ed., *Histoire de France des origines à la Révolution*. Paris: Hachette, 1911.

―――― *Catherine de Médicis (1519–89)*. Paris: Hachette, 1920.

―――― *La vie de Marguerite de Valois, reine de Navarre et de France (1553–1615)*. Paris: Hachette, 1928.

Mattingly, Garrett. *Renaissance Diplomacy*. Boston: Houghton Mifflin, 1955.

―――― *The Armada*. Boston: Houghton Mifflin, 1959.

―――― *The "Invincible" Armada and Elizabethan England*. Ithaca: Cornell University Press, 1963.

Maugis, Edouard. *Histoire du Parlement de Paris, de l'avènement des rois Valois à la mort d'Henri IV*. 2 vols., Paris: A. Picard, 1913–1914.

Maulde-la-Clavière, Marie Alphonse René de. *La diplomatie au temps de Machiavel*. 3 vols., Paris: Ernest Leroux, 1892–1893.

Merriman, Roger Bigelow. *The Rise of the Spanish Empire in the Old World and in the New*. Vol. IV, *Philip the Prudent*. New York: Macmillan, 1934.

Mesnard, Pierre. *L'essor de la philosophie politique au XVIᵉ siècle*. Paris: Boivin, 1936.

Meyer, Arnold Oskar. *England and the Catholic Church under Queen Elizabeth*, trans. J. R. McKee. London: Paul, Trench, Trübner, 1916.

Michelet, Jules. *La Ligue et Henri IV.* Vol. X of *Histoire de France au seizième siècle.* Paris: Chamerot, 1860.

Monty, Léopold. *Réformateurs et Jésuites: Guerres de religion en France.* Dijon: Imprimerie Darantière, 1876.

Moreau-Reibel, Jean. *Jean Bodin et le droit public comparé.* Paris: J. Vrin, 1933.

Morel-Fatio, Alfred. *Études sur l'Espagne.* 4 vols., Paris: E. Bouillon, 1922–25.

Moreuil, André de. *Résistance et collaboration sous Henri IV.* Paris: Pensée Moderne, 1960.

Motley, John Lothrop. *History of the United Netherlands.* 4 vols., New York: Harper, 1876–1900.

Mouton, Léo. *Un demi-roi, le duc d'Épernon.* Paris: Perrin, 1922.

Murray, R. H. *Political Consequences of the Reformation. Studies in Sixteenth Century Political Thought.* London: E. Benn, 1926.

Naef, Henri. *La conjuration d'Amboise et Genève.* Geneva: A. Jullien, George, 1922.

Neale, John E. *The Age of Catherine de Medici.* London: Jonathan Cape, 1943; New York: Barnes & Noble, 1959.

———— *Essays in Elizabethan History.* New York: St. Martin's Press, 1958.

———— *Elizabethan Government and Society: Essays presented to Sir John Neale,* ed. S. T. Bindoff, J. Hurstfield, and C. H. Williams. London: University of London, Athlone Press, 1961.

Noguères, Henri. *La Saint-Barthélemy, 24 août 1572.* Paris: Laffout, 1959.

Nouaillac, Joseph. *Villeroy, secrétaire d'état et ministre de Charles IX, Henri III, et Henri IV.* Paris: Bibliothèque de la Fondation Thiers, 1908.

Oman, Sir Charles. *History of the Art of War in the Sixteenth Century.* New York: Humanities Press, 1937.

Pastor, Ludwig von. *The History of the Popes from the Close of the Middle Ages.* 40 vols., London: Routledge & Kegan Paul; St. Louis: B. Herder, 1924–52.

Palm, Franklin Charles. *Politics and Religion in Sixteenth Century France. A Study of the Career of Henry of Montmorency-Damville, Uncrowned King of the South.* Boston: Ginn, 1927.

Piaget, E. *Histoire de l'établissement des Jésuites en France (1540–1640).* Leiden: E. J. Brill, 1893.

Picot, Georges M. R. *Histoire des États généraux.* 5 vols., Paris: Hachette, 1888.

Pirenne, Henri. *Histoire de Belgique,* vol. IV. Brussels: Lamertin, 1911.

Poëte, Marcel. *Une vie de cité, Paris de sa naissance à nos jours.* 4 vols., Paris: A. Picard, 1924–1931; esp. vol. III.

Poirson, M. A. *Histoire du règne de Henri IV.* 3 vols., Paris: Louis Colas, 1856.

Pollen, John Hungerford. *The English Catholics in the Reign of Queen Elizabeth.* London: Longmans, Green, 1920.

Prat, Jean Marie. *Recherches historiques et critiques sur la Compagnie de Jésus en France du temps du P. Coton (1564–1626).* 5 vols., Lyon: Briday, 1876–78.

Ranke, Leopold von. *Civil Wars and Monarchy in France in the Sixteenth and Seventeenth Centuries,* tr. M. A. Garvey. 2 vols., New York: Harper, 1854.

Read, Conyers. *Mr. Secretary Walsingham and the Policy of Queen Elizabeth.* 3 vols., Oxford: Clarendon Press, 1925.

——— *Mr. Secretary Cecil and Queen Elizabeth.* New York: Alfred A. Knopf; London: Jonathan Cape, 1955.

——— *Lord Burghley and Queen Elizabeth.* New York: Alfred A. Knopf; London: Jonathan Cape, 1960.

Recueil des actions et parolles memorables de Philippe Second, Roy d'Espagne. Cologne: Pierre Marteau, 1671.

Reynolds, Beatrice. *Proponents of Limited Monarchy in Sixteenth Century France: Francis Hotman and Jean Bodin.* New York: Columbia University Press, 1931.

Richard, P. *La Papauté et la Ligue française: Pierre d'Epinac, archévêque de Lyon (1573–1599).* Paris: A. Picard, 1901.

Robiquet, Paul. *Paris et la Ligue, sous le règne de Henri III.* Paris: Hachette, 1886.

——— *Histoire municipale de Paris.* 3 vols., Paris: Hachette, 1904.

Rocquain, Félix. *La France et Rome pendant les guerres de religion.* Paris: Edouard Champion, 1924.

Romanini, Vesin de. *La cryptographie dévoilée.* Brussels: Deprez-Parent, 1840.

Romier, Lucien. *Les origines politiques des guerres de religion.* 2 vols., Paris: Perrin, 1913.

——— *Le royaume de Catherine de Médicis: La France à la veille des guerres de religion.* 2 vols., Paris: Perrin, 1922.

——— *Catholiques et Huguenots à la cour de Charles IX.* Paris: Perrin, 1924.

——— *La conjuration d'Amboise.* Paris: Perrin, 1923.

Ruble, Alphonse de. *Antoine de Bourbon et Jeanne d'Albret.* 4 vols., Paris: Labitte, 1881–1886.

——— *Jeanne d'Albert et la guerre civile.* Paris: E. Paul et Guillemin, 1897.

——— *Le traité de Cateau-Cambrésis (2 et 3 avril 1559).* Paris: Labitte and E. Paul, 1889.

Salmon, J. H. M. *The French Religious Wars in English Thought.* New York: Oxford University Press, 1959.

Saulnier, Eugène. *Le rôle politique du Cardinal de Bourbon.* Paris: H. Champion, 1912.

Saunders, Jason L. *Justus Lipsius: the Philosophy of Renaissance Stoicism.* New York: Liberal Arts Press, 1955.

Sedgwick, Henry Dwight. *The House of Guise.* London: Lindsay Drummond, 1938.

Sée, Henri. *Histoire économique de la France.* 2 vols., Paris: A. Colin, 1948–51.

Sichel, Edith. *The Later Years of Catherine de' Medici.* London: Archibald Constable, 1908.

Sutherland, N. M. *The French Secretaries of State in the Age of Catherine de Medici.* London: University of London, Athlone Press, 1962.

Thompson, James Westfall. *The Wars of Religion in France, 1559–1576: The Huguenots, Catherine de Medici, Philip II.* New York: Frederick Ungar, 1909.

Tilley, Arthur. *The French Wars of Religion.* London: Society for the Promotion of Christian Knowledge, 1919.

———— *The Literature of the French Renaissance.* 2 vols., New York: Hafner Publishing Co., 1959.

Ulph, Owen. "The Estates General and the Catholic League, 1576–1593," unpub. dissertation, Stanford University, 1947.

Vaissière, Pierre de. *Henri IV.* Paris: Arthème Fayard, 1928.

———— *Messieurs de Joyeuse (1561–1615): Portraits et documents inédits.* Paris: A. Michel, 1926.

Vallina, Inocencio de la. *Relaciones políticas entre España y Francia durante el reinado de Felipe II.* Oviedo, 1893.

Valois, Noël. *Le conseil du roi aux XIVᵉ, XVᵉ, et XVIᵉ siècles.* Paris, 1888.

Van der Essen, Léon. *Alexandre Farnèse, prince de Parme, gouverneur générale des Pays-Bas (1545–1592).* 5 vols., Brussels: Librairie Nationale d'Art et d'Histoire, 1937.

Van Dyke, Paul. *Catherine de Médicis.* 2 vols., New York: Scribners, 1922–27.

Viénot, Jean. *Histoire de la Réforme française des origines à l'Edit de Nantes.* Paris: Fischbacher, 1926.

Vitet, Ludovic. *La Ligue, précédée des états d'Orléans.* 2 vols., Paris: Calumaun-Lévy, 1902.

———— *Les états de Blois, ou la mort de MM. de Guise. Scènes historiques, décembre 1588.* Paris: H. Fournier, 1829.

Vivent, Jacques. *La tragédie de Blois: le Roi de France et le Duc de Guise (1585–1588).* Paris: Hachette, 1946.

Weber, Bernard C. *The Youth of Mary Stuart, Queen of Scots.* Philadelphia: Dorrance and Co., 1941.

Weill, Georges. *Les théories sur le pouvoir royal en France pendant les guerres de religion.* Paris: Hachette, 1892.

Whitehead, Arthur W. *Gaspard de Coligny, Admiral of France.* London: Methuen, 1904.

Wiedner, Donald L. "Coins and Accounts in Western European and Colonial History, 1250–1936," unpub. dissertation, Harvard University, 1958.

Wilkinson, Maurice. *A History of the League or Sainte Union, 1576–1595.* Glasgow: Jackson, Wylie, 1929.

Yates, Frances A. *The Valois Tapestries.* London: The Warburg Institute, 1959.

Zeller, Gaston. *Les institutions de la France au XVIe siècle.* Paris: Presses Universitaires de France, 1948.

—— *Les temps modernes.* Vol. II of Pierre Renouvin, ed., *Histoire des relations internationales.* Paris: Hachette, 1953.

ARTICLES

Alcocer, Mariano. "Criptografía español," *Boletin de la Academia de Historia,* 105:336–460 (1934); and 107:603–676 (1935).

Armstrong, Edward. "The Political Theory of the Huguenots," *English Historical Review,* 4:13–40 (1889).

Baguenault de Puchesse, Gustave. "La politique de Philippe II dans les affaires de France, 1559–1598," *Revue des Questions Historiques,* 25:1–66 (1879).

—— "Le traité signé à Nemours en 1585, d'après des documents inédits," *Annales de la Société Historique et Archeologique du Gatinas,* 19:305–317 (1901).

—— "Les negociations de Catherine de Médicis à Paris après la Journée des Barricades," *Academie des Sciences Morales et Politiques,* new ser., 1:697–709 (1903).

Baldwin, Summerfield. "Jean Bodin and the League," *Catholic Historical Review,* 23:160–184 (1937).

Barker, Ernest. "The Authorship of the Vindiciae contra Tyrannos," *Cambridge Historical Journal,* 3:164–181 (1930).

—— "A Huguenot Theory of Politics: the *Vindiciae contra Tyrannos,*" *Proceedings of the Huguenot Society of London,* 14:37–61 (1930).

Barthélemy, Edouard de. "Catherine de Médicis, le duc de Guise et le traité de Nemours, d'après des documents inédits," *Revue des Questions Historiques,* 27:464–495 (1880).

Bouard, Michel de. "Sixte-Quint, Henri IV et la Ligue: la légation du cardinal Caetani en France (1589–1590)," *Revue des Questions Historiques,* 20:59–140 (1932).

Bremond d'Ars, Guy de. "La Saint-Barthélemy et l'Espagne, d'après la correspondance de Jean de Vivonne de Saint-Gouard," *Revue des Questions Historiques*, 35:386–412 (1884).

—— "Les conférences de Saint-Brice entre Henri de Navarre et Catherine de Médicis, 1586–87," *Revue des Questions Historiques*, 36:496–523 (1884).

Brown, Horatio F. "The Assassination of the Guises as Described by the Venetian Ambassador," *English Historical Review*, 10:304–332 (1895).

Butler, D. and J. H. Pollen. "Doctor Gifford in 1586," *The Month*, 103:243–258, 348–367 (1904).

Calendini, Louis. "Notes sur le traité de Vervins," *Revue Henri IV*, 1:86–88 (1905).

Colombier, Henri. "Les Jésuites ligueurs d'après M. l'Abbé Houssaye," *Études religieuses, philosophiques, historiques et littéraires, par les pères de la compagnie de Jésus*, 5:759–766 (1874).

Descloseaux, A. "Combats près d'Arques, 1589 et la bataille d'Ivry, 1590," *Revue Historique*, 52:43–56 (1893).

Devos, J. P. "La poste au service des diplomates espagnoles, 1555–1598," *Bulletin, Commission Royale d'Histoire*, 103:205–257 (1938).

Drouot, Henri. "La mission du légat Caetano et sa traversée de la Bourgogne (nov. 1589–janv. 1590)," *Revue d'Histoire Moderne*, 3:371–388 (1928).

—— "L'influence de Lyon et la Ligue en Bourgogne: Macon en 1588–1589," *Annales de Bourgogne*, 9:177–208 (1937).

—— "La royauté du cardinal de Bourbon et les ligueurs bourguignons (1589–1590)," *Annales de Bourgogne*, 5:30–44 (1933).

Dufour, Alain. "Le Catéchisme du docteur Pantalon et de Zani, son disciple (1594)," *Aspects de la propagande religieuse* (Geneva: E. Droz, 1957), pp. 361–372.

Dur, Philip. "The Right of Taxation in the Political Theory of the French Religious Wars," *Journal of Modern History*, 17:289–303 (1945).

Fabre, Frédéric. "The English College at Eu, 1582–1592," *Catholic Historical Review*, 37:257–280 (1951).

Felice, Philippe de. "Le Colloque de Poissy, 1561," *Bulletin de la Société de l'Histoire du Protestantisme Française*, 107:133–145 (1961).

Ferrière, Hector de la. "L'entrevue de Bayonne," *Revue des Questions Historiques*, 34:457–522 (1883).

—— "Catherine de Médicis et les Politiques," *Revue des Questions Historiques*, 56:404–439 (1894).

Frame, Donald M. "New Light on Montaigne's Trip to Paris in 1588," *Romanic Review*, 51:161–181 (1960).

Frémy, Edouard. "La médiation de l'Abbé de Feuillants entre la Ligue et Henri III, 1588-1589," *Revue d'Histoire Diplomatique,* 6:228-243, 449-473 (1892).

Gandy, Georges. "La Saint-Barthélemy; ses origines, son vrai caractère, ses suites," *Revue des Questions Historiques,* 1:11-94, 321-391 (1866).

Garnier, Armand. "Un scandale princier au XVIe siècle," *Revue du XVIe Siècle,* 1:153-189, 355-391, 561-612 (1913).

Gérard, Albert. "La révolte et la siège de Paris, 1589," *Mémoires de la Société de l'Histoire de Paris et de l'Isle-de-France,* 33:65-150 (1906).

Giraud, Charles. "Sixte-Quint, son influence sur les affaires de France au XVIe siècle," *Revue des Deux Mondes,* 101:462-486, 624-650, 848-877 (1872).

Halkin, Léon-E. "La physionomie morale de Philippe II, d'après ses derniers biographes," *Revue Historique,* 179:355-367 (1937).

Hamilton, E. Blanche. "Paris under the Last Valois Kings," *English Historical Review,* 1:260-276 (1886).

Hauser, Henri. "The European Financial Crisis of 1559," *Journal of Economic and Business History,* 2:241-255 (1930).

Kingdon, Robert M. "The Political Resistance of the Calvinists in France and the Low Countries," *Church History,* 27:220-233 (1958).

Koenigsberger, Helmuth G. "The Organization of Revolutionary Parties in France and the Netherlands during the 16th Century," *Journal of Modern History,* 27:335-351 (1955).

Lecler, Joseph. "Aux origines de la Ligue: premiers projets et premiers essais (1561-1570)," *Études,* 227:188-208 (1936).

L'Epinois, Henri de. "La politique de Sixte-Quint en France: preliminaires de la lutte entre Henri III et la maison de Lorraine," *Revue des Questions Historiques,* 27:151-213 (1880).

——— "La politique de Sixte-Quint: négociations diplomatiques avec la France pendant les premiers mois de 1588, d'après des documents inédits conservés aux archives du Vatican," *Revue des Questions Historiques,* 14:387-435 (1874).

——— "La reconciliation de Henri III et du duc de Guise, mai-juillet, 1588," *Revue des Questions Historiques,* 39:52-94 (1886).

——— "La légation du cardinal Caetani en France," *Revue des Questions Historiques,* 30:460-525 (1881).

——— "Les derniers jours de la Ligue. La France en 1592 — États de 1593 — Absolution d'Henri IV." *Revue des Questions Historiques,* 34:34-114 (1883).

Mackie, John Duncan. "The Will of Mary Stuart," *Scottish Historical Review,* 11:338-344 (1914).

——— "Scotland and the Spanish Armada," *Scottish Historical Review,* 12:1-24 (1914).

Manfroni, C. "La legazione del cardinale Caetani in Francia (1589–1590)," *Rivista Storica Italiana*, 10:190–270 (1893).

Mantel, Alfred. "Der Anteil der Reformierten schweizer am navarresischen Feldzug von 1587," *Jahrbuch für Schweizerische Geschichte*, 40:3–52 (1915).

Mathorez, J. "Notes sur les Espagnols en France depuis le XVIe siècle jusqu'au règne de Louis XIII," *Bulletin Hispanique*, 16: 337–371 (1914).

———— "Les Espagnols et la crise national française à la fin du XVIe siècle," *Bulletin Hispanique*, 18:86–113 (1916).

Mattingly, Garrett. "William Allen and Catholic Propaganda in England," *Aspects de la propagande religieuse* (Geneva: E. Droz, 1957), pp. 325–339.

Maury, Alfred. "La commune de Paris de 1588," *Revue des Deux Mondes*, 95:132–175 (1871).

Mesnard, Pierre. "La pensée religieuse de Bodin," *Revue du XVIe Siècle*, 16:77–121 (1929).

Moreau-Reibel, Jean. "Bodin et la Ligue d'après des lettres inédites," *Humanisme et Renaissance*, 2:422–440 (1935).

Morel-Fatio, Alfred. "Don Bernardino de Mendoza," *Bulletin Hispanique*, 8:20–70, 129–147 (1906).

Mousset, Albert. "Les droits de l'infante Isabelle-Claire-Eugénie à la couronne de France," *Bulletin Hispanique*, 16:46–79 (1914).

Neale, John E. "Elizabeth and the Netherlands, 1586–87," *English Historical Review*, 45:373–396 (1930).

———— "The Fame of Sir Edward Stafford," *English Historical Review*, 44:203–220 (1929).

Nouaillac, Joseph. "La fin de la Ligue: Villeroy négociateur des Politiques. Essai d'histoire des négociations de 1589 à 1594," *Revue Henri IV*, 1:37–58, 69–81 (1905); 1:197–217 (1906).

Philippson, Martin. "Philipp II. von Spanien und das Papstthum," *Historische Zeitschrift*, 39:269–315, 419–457 (1878).

Pigafetta, Filippo. "Relation du siège de Paris par Henri IV," tr. A. Dufour, *Mémoires de la Société de l'Histoire de Paris et de l'Isle-de-France*, 2:1–105 (1876).

Pinette, G. L. "Freedom in Huguenot Doctrine," *Archiv für Reformationsgeschichte*, 50:200–233 (1959).

Poole, Mrs. Reginald. "A Journal of the Siege of Rouen in 1591," *English Historical Review*, 17:527–537 (1902).

Potter, John M. "The Conference at Bayonne, 1565," *American Historical Review*, 35:798–803 (1930).

Read, Conyers. "Walsingham and Burghley in Queen Elizabeth's Privy Council," *English Historical Review*, 28:34–58 (1913).

———— "The Fame of Sir Edward Stafford," *American Historical Review*, 20:292–313 (1915); 35:560–566 (1930).

Rocquain, Félix. "Les Espagnols en France sous Henri IV: le roi et la nation," *Séances et Travaux de l'Académie des Sciences Morales et Politiques*, new ser., 86:135–155 (1916).

Romier, Lucien, 'La mort de Henri II,' *Revue du XVIe Siècle*, 1:99–152 (1913).

——— "La Saint-Barthélemy: les événements de Rome et la préméditation du massacre," *Revue du XVIe Siècle*, 1:529–560 (1913).

Ruble, Alphonse de. "Le Colloque de Poissy (sept.-oct. 1561)," *Mémoires de la Société de l'Histoire de Paris et de l'Isle-de-France*, 16:1–56 (1889).

Saint-Priest, Alexis de. "Les Guises," *Revue des Deux Mondes*, 20: 785–847 (1851).

Salmon, J. H. M. "Catherine dei Medici and the French Wars of Religion," *History Today*, 6:297–306 (1956).

Saulnier, Eugène. "Le cardinal de Bourbon entre des ducs de Guise et de Nevers," *Revue d'Histoire Diplomatique*, 24: 161–182 (1910).

Schelven, A. A. van. "Beza's De Iure Magistratuum in Subditos," *Archiv für Reformationsgeschichte*, 45:62–81 (1954).

Smith, David B. "François Hotman," *Scottish Historical Review*, 13: 328–365 (1916).

Solano, Fernando. "El tratado de Cateau-Cambrésis (1559)," *Universidad* (Zaragoza), 36:295–353 (1959).

Suárez Inclán, Julián. "Liberación de Paris en 1590," *Nuestro Tiempo*, 1:100–108 (1900).

Sutherland, N. M. "Calvinism and the Conspiracy of Amboise," *History*, 47:111–138 (1962).

Thickett, D. "Estienne Pasquier and His Part in the Struggle for Tolerance," *Aspects de la propagande religieuse*. Trauvaux d'Humanisme et Renaissance, no. XXVIII (Geneva: E. Droz, 1957), pp. 377–402.

Tilley, Arthur. "Some Pamphlets of the French Wars of Religion (1560–94)," *English Historical Review*, 14:451–470 (1899).

Törne, P. O. de. "Philippe II et Henri de Guise: le début de leurs relations (1578)," *Revue Historique*, 167:323–335 (1931).

"Troisième centenaire de l'Edit de Nantes," *Bulletin de la Société Historique du Protestantisme Française*, 47:169–392 (1898).

Ulph, Owen. "Jean Bodin and the Estates General of 1576," *Journal of Modern History*, 19:289–296 (1947).

Valois, Noël. "Les États de Pontoise," *Revue d'Histoire de l'Église de France*, 29:237–256 (1943).

Van Dyke, Paul. "The Estates of Pontoise," *English Historical Review*, 28:472–495 (1913).

Viñas, A. "Felipe II y la Jornada de las Barricadas," in *Hommage à*

Ernest Martinenche; Études hispaniques et américaines. Paris: Editions d'Artrey, 1939, pp. 514–533.

Waddington, A. "La France et les protestants allemands sous Charles IX et Henri III," *Revue Historique,* 42:241–277 (1890).

Weber, Bernerd C. "Personalities and Politics at the Court of Henry II of France, 1547–1559," *Studies in Modern European History in Honor of Franklin Charles Palm.* New York: Bookman Associates, 1956, pp. 250–264.

———— "The Council of Fontainebleau," *Archiv für Reformationsgeschichte,* 45:43–62 (1954).

Wernham, Richard B. "Queen Elizabeth and the Siege of Rouen, 1591," *Transactions of the Royal Historical Society,* 4th ser., 15: 163–179 (1932).

Wilkinson, Maurice. "A Provincial Assembly during the League," *Transactions of the Royal Historical Society,* 3rd ser., 9:65–76 (1915).

———— "The Wars of Religion in the Périgord," *English Historical Review,* 21:650–672 (1906).

Ysselsteyn, G. T. van. "L'auteur de l'ouvrage Vindiciae contra Tyrannos, publie sous le nom de Stephanus Junius Brutus," *Revue Historique,* 167:46–59 (1931).

Zeller, B. "Le mouvement Guisard en 1588: Catherine de Médicis et la Journée des Barricades," *Revue Historique,* 41:253–276 (1889).

Zeller, Gaston. "Saluces, Pignerol et Strasbourg: La politique des frontières au temps de la prépondérance espagnole," *Revue Historique,* 193:97–110 (1942).

NOTES

✦ ✦ ✦ ✦

CHAPTER I. The Wars of Religion in France

1. Philip to the Princess Dowager of Portugal, Regent of Spain, Brussels, 10 February 1588, in *Calendar of Letters, Despatches and State Papers Relating to the Negotiations between England and Spain*, ed. Royall Tyler (London, 1954), XIII, 353–354.

2. Charles Weiss, ed., *Papiers d'état du Cardinal de Granvelle, d'après les manuscrits de la bibilothèque de Besançon* (Paris, 1841–52), V, 453–454.

3. Fernando Solano, "El tratado de Cateau-Cambrésis (1559)," *Universidad*, 36:295–353 (1959); and Alphonse de Ruble, *Le traité de Cateau-Cambrésis* (Paris, 1889). See Lucien Romier, *Les origines politiques des guerres de religion* (Paris, 1913), II, 287–290, 304–314, 332–345 on the peace negotiations. Full text of the treaty is in Jean Dumont, ed., *Corps universel diplomatique du droit des gens . . .* (Amsterdam, 1726–1731), V, 31–41.

4. Granvelle to Philip II, 14 July 1563, Weiss, *Papiers d'état*, VII, 124; and Philip II to Alva, 14 December 1563, L. P. Gachard, ed., *Correspondance de Philippe II sur les affaires des Pays-Bas* (Brussels, 1848–79), I, 277. Also cf. H. G. Koenigsberger, "The Organization of Revolutionary Parties in France and the Netherlands during the Sixteenth Century," *Journal of Modern History*, 27:336–340 (1955); and Robert M. Kingdon, "The Political Resistance of the Calvinists in France and the Low Countries," *Church History*, 27:220–228 (1958).

5. *Calendar of Letters and State Papers, Relating to English Affairs, of the Reign of Elizabeth, Preserved Principally in the Archives of Simancas* ed. Martin A. S. Hume [hereafter cited *C.S.P., Span.*] (London, 1895), III, 579; and Roger B. Merriman, *The Rise of the Spanish Empire*, 4 vols. (New York, 1918–34), vol. IV, *Philip the Prudent*, p. 26.

6. "Relation de Frédéric Baboaro, faite an retour de son ambassade auprès de Charles-Quint et de Philippe II, en 1557," in L. P. Gachard, ed., *Relations des ambassadeurs vénitiens sur Charles-Quint et Philippe II* (Brussels, 1855), p. 35.

7. "Relation de Michel Suriano, faite au retour de son ambassade auprès de Philippe II, en 1559," *ibid.*, pp. 123–124.

8. Valentín Vásquez, *España y Francia ante la tercera apertura del Concilio de Trento*, cited in Pedro Aguado Bleye, *Manual de historia de España* (Madrid, 1954), II, 576–578. Cf. Martin Philippson, "Philipp II. von Spanien und das Papstthum," *Historische Zeitschrift*, 39:293–295 (1878).

9. Edmond Cabié, ed., *Ambassade en Espagne de Jean Ebrard, seigneur de Saint-Sulpice de 1562 à 1565* (Paris, 1903), pp. 279, 281–282, 285, 299.

10. Philip to Pius V, Madrid, 26 January 1566, in Luciano Serrano, ed., *Correspondencia diplomatica entre España y la Santa Sede durante el pontificado de S. Pio V* (Madrid, 1914), I, 113–114. Ludwig von Pastor, *History of the Popes*, 40 vols. (St. Louis and London, 1924–52), XVII, 12–17, 36–37.

11. *Documentos del Archivo de Alba* (Madrid, 1891), pp. 284–286, as cited in Pastor, *History of the Popes*, XIX, 364.

12. Alexander von Hübner, *The Life and Times of Sixtus V* (London, 1872), I, 379–382, and esp. II, 20–37; also Pastor, *History of the Popes*, XXI, 262–273, 340–351. See Paul Herre, *Papsttum und Papstwahl im Zeitalter Philipps II* (Leipzig, 1907), pp. 458–652 on Philip's relations with the popes of the 1590's.

13. James Westfall Thompson, *The Wars of Religion in France, 1559–1576* (New York, 1909), pp. 81, 89, 115, and notes.

14. Conyers Read, *Mr. Secretary Cecil and Queen Elizabeth* (New York, 1955), pp. 125–126. Also see Merriman, *Philip the Prudent*, pp. 272–273, and Arnold O. Meyer, *England and the Catholic Church under Queen Elizabeth* (London, 1916), p. 58.

15. *Calendar of State Papers, Foreign Series, of the Reign of Elizabeth, Preserved in the Public Record Office*, ed. Sophie Crawford Lomas (London, 1927), March 12, 1563 [hereafter cited *C.S.P., For.*]. Cabié, ed., *L'Ambassade de St.-Sulpice*, Robertet to St.-Sulpice, 24 July 1563, p. 142; Lansac to St.-Sulpice, 15 November 1563, p. 177; Charles IX to Mr. de Foix (French ambassador in England), 7 December 1563, pp. 194–195.

16. Count made by Beza in response to the request of Catherine de' Medici. Théodore Bèze, *Histoire ecclésiastique* (Paris, 1883), I, 745. This figure has been accepted as reasonably accurate by modern scholars. See Lucien Romier, *Le Royaume de Catherine de Médicis* (Paris, 1922), II, 180; Thompson, *Wars of Religion*, p. 230; and Robert Kingdon, *Geneva and the Coming of the Religious Wars in France, 1555–1563* (Geneva, 1956), p. 79.

17. Henry M. Baird, *History of the Rise of the Huguenots of France* (New York, 1879), I, 560. Thompson refers (without documentation) to the claim of the church at Orléans to 7000 members,

Wars of Religion, p. 230, but gives his own estimate of slightly under 400 as the average size of the Huguenot congregations in 1562; *ibid.*, pp. 230–231. This figure, however, seems to me rather large.

18. The lower figure was the estimate of Guido Giannetti, Venetian ambassador to England, 14 March 1562, *C.S.P., For.*, IV, 555–556. The higher number is contained in a remonstrance of King Charles IX to Pope Pius IV, in Louis de Bourbon, prince of Condé, *Mémoires de Condé, ou recueil pour servir à l'histoire de France, contenant ce qui s'est passé de plus memorable dans ce Royaume sous les Regnes de François II et Charles IX*, 6 vols. (London, 1740; Paris, 1743) [hereafter cited *Mémoires de Condé*], II, 812. Cf. *C.S.P., For.*, V, 623–625.

19. See, in particular, Kingdon, *Geneva*, and his "The Political Resistance of the Calvinists," pp. 220–233.

20. Romier, *Le Royaume*, II, 152–179 analyzes the extent of protestant penetration and their relative position in each of the provinces. Guienne, Languedoc, Gascony, Navarre, Béarn, Provence, Normandy, Poitou, and Orléanais apparently had the largest unmber of Huguenots, concentrated mainly in the cities of Bergerac, Nérac, Dieppe, Poitiers, Lyon, and Orléans. Cf. Kingdon, *Geneva*, pp. 54–55. Montluc estimated, in 1561, that one-tenth of the population of Guienne was Protestant, 25 March 1561, letter 48, Blaise de Montluc, *Commentaires et lettres* (Paris, 1864–72), IV, 115. The aldermen of Amiens declared that three-fourths of the inhabitants of that city were Protestant in 1567, Alexis-Auguste du Bois, *La Ligue: documents relatifs à la Picardie d'après les registres de l'échevinage d'Amiens* (Amiens, 1859), p. 5.

21. Champagne and Burgundy were the strongholds of Guise-Catholic influence, with the Ile-de-France, Picardy (except Amiens), and Nivernais also remaining staunchly Catholic, Romier, *Le Royaume*, II, 152–155, 164–167. Lorraine, which was only partially attached to the kingdom of France at this time, was also loyal to the Roman church.

22. *Ibid.*, pp. 264–269; Koenigsberger, "Organization of Revolutionary Parties," pp. 337–338; Gaston Zeller, *Les institutions de la France au XVIe siècle* (Paris, 1948), pp. 364–368; and Pierre Imbart de la Tour, *Les origines de la réforme*, 4 vols. (Paris, 1905–35), IV, 447–457. Thompson believes, however, that the strength of this Huguenot organization before 1572 has been exaggerated except in the province of Guienne, *Wars of Religion*, p. 324.

23. Romier, *Le Royaume*, I, 170–175; also Henri Hauser, *La prépondérance espagnole, 1559–1660* (Paris, 1948), pp. 197–203; Zeller, *Les institutions*, pp. 15–16; and Henri Sée, *Histoire économique de la France*, 2 vols. (Paris, 1948–1951), I, 135–137.

24. J. Russell Major, *The Estates General of 1560* (Princeton, 1951), pp. 17–18, 22–23. See Edward Armstrong, *The French Wars*

of Religion: Their Political Aspects (Oxford, 1904), pp. 10–13; and Davis Bitton, "The French Nobility as Seen by Contemporaries, 1560–1630," unpub. dissertation, Princeton University, 1961, pp. 1–5, 203–206.

25. Kingdon, *Geneva*, pp. 6, 108. Romier, *La Royaume*, II, 258–259.

26. Alphonse de Ruble, *Antoine de Bourbon et Jeanne d'Albret*, 4 vols. (Paris, 1881–86), I, 147–210; III, 225, 312–314; IV, 2–3, 17–19, 88.

27. See, in particular, J. Russell Major, *Representative Institutions in Renaissance France, 1421–1559* (Madison, 1960), pp. 3–20; and J. N. Figgis, *Political Thought from Gerson to Grotius: 1414–1625* (New York, 1960), p. 12. Also cf. Noël Valois, *Le conseil du roi aux XIVe, XVe et XVIe siècles*, 2 vols. (Paris, 1888); and Roger Doucet, *Les institutions de la France au XVIe siècle*, 2 vols. (Paris, 1948), esp. I, 102–229.

28. Pierre Champion, *Charles IX, la France et le controle de l'Espagne*, 2 vols. (Paris, 1939), II, 112–125, esp. p. 118; Philippe Erlanger, *Le massacre de la Saint-Barthélemy* (Paris, 1960), pp. 231–234; John E. Neale, *The Age of Catherine de Medici* (New York, 1959), p. 81; Paul Van Dyke, *Catherine de Médicis*, 2 vols. (New York, 1922–27), II, 81–84; and Jean Héritier, *Catherine de Médicis* (Paris, 1959), pp. 412–416.

29. Louis-Raymond Lefèvre, *Le Tumulte d'Amboise* (Paris, 1949). On the conspiracy and its connections with Calvin, cf. Lucien Romier, *La conjuration d'Amboise* (Paris, 1923); and Henri Naef, *La conjuration d'Amboise et Genève* (Geneva, 1922). For Navarre's complicity see Ruble, *Antoine de Bourbon*, II, 217–229. An interesting contemporary justification can be found in Louis Regnier de la Planche, *Histoire de l'estat de France*, in J. A. C. Buchon, ed., *Choix de chroniques et mémoires sur l'histoire de France (XVIe siècle)*, (Paris, 1836), pp. 245–274.

30. Albert Buisson, *Michel de l'Hospital, 1503–1573* (Paris, 1950), pp. 66–80. This attitude is reflected in his opening speech at the Estates General of Orléans in December 1560, when he recounted the dangers of religious diversity: "La division des langues ne faict la séparation des royaumes, mais celle de la religion et des loyx, qui d'ung royaume en faict deux. De là sort le vieil proverbe, une foy, une loy, un roy." Michel de l'Hôpital, *Oeuvres complètes de Michel de l'Hospital*, ed. P. J. S. Dufey, 5 vols. (Paris, 1824–25), I, 398.

31. See in particular, *ibid.*, I, 441–453; II, 175–215, also Buisson, *Michel de l'Hospital*, pp. 213–226.

32. Bernerd C. Weber, "The Council of Fontainebleau (1560)," *Archiv für Reformationsgeschichte*, 45:43–62 (1954), is a perceptive and well-documented study of the assembly. Cf. Major, *The Estates General of 1560*, chap. 3; and, on the Edict of Amboise, Joseph Lecler,

Histoire de la tolérance au siècle de la réforme, 2 vols. (Aubier, 1955), II, 63–72.

33. Major, *The Estates General of 1560,* chap. 6; also Georges Picot, *Histoire des États généraux,* 5 vols. (Paris, 1888), II, 9–53.

34. Paul Van Dyke, "The Estates of Pontoise," *English Historical Review,* 28:472–495 (1913). Cf. Noël Valois, "Les états de Pontoise (août 1561)," *Revue d'Histoire de l'Église de France,* 29:237–256 (1943); and Lucien Romier, *Catholiques et huguenots à la cour de Charles IX* (Paris, 1924), pp. 173–188.

35. For a contemporary Protestant insight into the doctrinal discussion, see Pierre de la Place, *Commentaires de l'estat de la religion et république,* in Buchon, *Choix de chroniques et mémoires,* pp. 154–201. Two old but basic studies of the colloquy are Alphonse de Ruble, "Le Colloque de Poissy (sept.-oct., 1561)," *Mémoires de la Société de l'Histoire de Paris et de l'Ile-de-France,* 16:1–56 (1889), and H. Klipffel, *Le Colloque de Poissy: Étude sur la crise religieuse et politique de 1561* (Paris, 1867). See also the recent article by Philippe de Felice, "Le Colloque de Poissy, 1561," *Bulletin de la Société de l'Histoire du Protestantisme Française,* 107:133–145 (1961).

36. Philip II to Chantonnay, 1 October 1561, Archivo General de Simancas, Sección de Estado, K. 1495, fol. 80, in Thompson, *Wars of Religion,* p. 116.

37. Romier, *Catholiques et Huguenots,* pp. 325–328, 341–345; and Kingdon, *Geneva,* pp. 107–109.

38. See, in particular, Georges Gandy, "La Saint-Barthélemy; ses origines son vrai caractère, ses suites," *Revue des Questions Historiques,* I:11–94, 321–391 (1866); Romier, "La Saint-Barthélemy, les événements de Rome et la préméditation du massacre," *Revue de XVIe Siècle,* I:529–560 (1913); Henri Noguères, *La Saint-Barthélemy, 24 août 1572* (Paris, 1959) (A very journalistic narrative); and most recently, Erlanger's *Le massacre de la Saint-Barthélemy* (1960). These last two were translated into English in 1962.

39. J. H. M. Salmon, *The French Religious Wars in English Thought* (Oxford, 1959). Also see Georges Weill, *Les théories sur le pouvoir royal en France pendant les guerres de religion* (Paris, 1891), pp. 99–121; John W. Allen, *A History of Political Thought in the Sixteenth Century* (New York, 1928), pp. 302–331; and G. L. Pinette, "Freedom in Huguenot Doctrine," *Archiv für Reformationsgeschichte,* 50: 200–233 (1959).

40. Simon Goulart, ed., *Mémoires de l'estat de France sous Charles IX,* 3 vols. in 6 (Meidelbourg, 1578), pp. 375–483. Cf. David Baird Smith, "François Hotman," *Scottish Historical Review,* 13:328–365 (1916); and Beatrice Reynolds, *Proponents of Limited Monarchy in Sixteenth Century France: Francis Hotman and Jean Bodin* (New York, 1931), pp. 41–104.

41. Its first publication was in French at Lyon, but the later Latin editions of 1576, 1580, and 1589 were more widely circulated. See A. A. van Schelven, "Beza's De Iure Magistratuum in Subditos," *Archiv für Reformationsgeschichte,* 45:62–81 (1954).

42. Eusèbe Philadelphe Cosmopolite, *Le Reveil-Matin des Français et de leurs voisins* (1574). See also the *Dialogue de l'authorité des princes et de la liberté des peuples* [*d'Archon et Politie*] (1576); *Le Tocsin contre les massacreurs et auteurs des confusions de la France* (1577); *Ethices christianae liber secundus* (1577); and *Le miroir des Français* (1581).

43. *Discours sur les moyens de bien gouverner et maintenir en bonne paix un royaume ou autre principauté, divisés en trois livres, à savoir du Conseil, de la Religion, et de la Police, que doit tenir un Prince — contre Nicholas Machiavel Florentin.*

44. *Remonstrance au roy tres chrestien Henry III* (Francfort, 1574); *Apologie ou défense pour les chrestiens de France qui sont de la religion évangelique ou réformée . . . à ceux qui ne veulent vivre en paix et concorde avec eux* (Geneva, 1578 and 1584); *Le bureau du concile de Trente . . .* (Geneva, 1586); and probable co-author, with Henri Estienne, of the *Discours marveilleux de la vie, action et déportements de Catherine de Médicis* (1575).

45. See Ernest Barker, "A Huguenot Theory of Politics: the *Vindiciae contra Tyrannos*," *Proceedings of the Huguenot Society of London,* 14:37–61 (1930); and Harold J. Laski's introduction to the London edition of 1924, *A Defence of Liberty Against Tyrants.*

46. The treatise was published under the pseudonym Stephanus Junius Brutus. On the conflicting evidence for authorship, cf. Ernest Barker, "The Authorship of the Vindiciae contra Tyrannos," *Cambridge Historical Journal,* 3:164-181 (1930), who believes it was written by Hubert Languet; Albert Elkan, *Die Publizistik der Bartholomäusnacht und Mornays "Vindiciae contra Tyrannos"* (Heidelberg, 1905), who gives the nod to Du Plessis-Mornay; and G. T. van Ysselstein, "L'auteur de l'ouvrage 'Vindiciae contra Tyrannos,'" *Revue Historique,* 167:46–59 (1931), who maintains they were co-authors.

47. Laski, *Defence of Liberty,* pp. 37–38.

CHAPTER II. Foundations of the Catholic League

1. Martha W. Freer, *Henry III, King of France and Poland: His Court and Times,* 3 vols. (London, 1858), III, 370–371.

2. Jacques-Auguste De Thou, *Histoire universelle, depuis 1543 jusqu'en 1607,* 16 vols. (London, 1734), X, 674–678, *passim.* I have also made use of the Basle edition of 1742, whenever the edition is

not cited, reference will be to the latter. Pierre de l'Estoile, *Mémoires-Journaux*, 12 vols. (Paris, 1875-1896), vol. I, *Journal de Henri III (1574-1580)*, pp. 93-94, 180-181, 219-221, 231-255; II, 21-24. Pierre de Brantôme, *Oeuvres complètes*, 11 vols. (Paris, 1864-1882), *passim*. Also see Armand Baschet *La diplomatie vénitienne* (Paris, 1862), pp. 566-569; and Charles Lenient, *La satire en France* (Paris, 1866), pp. 350-368.

3. Leo Mouton, *Un demi-roi, le duc d'Epernon* (Paris, 1922).

4. Quoted in Philippe Erlanger, *Henri III*, 9th ed. (Paris, 1948), p. 189.

5. On the Politiques, particularly between 1564 and 1576, see Francis De Crue, *Le parti des Politiques au lendemain de la Saint-Barthélemy: La Môle et Coconat* (Paris, 1892); also Lecler, *Histoire de la tolérance*, II, 72-99, *passim*.

6. Laski, *Defence of Liberty*, p. 33.

7. See the penetrating analysis of French legalist writing, including that of the Politiques, in William F. Church, *Constitutional Thought in Sixteenth Century France* (Cambridge, Mass., 1941), pp. 194-335. Also cf. Figgis, *Gerson to Grotius*, pp. 122-150; and Allen, *Political Thought*, pp. 280-301, 367-444. D. Thickett's provocative study, "Estienne Pasquier and His Part in the Struggle for Toleration," *Aspects de la propagande religieuse*, Travaux d'Humanisme et Renaissance, no. XXVIII (Geneva, 1957), pp. 377-402, is also valuable, as is Edmond Beame's dissertation, "The Development of Politique Thought during the French Religious Wars," University of Illinois, 1958, which emphasizes politique constitutional thought.

8. *Methodus ad facilem historiarum cognitionem* (Paris, 1566). For a recent and careful examination of this work see Vittorio de Caprariis, *Propaganda e pensiero politico in Francia during le guerre di religione* (Naples, 1959), I, 316-371.

9. *Les six livres de la République* (Paris, 1576). A forthright and perceptive, although unusual, examination of Bodin's political theory can be found in Reynolds' *Proponents of Limited Monarchy*, pp. 105-193. Also see Elisabeth Feist, *Weltbild und Staatsidee bei Jean Bodin* (Halle, 1930); Jean Moreau-Reibel, *Jean Bodin et le droit public comparé* (Paris, 1933); and especially Pierre Mesnard, "La pensée religieuse de Bodin," *Revue du XVIᵉ Siècle*, 16:77-121 (1929). Of related interest is Julian H. Franklin's *Jean Bodin and the Sixteenth Century Revolution in the Methodology of Law and History* (New York, 1963).

10. Bodin, *République*, book II, chap. V.

11. Franklin C. Palm, *Politics and Religion in Sixteenth Century France: A Study of the Career of Henry of Montmorency-Damville, Uncrowned King of the South* (Boston, 1927). De Thou, *Histoire universelle* (1734), VII, 38, 412-413.

12. Goulart, *Mémoires de l'estat*, III, 139–143. De Crue, *Le parti des Politiques*, pp. 12–15.

13. De Thou, *Histoire universelle* (1734), VII, 247–248. Lecler, *Histoire de la tolérance*, II, 86–87, and notes. An abstract of the Declaration of Nîmes, 25 April 1575, which formally linked the two parties, can be seen in C.S.P., *For.*, XI, 48–49. Cf. Léonce Anquez, *Histoire des assemblées politiques des Réformées de France* (Paris, 1859), pp. 16–28.

14. "Traicté d'association . . ." 1575, Bib. Nat., Lb^{34} 102 B$_3$, as quoted in Lecler, *Histoire de la tolérance*, II, 87.

15. Henri Hauser, *François de la Noue* (Paris, 1892), p. 65.

16. Bibliothèque Nationale, collection Brienne, p. 207, fol. 134. Also see Claude Devic and Jean Joseph Vaissete, *Histoire générale de Languedoc*, 15 vols. (Toulouse, 1872–1904), XII, 1112–1138; and Daniel, *Histoire de France*, XI, 40–42, cited in Palm, *Politics and Religion*, pp. 104–106. See the letters to Condé while in Germany in Goulart, *Mémoires de l'estat*, III, 405–412.

17. These towns were Aigues-Mortes and Beaucaire in Languedoc, Périgueux and Le Mas de Verdun in Guyenne, La Rochelle in Poitou, Yssoire in Auvergne, Nions and Serres in Dauphiné, and Cannes in Provence. See De Thou, *Histoire universelle* (1734), VII, 416–417.

18. J. H. Mariéjol, *La réforme et la Ligue, l'edit de Nantes*, vol. VI, part I of *Histoire de France des origines à la Révolution*, ed. Ernest Lavisse (Paris, 1911), p. 174. De Thou, *Histoire universelle* (1734), VII, 423–427.

19. Pierre-Victor Palma Cayet, *Chronologie novenaire, contenant l'histoire de la guerre sous la règne du Très Chrestien Roy de France et de Navarre Henry IV . . .*, 1st series, vol. XXXVIII of Charles Bernard Petitot, ed., *Collection complète des mémoires relatifs à l'histoire de France* (Paris, 1823), pp. 254–257.

20. At least this was the opinion of the Protestant chronicler, Agrippa d'Aubigné, *Histoire universelle* (Paris, 1886), V, 96–97. Cf. Jean Loutchitzki, ed., *Documents inédits pour servir à l'histoire de la réforme et de la Ligue*, vol. XIV of *Universitetskiya Izvestiya* (Kiev, 1874), pp. 39–42.

21. Palma Cayet, *Chronologie novenaire*, pp. 254–255.

22. See Koenigsberger, "The Organization of Revolutionary Parties," pp. 345–351.

23. Palma Cayet, *Chronologie novenaire*, pp. 255–257. Text of the subsequent Treaty of Péronne, 13 February 1577, in which Humières restated the League position in somewhat milder terms, can be found in Louis Maimbourg, *The History of the League*, tr. Dryden (London, 1684), pp. 42–57.

24. Blaise de Montluc, *Commentaires et lettres* (Paris, 1864–72), II, 417. Also Gaullieur, *Histoire de la réformation à Bordeaux et dans*

le ressort du parlement de Guyenne (Paris, 1848), vol. I, cited in Thompson, *Wars of Religion*, p. 214.

25. Devic and Vaissete, *Histoire générale de Languedoc*, V, 249 ff.

26. "Extraits des deliberations du conseil de la ville de Toulouse," in Loutchitzki, *Documents inédits*, XIV, 25–30.

27. For a good sketch of these early leagues and their background see Thompson, *Wars of Religion*, pp. 212–223; and especially Joseph Lecler, "Aux origines de la Ligue: premiers projets et premiers essais (1561–1570)," *Études*, 227:188–208 (1936).

28. Thompson, *Wars of Religion*, pp. 216–223.

29. Marguerite de Valois, *Mémoires de Marguerite de Valois, reine de France et de Navarre*, in Petitot, *Collection*, XXXVII, 97. De Thou, *Histoire universelle* (1734), VII, 458–459.

30. Palma Cayet, *Chronologie novenaire*, pp. 261–262. Cf. Mariéjol, *La réforme et la Ligue*, p. 177.

31. "Lettres patentes de Henri III données à Blois, le 16 avril 1577," Archives Nationales, fonds du Parlement de Paris, vol. X 8633, fol. 342.

32. In addition to Picot's *Histoire des États généraux*, II, 377–378, see M. A. Boullée, *Histoire complète des États-généraux et autres assemblées representatives de la France*, 2 vols. (Paris, 1845), I, 274–316; Owen Ulph, "The Estates General and the Catholic League, 1576–1593," unpublished dissertation, Stanford University, 1947, pp. 84–162; and especially Edmond Charleville, *Les États généraux de 1576: Le fonctionnement d'une tenue d'états* (Paris, 1901), pp. 177–180.

33. Owen Ulph, "Jean Bodin and the Estates General of 1576," *Journal of Modern History*, 19:289–296 (1947). Picot, *Histoire des États généraux*, II, 320–322. De Thou, *Histoire universelle* (1734), VII, 474–481.

34. Dumont, *Corps universel diplomatique*, V, 302–311.

35. L'Estoile, *Journal de Henri III*, I, 276; also Michaud et Poujaulat, eds., *Nouvelle collection des mémoires relatifs à l'histoire de France* (Paris, 1854), XIV, 90–91.

36. Particularly, Conyers Read, *Lord Burghley and Queen Elizabeth* (New York and London, 1960), pp. 306–310; also Conyers Read, *Mr. Secretary Walsingham and the Policy of Queen Elizabeth*, 3 vols. (Oxford, 1925), III, 71–86.

37. C.S.P., For., XIX, 95–98.

38. *Le droict de monseigneur le cardinal de Bourbon à la couronne de France défende et maintenu par les princes et catholiques françois* (Paris, 1589), and *De la succession du droict et prérogative de premier prince du sang de France, déférée par le loy du royaume à monseigneur Charles, cardinal de Bourbon, par la mort de monseigneur François de Valois, duc d'Anjou* (Paris, 1588). Cited in Eugène Saul-

nier, *Le rôle politique du cardinal de Bourbon* (Paris, 1912), pp. 104–106.

39. For a good contemporary account of the League organization see Nicolas Poulain, "Le procez-verbal, qui contient l'histoire de la Ligue, depuis le second janvier 1585 jusques au jour des barricades, escheues le 12 may 1588," in L. Cimber et F. Danjou, ed., *Archives curieuses de l'histoire de France* (Paris, 1834–50), 1st ser., XI, 289–323.

40. Marcel Poëte, *Une vie de cité Paris*, 5 vols. (Paris, 1931), III, 228; and Paul Robiquet, *Paris et la Ligue sous Henri III* (Paris, 1886), p. 213.

41. There is evidence that the term *les Seize* was also used in reference to all of the more radical Leaguers of Paris and not just to the actual governing council. This usage seems to have been more common with the enemies of the League. See the *Satyre Ménippée de la vertu du catholicon d'Espagne, et de la tenu des Estats de Paris* (Ratisbone, 1752), III, 420 ff; and Arthur Tilley, "Some Pamphlets of the French Wars of Religion," *English Historical Review*, 14:469 (1899). Maimbourg, *History of the League*, p. 99.

42. Jean Baptiste Honoré Raymond Capefigue, *Histoire de la Réforme, de la Ligue, et du règne de Henri IV*, 8 vols. (Paris, 1834), IV, 243–245.

43. Victor de Chalambert, *Histoire de la Ligue sous les règnes de Henri III et Henri IV* (Paris, 1898), pp. 14–16. Also Edward Armstrong, *The French Wars of Religion* (Oxford, 1904), p. 66.

44. Poëte, *Une vie de Cité*, pp. 242–243.

45. Poulain, "Le procez-verbal," in Cimber et Danjou, *Archives curieuses*, XI, 295.

46. Chalambert, *Histoire de la Ligue*, p. 12.

47. Especially Charles Labitte, *De la démocratie chez les prédicateurs de la Ligue* (Paris, 1841), pp. lxxii–lxxiv.

48. Figgis, *Gerson to Grotius*, p. 188.

49. Weill, *Les théories*, pp. 7, 199, *passim*. Laski, *Defence of Liberty*, p. 49.

50. See *Dialogue d'entre le Maheustre et le Manant*, for example. Published in *Satyre Ménippée* (1711 ed.), III, 367–585.

51. Anonymous, "Causes qui ont contraint les Catholiques à prendre les armes," in Goulart, *Mémoires de la Ligue*, III, 523–529.

52. "Remontrance du clergé de France" (1585), *ibid.*, I, 247.

53. "Avertissement des avertissement au peuple trè chrétien" (1587), *ibid.*, II, 121.

54. Quoted in Weill, *Les théories*, pp. 207–208.

55. *Apologie ou défense des catholiques unis les uns avec les autres, contre les impostures des catholiques associés à ceux de la prétendue religion* (Paris, 1586).

56. See Allen, *Political Thought*, p. 351.

57. Hübner, *Sixtus Fifth*, II, 145–160.

58. Quoted in Armstrong, *French Wars of Religion*, p. 65.

59. *Recueil des choses mémorables passées et publiées pour le fait de la religion et état de la France* (Strasbourg, 1566), cited in Anquetil, *L'esprit de la Ligue*, I, 77–78, 80–81.

60. De Thou, *Histoire universelle* (1734), IV, 124–126. Ruble, *Antoine de Bourbon*, III, 225–227, 255–258; IV, 88.

61. See Real Academia de la Historia, *Archivo documental español*, vol. VII, *Negociaciones con Francia, 1565* (Madrid, 1953); also Kervyn de Lettenhove, *La conférence de Bayonne en 1565* (Brussels, 1883); M. F. Combes, *L'entrevue de Bayonne de 1565 et la question de la Saint Barthélmy, d'après les archives de Simancas* (Paris, 1882); and John M. Potter, "The Conference at Bayonne, 1565," *American Historical Review*, 35:798–803 (1930). For De Thou's suspicions see *Histoire universelle* (1734), V, 33–36.

62. On these negotiations see P. O. de Törne, "Philippe II et Henri de Guise. Le début de leurs relations (1578)," *Revue Historique*, 167:323–335 (1931).

63. Particularly close ties were made in 1580–81. See *C.S.P., Span.*, III, 4–5, 71, *passim*.

64. Chalambert, *Histoire de la Ligue*, p. 13.

65. Dumont, *Corps universel diplomatique*, V, 441–443.

66. These secret articles, "Instrumentum de dedendo Antonio Portugalensi," and "Instrumentum donationis factae à Cardinale Bourbonio in favorem Regis Catholici," are not present in Dumont, but are given by Tassis in his *Commentaries* (Jean Baptiste de Tassis, *Commentariorum de tumultibus Belgicis sui temporis*, in Hoynck van Papendrecht, *Analecta Belgica* (Brussels, 1743), vol. II, pt. II, pp. 119–600). According to Ranke, "A brochure, entitled '*Ragguaglio delle Prattiche tenute con il Re di Spagna degli Signori Guisi*,' was circulated at the time, and may still be found in collections of political papers. According to its authority the greater part of the stipulated sum was not to be paid until the League had delivered either the city of Marseilles or Lyons into the hands of the King of Spain. There is no authentic proof of this condition, nor any trace of it in the actual treaty." Leopold von Ranke, *Civil Wars and Monarchy in France in the Sixteenth and Seventeenth Centuries* (New York, 1854), p. 341.

CHAPTER III. Mendoza and France

1. Forneron incorrectly gives April 1585 as the date of his arrival, and this error has passed on into many modern and contemporary

works. Henri Forneron, *Histoire de Philippe II* (Paris, 1887), III, 233.

2. Philip to Tassis, Madrid, 12 March 1584, Archivo General de Simancas, Sección de Estado, legajo K. 1448, folio 5 [hereafter cited Simancas]. Cf. Longlée to Villeroy, Madrid, 1 May 1584, Bibliothèque Nationale, Fonds français, 16109, folio 108. Documents for the first few months of Mendoza's embassy are very scarce, but after February 1585 they are more plentiful and for the rest of the period abundant.

3. Philip to Mendoza, 28 August 1584, Simancas, K. 1448, fol. 14.

4. "Dezid este alos amigos para que sepan quan cerca esta la resolucion la qual va con las consideraciones que vos avaeis advertido desu autoridad y reputacion." Philip to Tasis, 23 September, fol. 18.

5. Tassis, *Commentarii* (1583), p. 144, quoted in Alfred Morel-Fatio, *Études sur l'Espagne* (Paris, 1925), pp. 415–416; and Philip to Tassis, El Pardo, 8 October 1584, Simancas, K. 1448, fol. 20.

6. Idiáquez to Granvelle, Du Prado, 6 October 1584, in Charles Piot, ed., *Correspondance du cardinal de Granvelle* (Brussels, 1877–96), XI, 317–319.

7. Stafford to Walsingham, *C.S.P., For.*, 8 November 1584, n.s., XIX, 124–125.

8. There is no biography of Mendoza available at the present time. The only summary of his early life which makes some use of source materials is the article by Morel-Fatio in vol. VIII (1916) of the *Bulletin Hispanique*. This article was republished in 1925 in vol. IV of his *Études*. For the following brief sketch on Mendoza's early life I am also indebted to a variety of printed materials from the Biblioteca Nacional in Madrid.

9. Juan Catalina García, *Biblioteca de escritores de la provincia de Guadalajara y bibliografía de la misma hasta el siglo XIX* (Madrid, 1899), p. 330. Gerónimo de Quintana, *Historia de la villa de Madrid* (Madrid: Biblioteca Nacional, V 1629, fol. 295).

10. *Colección de documentos inéditos para la historia de España* [hereafter cited *C.D.I.*] (Madrid, 1842–95), XXVI, 373. Gachard, *Correspondance de Philippe II*, I, 570. Morel-Fatio, *Études*, p. 485.

11. Bernardino de Mendoza, *Comentarios de lo sucedido en las guerras de los Paises-Bajos, desde el año de 1567 hasta el de 1577*, published in *Biblioteca de Autores Españoles*, vol. XXVIII, part II (Madrid, 1884, 1948), pp. 389–570.

12. *Ibid.*, bk. II, chap. i, p. 403; and Gachard, *Correspondance de Philippe II*, III, 105.

13. Mendoza, *Comentarios*, p. 405.

14. Requesens to Philip, in Gachard, *Correspondance de Philippe II*, III, 105; Mendoza, *Comentarios*, bk. VI, chap. ii, p. 452; bk. VIII, chap. viii, p. 476; bk. IX, chap xii, p. 486; and Alba to Philip, in *C.D.I.*, XXXVII, 298, 545. Even the Politique, De Thou, recognized and

commented on his military prowess at Mook. *Histoire universelle* (1734), VII, 184–187.

15. Gachard, *Correspondance de Philippe II*, II, 319, 326, 354.

16. *Ibid.*, III, 133–134. Cf. Mendoza, *Commentarios*, bk. XII, p. 516. Also see De Thou, *Histoire universelle* (1734), VII, 236.

17. *C.D.I.*, XCI, 181.

18. Bibliothèque Nationale, MS Espagnol, 132, fol. 14, in Morel-Fatio, *Études*, p. 385. On the presentation of his credentials see *C.D.I.*, XCI, 194, 201.

19. Meyer, *England and the Catholic Church*, pp. 258–259. Read, *Lord Burghley*, pp. 237–245.

20. *C.D.I.*, XCI, 469, 515–517; and Merriman, *Rise of the Spanish Empire*, IV, 501.

21. *C.D.I.*, XCII, 528–533; and Read, *Walsingham*, II, 370–390.

22. Mendoza to Philip II, 30 January 1584, *C.S.P., Span.*, III, 516.

23. Catherine de' Medici to Longlée, in *Lettres de Catherine de Médicis*, ed. Baguenault de Puchesse, vol. XVIII of *Collection de documents inédits sur l'histoire de France* (Paris, 1835), VIII, 224–225.

24. *C.S.P., For.*, 17 November 1584, n.s., XIX, 141.

25. Catherine de' Medici, *Lettres*, VIII, 226.

26. Catherine to Longlée, 13 January 1585, *ibid.*, pp. 132–133.

27. Catherine to Balagny, 31 January 1585, *ibid.*, pp. 236–237. Also "Proposition et memoir au Roi de France par députes des Etats de Flandre," Simancas, K. 1563, fol. 50. Cf. J. L. Motley, *History of the United Netherlands* (New York and London, 1900), I, 95.

28. Stafford to Walsingham, 12 January 1585, *C.S.P., For.*, XIX, 228.

29. As reported by the interested, though not always reliable, observer of events in Paris during this period, Pierre de l'Estoile, in his *Journal de Henri III*, vol. II (1581–1586) of *Mémoires-Journaux* (Paris, 1875), pp. 180–181.

30. Mendoza to Parma, 27 February 1585, *C.S.P., For.*, XIX, 285–287. Also reported by Cardinal Granvelle on the basis of a note to him from Mendoza; Granvelle to Marguerite of Parma, 1 April 1585, Archives Farnésiennes à Naples, fascicule 1735, in Piot, *Correspondance de Granvelle*, XII, 29–30.

31. Mendoza to Philip, Simancas, K. 1563, fols. 24, 28–29, 31–32, 38–41, 46.

32. See *C.S.P., For.*, XIX, 286; and L'Estoile, *Journal de Henri III*, II, 181.

33. "Mandement du Roy sur la convocation et mostre des compagnies de sa gendarmerie . . . ," Simancas, K. 1563, fol. 47. This was followed two weeks later by a similar decree, "Lettres patentes du Roy portans defenses de faire des levées en ce Royaume sans commision de sa M," *ibid.*, fol. 52.

34. "Declaration des causes qui ont meu M. le Cardinal de Bourbon, et les princes, pairs, prélats, seigneurs, villes et communautez Catholiques de ce royaume de France, de s'opposer a ceux qui veulent subvertir la religion Catholique et l'Estat." Cimber et Danjou, *Archives curieuses*, XI, 7–19. Also see Charles Valois, ed., *Histoire de la Ligue: Oeuvre inédite d'un contemporain* (Paris, 1914), I, 83–85.

35. Goulart, *Mémoires de la Ligue*, I, 56–63.

36. De Thou, *Histoire universelle*, vol. IX, bk. lxxxi.

37. Mendoza to Philip, Simancas, K. 1563, fols. 60, 61, 63. Cf. Mariéjol, *La réforme et la Ligue*, p. 246.

38. *C.S.P., For.*, XIX, 206. L'Estoile, *Journal de Henri III*, III, 199.

39. These negotiations can be conveniently followed in the *Lettres de Catherine de Médicis*, VIII, 244–339.

40. Mendoza to Philip, Simancas, K. 1563, fol. 63. See Jean-H. Mariéjol, *Catherine de Médicis, 1519–1589* (Paris, 1922), pp. 371–376.

41. Mendoza to Philip, Simancas, K. 1563, fol. 78. Cf. Motley, *United Netherlands*, I, 124–129.

42. Catherine to Henry, 19 June 1585, *Lettres*, VIII, 323.

43. See Edouard de Barthélemy, "Catherine de Médicis, le duc de Guise et le traité de Nemours, d'après des documents inédits," *Revue des Questions Historiques*, 27:464–495 (1880).

44. Mendoza to Philip, 16 July 1585, Simancas, K. 1563, fol. 103.

45. Dumont, *Corps universel diplomatique*, V, 453 ff. Gustave Baguenault de Puchesse, "Le traité signé à Nemours en 1585, d'après des documents inédits," *Annales de la Société Historique et Archeologique du Gatinas*, 19:305–317 (1901).

46. Goulart, *Mémoires de la Ligue*, I, 178–182.

47. Philip to Mendoza, Monçon, 17 August 1585, Simancas, K. 1448, fol. 29A.

48. Mendoza to Philip, 16 July 1585, K. 1563, fol. 102.

49. K. 1448, fol. 29, *passim*, for example; also Joseph Lefèvre, ed., *Correspondance de Philippe II sur les affaires des Pays-Bas* (2e partie, 1577–1591), 4 vols. (Brussels, 1940–60), I, 266; III, 222, 282; and De Thou, *Histoire universelle* (1734), IX, 263–271. Cf. Louis Pierre Anquetil, *L'esprit de la Ligue*, 2 vols. (Paris, 1818), II, 54–55, 71–74, 84.

50. Philip to Mendoza, Simancas, 23 July 1585, K. 1448, fol. 26.

51. Guise to Mendoza, Châlons, 25 August 1585, K. 1563, fol. 126.

52. Nevers to the cardinal of Bourbon, 31 July 1585, in Duc de Nevers, *Mémoires* (Paris, 1625), I, 668–670. Also Saulnier, *La rôle politique*, pp. 146–156; and "Le cardinal de Bourbon entre des ducs de Guise et de Nevers," *Revue d'Histoire Diplomatique*, 24:161–182 (1910); and Capefigue, *Histoire de la Réforme*, IV, 202–205.

53. Henri de l'Epinois, "La politique de Sixte-Quint en France," *Revue des Questions Historiques*, 27:155–157 (1880).

54. "Declaration de notre Saint-Pere le Pape Sixte V, a l'encontre de Henri de Bourbon, soi-disant Roi de Navarre, et Henri semblable de Bourbon, prétendu prince de Condé, hérétiques contre leurs postérités et sucesseurs." Cimber et Danjou, *Archives curieuses,* XI, 47–58; and Goulart, *Mémoires de la Ligue,* I, 214–221.

55. Philip to Mendoza, Tortosa, 29 December 1585, Simancas, K. 1448, fol. 36; Mendoza to Philip, 24 October 1585, K. 1563, fol. 156.

56. Catherine to Villeroy, *Lettres,* XVIII, 352–353; Catherine to Bellièvre, p. 376.

57. "Remonstrance au Roy par la Cour de Parlement," in Goulart, *Mémoires de la Ligue,* I, 222–226.

58. "Copie de l'opposition faite par le Roi de Navarre et Mgr. le prince de Condé contre l'excommunication du Pape Sixte V," Cimber et Danjou *Archives curieuses,* XI, 59–61. Henri de l'Epinois suggests in *La Ligue et les papes* (Paris, 1886), p. 29, that Navarre's protest was so vigorously stated that it even impressed the pope favorably. For Navarre's reaction to the Treaty of Nemours, see "Declaration et protestation du Roi de Navarre, de monseigneur le prince de Condé et de Monsieur le duc de Montmorency, sur la paix faicte avec ceux de la maison de Lorraine, chefs et principaux autheurs de la Ligue, au prejudice de la maison de France," in Philippe du Plessis-Mornay, *Mémoires et correspondance* (Paris, 1824), III, 159–182.

59. Mendoza to Philip, Simancas, K. 1563, fol. 156.

CHAPTER IV. Mendoza and Guise

1. Philippe, comte de Cheverny, *Mémoires,* in Michaud et Poujoulat, *Nouvelle collection des mémoires sur l'histoire de France depuis le XIII siècle jusqu'à la fin du XVIIIe siècle* (Paris, 1836–39), X, 482–485. Also Vicomte de Turenne, *Mémoires,* in C. B. Petitot, ed., *Collection complète des mémoires relatifs à l'histoire de France* (Paris, 1820–29), 1st ser., XXXV, 217–224.

2. Philip to Mendoza, Monzon, 17 August 1585, Simancas, K. 1448, fol. 27. Cf. J. H. Mariéjol, *La vie de Marguerite de Valois* (Paris, 1928), pp. 234–238.

3. Guise to Mendoza, Troyes, 14 September 1585, Simancas, K. 1563, fol. 135; Guise to Philip, fol. 136.

4. Guise to Mendoza, Rheims, 1 October 1585, K. 1563, fol. 139. Cf. Mariéjol, *Catherine de Médicis,* pp. 386–387.

5. Philip to Mendoza, Tortosa, 29 December 1585, K. 1448, fol. 35; also Philip to Tassis, 4 January 1586, fol. 38.

6. Mendoza to Philip, 1 April 1586, K. 1564, fol. 41.

7. Dolfin to the Doge and Senate, 17 July 1586, *Calendar of State*

Papers and Manuscripts, relating to English Affairs, Existing in the Archives and Collections of Venice, ed. R. F. Brown [hereafter cited *C.S.P., Ven.*] (London, 1894), VIII, 181–182.

8. Lippomano to the Doge and Senate, 18 September 1586, *ibid.*, p. 205.

9. Philip to Mendoza, Madrid, 17 December 1586, Simancas, K. 1448, fol. 86. Cf. Devic and Vaissete, *Histoire générale de Languedoc;* XII, 421 ff; and Joseph Desormeaux, *Histoire de la maison de Montmorenci* 5 vols. (Paris, 1764), III, 123 ff.

10. Philip to Comendador Mayor de Castilla and Baron Sfondrato, Simancas, K. 1448, fol. 95.

11. Philip to Montmorency, S. Lorenzo, 12 May 1588, K. 1448, fols. 181, 182.

12. Instructions for the mission of Constantino, K. 1448, fols. 180, 185.

13. Philip to Mendoza, 12 May 1588, K. 1448, fol. 184.

14. Villeroy maintained that the only reason Navarre refused to leave the Protestant sect was the great influence of his fanatical counselors. Villeroy to Maisse, 4 January 1586, Bibilothèque Nationale, fonds français 16093, fol. 5.

15. Mendoza to Philip, 1 April 1586, Simancas, K. 1564, fol. 41.

16. B. de Xivrey et J. Gaudet, ed., *Recueil des lettres missives de Henri IV* (Paris, 1843–76), II, 214–215.

17. Filippo Cavriana, representative of the grand duke of Tuscany in Paris (and also personal physician of Catherine de' Medici), although he generally seems to have been on good terms with Mendoza, gave one of the harshest appraisals of Mendoza's character: ". . . consigliata a ciò dall'ambasciatore di Spagna, il quale, a guisa del demonio, accompagna gli uomini al pericolo, poi ne gli lascia perire." Cavriana to Bélisario Vinta, 18 May 1587, in Abel Desjardins, ed., *Négociations diplomatiques avec la Toscane* (Paris, 1872), IV, 687.

18. Mendoza to Philip, 11 May 1586, Simancas, K. 1564, fol. 54.

19. *Ibid.* Cf. Joseph Croze, *Les Guises, les Valois, et Philippe II* (Paris, 1866), I, 313–316, and Mariéjol, *La réforme et la Ligue,* pp. 254–255.

20. Simancas, K. 1564, fol. 54.

21. See S. H. Ehrman, ed., *The Letters and Documents of Armand de Gontaut, Baron de Biron, Marshal of France* (Berkeley, 1936), Biron to Henry, June 14, 20, and 22; Henry to Biron, June 29, II, 386–397.

22. Henry IV, *Lettres missives,* II, 228–229.

23. De Thou, *Histoire universelle* (1734), IX, 585. On the negotiations, see Guy de Bremond d'Ars, "Les conférences de Saint-Brice entre Henri de Navarre et Catherine de Médicis, 1586–87," *Revue des Questions Historiques,* 36:496–523 (1884).

24. Catherine to Matignon, 7 March 1587, Bibliothèque Nationale, fonds français, 3301.

25. Henry III to Catherine, Bibliothèque Nationale, collection Brienne, 214, fol. 152, in Goulart, *Mémoires de la Ligue*, II, 189–191. Cf. Mariéjol, *Catherine de Médicis*, pp. 384–388.

26. Mendoza to Philip, 23 July 1586, Simancas, K. 1564, fol. 114.

27. See, for example, De Thou, *Histoire universelle* (1734), V, 676–677, 686–687; IX, 471–472, *passim*.

28. Guise to Mendoza, 16 July, K. 1564, fol. 105. Cf. Croze, *Les Guises*, I, 375.

29. Letters and articles presented by Robert Bruce, Simancas, K. 1564, fol. 104.

30. Mendoza to Philip, 23 July 1586, K. 1564, fol. 114. Cf. Alexandre Teulet, ed., *Relations politiques de la France et de l'Espagne avec l'Ecosse au XVIᵉ siècle* (Paris, 1862), V, 367–369; and J. H. Pollen, *The Counter Reformation in Scotland* (London, 1921), pp. 34–35.

31. Philip to Guise, San Lorenzo, 28 September 1586, Simancas, K. 1448, fol. 73; Philip to Mendoza, fol. 74.

32. Lefèvre, *Correspondance de Philippe II*, III, 152–153.

33. Mendoza to Parma, 15 October 1586, Simancas, K. 1564, fol. 191.

34. Read, *Lord Burghley*, pp. 334–339.

35. Parma to Mendoza, Brussels, 27 November 1586, Simancas, K. 1564, fol. 232.

36. See introduction to J. H. Pollen, ed., *Mary Queen of Scots and the Babington Plot* (Edinburgh, 1922), pp. cc–ccxii. Also J. B. Black, *The Reign of Elizabeth*, 2nd ed. (Oxford, 1959), pp. 378–386.

37. Morgan to Mary, 10 April 1586, in Historical Manuscripts Commission, *Calendar of the Manuscripts of the Most Hon. the Marquis of Salisbury, K.G., preserved at Hatfield House* (London, 1889), pt. III, p. 137 [hereafter cited *Cecil Papers*]. Read, *Walsingham*, III, 1–10; *Lord Burghley*, pp. 342–345. D. Butler and J. H. Pollen, "Doctor Gifford in 1586," *The Month*, 103:243–258, 348–367 (1904).

38. *Italics mine.* For an interesting, but inconclusive, case against the authenticity of Mary's Will and the Hispano-Scottish conjunction over rights to the English throne, see John Duncan Mackie, "The Will of Mary Stuart," *Scottish Historical Review*, 11:338–344 (1914), and "Scotland and the Spanish Armada," *ibid.*, 12:1–24 (1914).

39. Mary Stuart to Mendoza, Charley, 20 May 1586, Simancas, K. 1564, fol. 72. For Martin A. S. Hume's translation of this letter, which differs slightly from mine, see *C.S.P., Span.*, III, 581–582.

40. Philip to Mendoza, S. Lorenzo, 18 July 1586, K. 1448, fol. 49. Also cf. *C.S.P., Span.*, III, 590–591, and Morgan to Mary, *Cecil Papers*, pt. III, p. 147.

41. See John Pickering's notes on the case against Mary Stuart,

Egerton MS, 2124, fols. 50–54, in Convers Read, ed., *The Bardon Papers: Documents Relating to the Imprisonment and Trial of Mary Queen of Scots* (London, 1909), Camden Society, 3rd ser., XVII, 53–56. Cf. Read, *Walsingham*, III, 18–21.

42. Babington to Mary, 3 August 1586, Read, *Bardon Papers*, pp. 40–41.

43. Charges against Mary Stuart, November 1586, Egerton MS, 2124, fols. 48–49, *ibid.*, pp. 77–80. Cf. Pollen, *Mary Queen of Scots*, pp. clx–clxxiii, 114–115.

44. Mary to Mendoza, Chartley, 27 July 1586, Simancas, K. 1564, fol. 119. Cf. *C.S.P., Span.*, III, 614.

45. Mendoza to Philip, 19 July 1586, K. 1564, fol. 108. Cf. Read, *Walsingham*, III, 2–47. *Cecil Papers*, pt. III, pp. 346–349.

46. Read, *The Bardon Papers*, p. 28. For a short but fascinating account of this cloak-and-dagger episode see Fletcher Pratt, *Secret and Urgent* (Garden City, N.Y., 1942). Cf. Read, *Walsingham*, III, 10–13; and Pollen, *Mary Queen of Scots*, pp. civ–clxxiii.

47. On the execution see Garrett Mattingly, *The Armada* (Boston, 1959), pp. 1–5. Cf. Read, *Walsingham*, III, 48–65; and Pollen, *Mary Queen of Scots*, pp. clxxvii–cxcviii.

48. Late in June, Philip sent 100,000 escudos to Guise to begin the campaign against Navarre. Philip to Tassis, Monzon, 30 June 1585, Simancas, K. 1563, fol. 85. He followed this with another extension of credit in July, fol. 112.

49. Philip to Mendoza, S. Lorenzo, 25 June 1586, K. 1448, fol. 44. Cf. Croze, *Les Guises*, I, 301–302.

50. Guise to Mendoza, Rheims, 1 October 1585, K. 1563, fol. 139.

51. Guise to Mendoza, K. 1563, fol. 155. Forneron, *Histoire de Philippe II*, III, 248.

52. Guise to Mendoza, 10 November 1586, K. 1564, fol. 221.

53. I have translated this from the French text given in Capefigue, *Histoire de la Réforme*, IV, 307. Capefigue infers that this letter to Guise is located in the Simancas collection, but I have been unable to find it there.

54. Guise to Mendoza, 22 September 1586, Simancas, K. 1564, fol. 158, and September 27, fol. 164. See, Read, *Walsingham*, III, 196–201; and *Lord Burghley*, pp. 382–386.

55. "Accort et capitulation faict entre le Roy de Navarre et le duc de Cazimir pour la levée de l'armee des reistres venus en France en 1587," Simancas, K. 1565, fol. 14 bis. Cf. Henry IV, *Lettres missives*, VIII, 304 ff.

56. Simancas, K. 1565, fol. 57. See De Thou, *Histoire universelle*, VII, 17, *passim*. The different accounts of the invasion vary considerably in their estimates of the size of the forces. Cf. Mariéjol, *La réforme et la Ligue*, pp. 255–262; Henri Forneron, *Les ducs de Guise*

et leur époque (Paris, 1877), II, 316 ff.; and Du Plessis-Mornay, *Mémoires et correspondance*, IV, 82, 119.

57. Simancas, K. 1566, fol. 69. Cf. Henry IV, *Lettres missives*, VIII, 304, which gives the English amount as only one-half that reported by Mendoza. Without reference to Mendoza's figures, Conyers Read corroborates the English sum by reference to B.M., Lansdowne MSS, 50, no. 4, cited in his *Lord Burghley*, p. 383. Mariéjol upholds Mendoza's figures on the Danish contribution, *La réforme et la Ligue*, p. 256.

58. Mendoza to Philip, Simancas, K. 1565, fol. 13. Alfred Mantel, "Der Anteil der reformierten Schweizer am navarresischen Feldzug von 1587," *Jahrbuch für Schweizerische Geschichte*, 40:3–52 (1915).

59. Bibliothèque Nationale, fonds fr. 15892, fol. 114 gives a detailed breakdown of the invading force, written by Secretary Bellièvre. Cf. Croze, *Les Guises*, II, 23–39.

60. Guise to Mendoza, 2 October 1587, Simancas, K. 1565, fol. 61. D'Aubigné maintains that Châtillon only managed to raise 2000 men. *Histoire universelle*, VII, 171.

61. Mendoza to Philip, K. 1565, fol. 106.

62. Guise to Henry III, 20 November 1586, in Croze, *Les Guises*, II, 393–394. Guise to Mendoza, Simancas, K. 1564, fol. 231; Guise to Pfyffer, fol. 181.

63. Mendoza to Philip, K. 1566, fols. 101, 102; to Parma, K. 1565, fol. 7; and Philip to Mendoza, K. 1448, fols. 104, 112, 138. Cf. D'Aubigné, *Histoire universelle*, VII, 169–170. Parma also financed the raising of some German and Swiss mercenaries for use by the duke of Lorraine in defending his territories. Parma to Philip, 30 May 1587, Lefèvre, *Correspondance de Philippe II*, III, 212.

64. Simancas, K. 1565, fols. 12, 20, 97; K. 1566, fol. 145.

65. Mendoza to Philip, K. 1566, fol. 70. Marshal Bassompierre, whose father was with Henry III's army at the time, maintained that Guise had no more than 1500 horse. Bassompierre, *Mémoires de maréchal de Bassompierre*, in Petitot, *Collection*, 2nd ser., XIX, 245.

66. Several good eyewitness accounts of the Battle of Coutras exist. See especially D'Aubigné (who was a squire of Navarre at the time), *Histoire universelle*, VII, 146–160. For modern reconstructions of the battle see Pierre de Vaissière, *Messieurs de Joyeuse* (Paris, 1926), pp. 224–264; Sir Charles Oman, *A History of the Art of War in the Sixteenth Century* (London, 1937), pp. 470–480; and Mattingly, *The Armada*, pp. 146–157.

67. Michel de la Huguerye, *Mémoires* (Paris, 1880), III, 185. Also his *Ephéméride de l'expedition des Allemands*, pp. 223 ff.

68. Bibliothèque Nationale, fonds fr. 3975, fol. 131. Cf. Simancas, K. 1565, fol. 97. Also see Alfred Mantel, "Der Anteil der reformierton Schweizer," pp. 29–36.

69. Guise to Mendoza, 30 October 1587, Simancas, K. 1565, fols. 94, 117, 118, 132. Guise reported that for the 2000 German dead and captured he had lost only 4 men. Cf. *Mémoires de Cheverny*, in Petitot, *Collection*, 1st ser., XXXVI, 99; and De Thou, *Histoire universelle*, VII, 39–41. Mattingly, *The Armada*, pp. 166–169.

70. M. de Saint Auban (Châtillon's lieutenant), *Mémoires*, in Petitot, *Collection*, 1st ser., XLIII, 472–482. D'Aubigné, *Histoire universelle*, VII, 190–193. Mendoza followed the campaign closely from Guise's numerous letters during October and December, and from some of these it appears that Mendoza frequently sent him suggestions on tactics. See Simancas, K. 1565, fol. 77.

71. Guise to Mendoza, 16 December 1587, K. 1565, fol. 140. Also see 11 December 1587, fol. 138, and fols. 144, 146, and the lengthy "memoir" on the entire campaign, fol. 156.

CHAPTER V. Diplomatic Procedure, I: Gathering Data

1. *C.S.P., Span.*, III, 513.

2. Philip to Mendoza, 10 March 1584, Simancas, K. 1448, fol. 4.

3. See the tribute to Mendoza given by his friend and military companion, Francisco de Aldena, in Morel-Fatio, *Études*, pp. 487–488. Also Simancas, K. 1564, fols. 98, 258, and K. 1565, fol. 89; and Guise to Mendoza, 6 April 1587, K. 1566, fol. 85.

4. Cavriana to Serguidi, Paris, 14 February 1588, Desjardins, *Négociations avec la Toscane*, IV, 757–760. Simancas, K. 1567, fol. 58; and Philip to Mendoza, Madrid, 7 July 1587, K. 1448, fol. 129.

5. Stafford to Walsingham, 2 December 1584, *C.S.P., For.*, XIX, 165. Catherine to Henry, 23 May 1588, Catherine de' Medici, *Lettres*, IX, 346–347. Cf. Edouard Frémy, *Essai sur les diplomates du temps de la Ligue d'après des documents nouveaux et inédits* (Paris, 1873), pp. 146–147.

6. Simancas, K. 1564, fol. 230; K. 1568, fols. 80, 83.

7. *Quenta de gastos extraordinarios*, K. 1564, fol. 98. Embassy papers and correspondence were the express responsibility of the ambassadors, not their secretaries. See Frémy, *Les diplomates*, p. 73.

8. Mendoza to Idiáquez, 21 June 1589, Simancas, K. 1569, fol. 64.

9. K. 1564, fol. 98.

10. K. 1567, fol. 82.

11. See Garrett Mattingly, *Renaissance Diplomacy* (Boston, 1955), pp. 37–39, 107. Cf. Anonymous, *Embajada española*, in *Camden Miscellany* (London, 1926), XIV, 49–55; and M. A. R. de Maulde-la-Clavière, *La diplomatie au temps de Machiavel*, 3 vols. (Paris, 1892), II, 175–176, 190–191. Also Frémy, *Les diplomates*, pp. 87–88, 90–91.

12. Mendoza to Philip, 12 February 1585, Simancas, K. 1563, fol. 30.

13. Mendoza to Philip, K. 1566, fol. 81; and Catherine to the Infanta, 17 November 1587, K. 1448, fol. 149.

14. Mendoza to Philip, 1 February 1586, K. 1564, fol. 13.

15. See Joseph Nouaillac, *Villeroy, secrétaire d'état et ministre* (Paris, 1908), and especially N. M. Sutherland, *The French Secretaries of State in the Age of Catherine de Medici* (London, 1962), pp. 185–308.

16. *Introduction aux mémoires de Henri III*, in Petitot, *Collection*, 1st ser., XX, 233. Cf. Sutherland, *The French Secretaries of State*, p. 229.

17. Mendoza to Philip, 11 May 1586, Simancas, K. 1564, fol. 56.

18. Henri de l'Epinois, "La politique de Sixte-Quint en France," *Revue des Questions Historiques*, 27:161–162 (1880).

19. Mendoza to Philip, 16 July 1585, Simancas, K. 1563, fol. 102.

20. *C.S.P., Span.*, III, 618.

21. *C.S.P., Ven.*, VIII, 181–182.

22. Desjardins, *Négociations avec la Toscane*, IV, 571, 687, *passim*.

23. *C.S.P., For.*, XIX, 141; also *Embajada española*, pp. 6–7, and Maulde-la-Clavière, *La diplomatie*, II, 181–182.

24. Stafford to Walsingham, 2 December 1584, *C.S.P., For.*, XIX, 165.

25. Mendoza to Idiáquez, 17 February 1586, Simancas, K. 1564, fol. 25.

26. Stafford to Walsingham, 29 September 1586, *C.S.P., For.*, XXI, 96.

27. Mattingly, *Renaissance Diplomacy*, pp. 109–110, 114, 242–246. Gaston Zeller, *Les temps modernes*, vol. II of Pierre Renouvin, ed., *Histoire des relations internationales* (Paris, 1953), pp. 9–12; and Maulde-la-Clavière, *La diplomatie*, II, 317.

28. Mendoza to Philip, 26 March 1587, Simancas, K. 1566, fol. 67.

29. The growing anti-Spanish sentiment in France can be noted from many sources. See, for example, De Thou, *Histoire universelle* (1734), VIII, 314; IX, 262–263, *passim*; L'Estoile, *Journal de Henri III*, II, 387–388; IV, 303; V, 297; Henry IV, *Lettres missives*, III, 252, *passim*; and the studies of this subject by J. Mathorez in "Notes sur les Espagnols en France depuis le XVIe siècle jusqu'au règne de Louis XIII," *Bulletin Hispanique*, 16:337–371 (1914), esp. p. 349, and "Les Espagnols et la crise nationale française a la fin du XVIe siècle," *ibid.*, 16:86–113 (1916). Also see the many writings and letters suggesting this feeling in Goulart, *Mémoires de la Ligue*, II, 106–112, *passim*, and Desjardins, *Négociations avec la Toscane*, IV, *passim*.

30. *Embajada española*, pp. 16–17. Maulde-la-Clavière, *La diplomatie*, III, 46–52.

31. See Robert Lechat, *Les refugiés anglais dans les Pays-Bas espa-*

gnols durant le règne d'Elisabeth (Louvain, 1914); J. H. Pollen, *The English Catholics in the Reign of Queen Elizabeth* (London, 1920); and Peter K. Guilday, *The English Catholic Refugees on the Continent* (London, 1914), vol. I.

32. Read, *Walsingham*, II, 258–339 gives some idea of the various factions among the exiles, and their political allegiances and activities. On Cardinal Allen's key role, see Garrett Mattingly, "William Allen and Catholic Propaganda in England," in *Aspects de la propagande religieuse* (Geneva, 1957), pp. 325–339.

33. See Mendoza to Philip, Simancas, K. 1563, fol. 144. Sources differ as to the exact amounts of these stipends; the *Dictionary of National Biography*, for example, states that Lord Paget received 180 crowns. Throughout the present study I have used, unless otherwise indicated, the figures given in Mendoza's correspondence and in his expense accounts.

34. Mendoza to Philip, 11 May 1586, Simancas, K. 1564, fol. 56.

35. Philip to Mendoza, El Pardo, 25 April 1586, K. 1564, fol. 49.

36. Mendoza to Philip, 27 September 1586, K. 1564, fol. 166.

37. See Lechat, *Les refugiés*, pp. 157–159, and Read, *Walsingham*, II, 381–385, 417–423. Cf. *The Dictionary of National Biography*, XIII, 929–930; XIV, 245–246; XIX, 808. Sporadic correspondence was also maintained between Mendoza and Sir Francis Englefield, Mary's agent in Spain. See *Cecil Papers*, pt. III, pp. 91, 129–130.

38. Lefèvre, *Correspondance de Philippe II*, III, 110, 122, 130, 141, *passim*.

39. See particularly *ibid.*, p. 130. Cf. Read, *Lord Burghley*, 334–339, 396.

40. "Cuenta de gastos extraordinarios," 31 December 1586, Simancas, K. 1564, fol. 256.

41. Don Antonio de Crato to Escobar, K. 1568, fol. 130; K. 1569, fols. 6, 92; and "Avisos de Londres por Sanson," K. 1564, fols. 79, 111, 134.

42. Idiáquez to Mendoza, 20 October 1586, K. 1448, fol. 80. Cf. *Cecil Papers*, pt. III, p. 87.

43. Mendoza to Philip, 16 July 1585, K. 1563, fol. 101.

44. Mendoza to Philip, 26 June 1586, K. 1564, fol. 96; and K. 1564, fol. 196, K. 1448, fol. 83.

45. Mendoza to Philip, K. 1568, fol. 113; K. 1564, fol. 258.

46. Stafford had been approached as early as February 1585 about helping the Catholics. His reply was ambivalent. See *Cecil Papers*, pt. III, p. 91.

47. Martin A. S. Hume began the controversy by correlating the name of Stafford with Mendoza's correspondent "Julio" and the "new confident," in his 1896 edition of *C.S.P., Span.* A. F. Pollard attacked Hume's classification of Stafford as a traitor in his own review of the

Calendar in the *English Historical Review*, 16:572–577 (1901). Conyers Read took issue with Pollard in an *American Historical Review* article entitled "The Fame of Sir Edward Stafford," in which he questioned the ambassador's integrity, and identified Stafford as a spy; 20:292–313 (1915). This view was in turn challenged by J. E. Neale who admitted Stafford's involvement, but attributed it to counterspying for Elizabeth. See *English Historical Review*, 44:203–220 (1929), and reprinted in his *Essays in Elizabethan History* (New York, 1958), pp. 146–169. Read published a perceptive rejoinder in the *American Historical Review*, 25:560–566 (1939), and added a few additional bits of evidence in his *Lord Burghley*, pp. 386–390, just prior to his death in 1960.

48. Mendoza to Philip, 11 May 1586, Simancas, K. 1564, fol. 54.

49. *Ibid.* Cf. Neale, "The Fame of Sir Edward Stafford," 44:204 (1929).

50. Read, *Lord Burghley*, p. 387. Also see Donald M. Frame, "New Light on Montaigne's Trip to Paris in 1588," *Romanic Review*, 51: 173–175 (1960).

51. Simancas, K. 1565, fol. 29. Cf. Read, "The Fame of Sir Edward Stafford," 303–307, and Walsingham and Burghley in Queen Elizabeth's Privy Council," *English Historical Review*, 27:51–52 (1913).

52. Philip to Mendoza, 28 February 1587, Simancas, K. 1448, fol. 104. Cf. *C.S.P., Span.*, III, 25.

53. Philip to Mendoza, 6 July 1587, K. 1448, fol. 124.

54. Philip to Mendoza, K. 1448, fol. 128.

55. Mendoza to Philip, 1 April 1586, K. 1564, fol. 41; and 19 July 1586, fol. 109.

56. Guise to Mendoza, 10 November 1587, K. 1565, fol. 104; and *Copie de l'écrit de Mayneville*, 18 February 1587, K. 1566, fol. 37.

57. Mendoza to Philip, 4 December 1587, K. 1565, fol. 131; and 27 December 1588, K. 1567, fol. 194.

58. Mendoza to Philip, 16 July 1585, K. 1563, fol. 101.

59. Mendoza to Philip, 11 September 1585, K. 1563, fols. 132, 168.

60. Guise to Mendoza, Villeneuve, 1 November 1585, K. 1563, fol. 166. Philip's instruction appears in a notation at the close of this note from Guise.

61. Mendoza to Philip, 1 July 1587, K. 1565, fol. 12.

62. K. 1565, fol. 17.

63. Ludovic Vitet, *La Ligue, précédée des états d'Orléans* (Paris, 1883), II, 319.

64. John R. Cousins, "The Jesuit Influence in the French Catholic League," unpub. thesis, Brigham Young University, 1961, pp. 145–148, *passim*.

65. See the useful study by E. Piaget, *Histoire de l'établissement des Jésuites en France (1540–1640)* (Leiden, 1893), pp. 107 ff.; also

Paul Robiquet, *Paris et la Ligue* (Paris, 1886), p. 197; Léopold Monty, *Reformateurs et Jésuites: guerres de religion en France* (Dijon, 1876); and Henri Fouqueray, *Histoire de la Compagnie de Jésus en France, des origines à la supression (1528–1762)* (Paris, 1913), II, 144.

66. *Annales de la société des soi-disans Jésuites: ou recueil historique chronologique de tous les actes, ecrits, etc.* (Paris, 1764), pp. 456–458, 514 [hereafter cited *Annales*]. Also Etienne Pasquier, *Le catéchisme des Jésuites* (Ville Franche, 1677), II, 89–90, 154, 187; De Thou, *Histoire universelle*, VIII, 42; and Piaget, *L'établissement des Jésuites*, pp. 110, *passim*.

67. *Ibid.*, p. 116. Frémy, *Les diplomates*, p. 137. L'Epinois, *La Ligue et les papes*, p. 16; and Robiquet, *Paris et la Ligue*, p. 197. See in particular the letters from Mathieu to the duke of Nevers, 5 and 11 February 1585, in *Mémoires du duc de Nevers*, I, 654 ff., one of which is quoted in Capefigue, *Histoire de la Réforme*, IV, 198–200.

68. J. Crétineau-Joly, *Histoire religieuse, politique et littéraire de la Compagnie de Jésus*, 6 vols. (Paris, 1845–46), II, 309. Andrew Steinmetz, *History of the Jesuits* (Philadelphia, 1848), II, 82–83.

69. Hippolyte Abord, *Histoire de la réforme et de la Ligue dans la ville d'Autun*, 3 vols. (Paris, 1855–86), II, 322. Labitte, *De la démocratie*, pp. 119–121. De Thou, *Histoire universelle*, VIII, 324. Pasquier, *Le catéchisme*, II, 91, 192. Much of Pigenat's manuscript correspondence is in the Bibliothèque Nationale, Nouv. acq. Lat. 1634, "Pièces relatives à l'ordre des Jésuites addresses la plupart à Odon Pigenat."

70. Père Barny, in *Annales*, p. 514; and Fouqueray, *Histoire de la Compagnie de Jésus*, II, 244: "Car le P. Pigenat ne fut point, comme le peint de Thou, 'un ligueur furieux aussi fanatique qu'un corybante,' ni, comme le prétend Arnauld, 'le plus cruel tigre qui fût dans Paris.' Au contraire, par sa prudence et sa modération, il empêcha le Conseil de se porter à des résolutions extrêmes ou criminelles."

71. Pasquier, *Le catéchisme*, II, 192. This is affirmed also by Piaget, *L'établissement des Jésuites*, pp. 115, 130; and Fouqueray, *Histoire de la Compagnie de Jésus*, II, 230.

72. Nicolas Poulain, *Le procez-verbal*, in Cimber et Danjou, *Archives curieuses*, XI, 295. Vitet, *La Ligue*, II, 319.

73. Louis Blond, *Les Jésuites a Paris: la maison professe Saint Louis de la rue Saint-Antoine* (1580–1763), Bibilothèque Nationale, fasc. 13, "Extrait des etablissements des Jésuites en France depuis quatre siècles" (n.p., 1955), p. 1262. Also Piaget, *L'établissement des Jésuites*, pp. 128, *passim*; Labitte, *De la démocratie*, pp. 114, 235, 245, 293 ff.

74. See especially *Annales*, pp. 456, 458, 498–499; De Thou, *Histoire universelle*, VIII, 322, 391, *passim*; H. Colombier, "Les Jésuites ligueurs d'après M. L'abbé Houssaye," *Études religieuses, philosophiques, historiques et littéraires, par des pères de la compagnie de Jésus*, 5:759–766 (1874); "Recueil curieux et historique touchant l'etablissement

et la conduite des Jésuites," in Archives Nationales, MS. 241, no. 3; Crétineau-Joly, *Histoire religieuse*, II, 334–335; Labitte, *De la démocratie*, pp. 195, 235–236; and Piaget, *L'établissement des Jésuites*, pp. 112, 117, 120–121, *passim*.

75. Henri Forneron, *Histoire de Philippe II*, 4 vols. (Paris, 1881–82), IV, 61.

76. *Annales*, pp. 606–607; Pasquier, *Le catéchisme*, II, 191–192.

77. *Annales*, pp. 456–458, 496, 513, 601–602; Frémy, *Les diplomates*, p. 138.

78. Stafford to Walsingham, 1 April 1585, *C.S.P., For.*, XIX, 390.

79. Fouqueray, *Histoire de la Compagnie de Jésus*, II, 122, 137, 155–158, 161–165, 188–197; Labitte, *De la démocratie*, p. 134; Piaget. *L'établissement des Jésuites*, pp. 105–110.

80. Stafford to Walsingham, *C.S.P., For.*, XX, 26; XXI, 124.

CHAPTER VI. Diplomatic Procedure, II: Communication

1. Philip to Mendoza, El Pardo, 29 April 1586, Simancas, K. 1448, fol. 42.

2. See Mattingly, *Renaissance Diplomacy*, pp. 111–112.

3. Mendoza to Philip, Simancas, K. 1569, fols. 133–135, and K. 1571, fols. 26–29.

4. "Pues conviene que se entiendan tan amenudo no os contentays con despachar correos de ordinario sino tambien embiad los despachos por diferentes partes que con esto llegaran alg⁰ˢ no obstante el cuydado que avisays que ay en el camino en que quiça se reportaran pues aca se ha dicho a los que estan de parte del Rey Chris^mo la sin razon que esto es y lo que se sentira que passe adelante." Philip to Mendoza, San Lorenzo, 24 May 1589, K. 1449, fol. 31.

5. Mattingly, *Renaissance Diplomacy*, pp. 247–248. On the French royal post see Maulde-la-Clavière, *La diplomatie*, III, 147–148; on couriers see pp. 148–157.

6. Mendoza to Philip, 9 June 1586, Simancas, K. 1564, fol. 86.

7. Summary of expenses, 25 October 1587, K. 1565, fol. 89.

8. "Los caminos estavan y estan muy peligrossos," explained Mendoza to Philip concerning the high rate paid to Blanchet, "y es necessario hazer algunos rodeos." Mendoza to Philip, 24 July 1586, K. 1564, fol. 258.

9. On the equivalents of sixteenth-century French money see Nancy Lyman Roelker, ed., *The Paris of Henry of Navarre as seen by Pierre de l'Estoile* (Cambridge, Mass., 1958), pp. 308–309; and Donald L. Wiedner, "Coins and Accounts in Western European and Colonial History," unpub. dissertation, Harvard University, 1958.

10. One escudo pistolet = fifty-eight sueldos; one sueldo = twelve dineros.

11. Philip to Mendoza, S. Lorenzo, 28 September 1587, K. 1448, fol. 141.

12. See J. P. Devos, "La poste au service des diplomates espagnoles, 1555–1598," *Bulletin, Commission Royale d'Histoire,* 103:205–257 (1938); also Antonio Ballesteros y Beretta, *Historia de España y su influencia en la historia universal* (Barcelona, 1919–1941), IV, 192–195; and Merriman, *Philip the Prudent,* p. 453.

13. See Arbelays to Idiáquez, Irún, 16 March 1589, Simancas, K. 1570, fol. 94.

14. Devos, "La poste au service des diplomates," pp. 238, 265–266.

15. Mendoza to Philip, Simancas, K. 1568, fol. 100 was sent on 4 September 1588 and received on 12 September.

16. Philip to Mendoza, S. Lorenzo, 2 October 1587, K. 1448, fol. 142.

17. Mendoza to Philip, K. 1568, fol. 66.

18. Philip's letter of 6 March 1588 reached Mendoza on March 17. K. 1567, fol. 82.

19. Trapetier occasionally made this trip; Simancas, K. 1564, fol. 98.

20. Devos, "La poste au service des diplomates," pp. 220, 228–230, 237–238.

21. Mendoza to Philip, 9 October 1585, K. 1563, fol. 151; Balbani to Idiáquez, Lyon, 17 September 1589, K. 1569, fol. 117; K. 1571, fol. 111; and Capelo to Mendoza, Rouen, 10 August 1588, K. 1567, fol. 101.

22. The following books on cryptography are particularly useful for sixteenth-century ciphers: André Lange, *Traité de cryptographie* (Paris, 1925); Etienne Bazeries, *Les chiffres secrets dévoilés* (Paris, 1901); Vesin de Romanini, *La cryptographie dévoilée* (Brussels, 1840); and Fleissner von Wostrowitz, *Handbuch der Cryptographie* (n.p., 1881).

23. Mattingly, *Renaissance Diplomacy,* p. 250.

24. Many variations of substitution and transposition ciphers are discussed in Lange, *Traité de cryptographie,* pp. 129–193. See Mattingly, *Renaissance Diplomacy,* pp. 248–250; and Maulde-la-Claviere, *La diplomatie,* III, 132–135.

25. Philip to Ferdinand, Brussels, 24 May 1556, in Mariano Alcocer, "Criptografía español," *Boletin de la Academia de Historia,* 105:338–340 (1934).

26. For examples of sixteenth-century Spanish ciphers see *ibid.,* pp. 336–460; 107:603–676 (1935); and especially J. P. Devos, *Les chiffres de Philippe II (1555–1598), et du despacho universal durant le XVII siècle* (Brussels, 1950), pp. 92–377.

27. Tassis to Idiáquez, Paris, 5 February 1584, Simancas, K. 1563, fol. 2. For a brief description of this cipher see appendix. Another of Tassis' ciphers is illustrated in Devos, *Les chiffres de Philippe II,* pp. 300–303.

28. See appendix, pp. 232–236 for an explanation of the operation of this important cipher, for which no key has survived.

29. Count Maurice of Nassau to Walsingham, 24 March 1585, *C.S.P., For.*, XIX, 356.

30. This cipher is illustrated in the appendix, pp. 236–237.

31. "Los caminos estan de manera que no sera poca duda si los despachos aciertan a passar, con esto ymvio a V.M. una cifra de algunas que hize en Inglaterra, la qual no va en rueda por no poderse acomodar en los despachos y lo que siento que passan los que escriven otras consumiendo dobla de tiempo en el escrivir que lo haran en esta aorrando anssimismo la mitad del travaxo. Me ha hecho ymvialla a V.M. que conmander provalla se vera si tiene las calidades que digo." Mendoza to Idiáquez, Simancas, 9 April 1587, K. 1566, fol. 91.

32. See appendix, p. 237.

33. Bazeries, *Les chiffres secrets*, pp. 32, 40, 217.

34. "Et ne doit esmouvoir que cela sera occasion à nous voz ennemis de changer leurs chiffres, et se tenir plus couverts, et à nous voz officiers plus empeschez à vous y servir. Ils en ont changé et rechangé, et néantmoins ont esté et seront toujours surpris en leurs finesses. Car vostre cause est juste et la leur inique. Et pour ce Dieu dissipera leurs conseils pour bénir les vostres, illuminant les espirits à ce qui fera de vostre service auquel s'affectionnera à jamais selon son devoir." Bibliothèque Nationale, MS, Les 500 de Colbert, 33, quoted in *ibid.*, p. 221.

35. Philip to Mendoza, Madrid, 30 January 1590, Simancas, K. 1449, fol. 98.

36. Mendoza to Idiáquez, K. 1571, fol. 96. Cf. K. 1582, fol. 43.

37. See Mattingly, *Renaissance Diplomacy*, pp. 147–148, 246.

38. Simancas, K. 1571, fol. 123B.

39. Mendoza to Idiáquez, 9 October 1585, K. 1563, fol. 151.

40. Mendoza to Idiáquez, K. 1564, fol. 5; and 6 March, fol. 33.

41. Lefèvre, *Correspondance de Philippe II*, III, 164, 247, 445.

42. Mendoza to Philip, 11 May 1586, Simancas, K. 1564, fol. 54. Twelve thousand escudos, which Mendoza received two weeks later, had been sent on the previous day.

43. "Cuenta de gastos extraordinarios," K. 1564, fol. 258.

44. K. 1565, fol. 89; K. 1567, fol. 82.

45. See K. 1564, fol. 98.

46. K. 1564, fol. 258.

CHAPTER VII. The Revolt Begins

1. Mendoza to Philip, 30 January 1588, Simancas, K. 1568, fol. 8.

2. Philip to Mendoza, 25 January 1588, K. 1448, fol. 160. Cf. Léo Mouton, *Un demi-roi, le duc d'Epernon* (Paris, 1922), pp. 182–183.

3. L'Estoile, *Journal de Henri III*, III, 119. De Thou, *Histoire universelle* (1734), X, 215–218.

4. L'Estoile, *Journal de Henri III*, III, 83.

5. "Sa Majesté nous la sera si couverte que nous ne la romprens peult-estre jamais, qu'avec une aparente injustice, et abandonnez d'ung chacun, ou qu'il atendra de nous la commencer, alors que six fois davantage de moyens ne pourront pas relever nos forces en l'estat, qu'elles sont maintenant." Guise to Mendoza, Joigny, Simancas, K. 1565, fol. 79.

6. "Aucuns articles proposes parles chefs de la Ligue en l'assable de Nancy, en Jan. 1588," Goulart *Mémoires de la Ligue*, II, 269–279.

7. Guise to Mendoza, 9 March 1588, Simancas, K. 1568, fol. 15.

8. Mendoza to Philip, 25 February 1588, K. 1567, fol. 27.

9. Poulain, *Le procez-verbal*, pp. 292–295.

10. Maurice Wilkinson, *The Holy League, or Sainte Union* (Glasgow, 1929), p. 34.

11. L'Estoile, *Journal de Henri III*, III, 118.

12. See extracts of the expenses of the king (1588) in Cimber et Danjou, *Archives curieuses*, X, 433. Cf. Poulain, *Le procez-verbal*, p. 306; De Thou, *Histoire universelle*, VI, 721; Chalambert, *Histoire de la Ligue* pp. 16, 50; and Capefigue, *La réforme et la Ligue*, IV, 254–265.

13. Mendoza to Philip, 7 and 8 May 1588, Simancas, K. 1567, fols. 70, 71. Poulain, *Le procez-verbal*, p. 297.

14. Simancas, K. 1567, fol. 47.

15. Poulain, *Le procez-verbal*, pp. 320–321. Chalambert, *Histoire de la Ligue*, pp. 71–72.

16. "Signor mio, questa è una delle maggiori rivolte e ribellioni che si udisse mai; e temo molto, che prima che sia un mese, io vi scriverò un accidente stranissimo." Cavriana to Serguidi, Paris, 7 May 1588, Desjardins, *Négociations avec la Toscane*, IV, 775.

17. Guise to Mendoza, 9 and 10 March 1588, Simancas, K. 1568, fol. 15.

18. "Pernon ha ydo a Normandia a tomar posession de aquel govierno. Este Rey le acompaño hasta San Germain donde se dispidio del con tanta ternura y lagrimas que muestra bien lo mucho que le ama," reported Mendoza to Philip on 8 May 1588, K. 1567, fol. 71. Also see Bibliothèque Nationale, fonds fr. 17294, fol. 421.

19. "Advis donné à M. le due de Guise quand il revint à la Cour apres les baricades," Bibliothèque Nationale, MSS Colbert, 30, in Loutchitzki, *Documents inédits*, XIV, 225–227.

20. Mendoza to Philip, 14 April 1588, Simancas, K. 1567, fol. 61 and several other dispatches of the ambassador leave very little doubt on this point. See Mendoza to Philip, 15 May, K. 1568, fol. 33.

21. Erlanger maintains that Mendoza went to Soissons in person to

order Guise to come to Paris "d'y provoquer l'explosion," but I have been unable to substantiate this from any of the sources. Erlanger, *Henri III*, p. 261.

22. Chateauneuf to Henry III, Bib. Nat., MSS Béthune, vol. 8880, fol. 16, in Capefigue, *La réforme et la Ligue*, V, 91–99. Cf. Read, *Walsingham*, III, 213–215.

23. Philip to Mendoza, Simancas, K. 1448, fol. 175.

24. Léon van der Essen, *Alexandre Farnèse, prince de Parme* (Brussels, 1937), V, 165–174.

25. Guise to Mendoza, March 1588, Simancas, K. 1567, fol. 56; and Mendoza to Philip, fol. 51.

26. Mendoza to Philip, 14 April 1588, K. 1567, fol. 61.

27. Simancas, K. 1567, fols. 15, 30, 33, 61; and K. 1568, fol. 15.

28. Mendoza to Philip, 15 March 1588, K. 1567, fol. 33.

29. Mendoza to Philip, 14 April 1588, K. 1567, fol. 61.

30. Philip to Parma, 24 April 1588, Lefèvre, *Correspondance de Philippe II*, III, 295.

31. Guise to Parma, 21 May 1588, Simancas, K. 1568, fol. 42.

32. Mendoza to Philip, 5 April 1588, K. 1567, fol. 51. See Mariéjol, *La réforme et la Ligue*, pp. 268–269; and Poulain, *Le procez-verbal*, pp. 295–297.

33. The following is only a brief outline of the Paris revolt which I have reconstructed from some of the best contemporary accounts. With these cf. "Histoire très véritable de ce qui est advenu en ceste ville de Paris depuis le 7 mai 1588 jusqu'au dernier jour de juing audit an," in Cimber et Danjou, *Archives curieuse*, XI, 325–350; "Amplification des particularités qui se passèrent à Paris quand M. de Guise s'en empara et que le Roy en sortit," *ibid.*, pp. 351–362; and "Histoire de la journée des barricades de Paris," *ibid.*, pp. 363–410. Also B. Zeller, "Le mouvement Guisard en 1588, Catherine de Médicis et la journée des barricades," *Revue Historique*, 61:253–276 (1889); and A. Viñas, "Felipe II y la Jornada de las Barricadas," in *Hommage à Ernest Martinenche* (Paris, 1939), pp. 514–533.

34. Mendoza to Philip, 15 May 1588, Simancas, K. 1568, fol. 31. The most vivid modern picture of the Day of the Barricades, which also makes use of Mendoza's account, is in Mattingly, *The Armada*, pp. 218–244.

35. L'Estoile, *Journal de Henri III*, III, 137.

36. Cavriana to Serguidi, 13 May 1588, Desjardins, *Négociations avec la Toscane*, IV, 779.

37. "Le dimostrazioni del Duca di Guisa furono piene d'affettuosa umiltà e di profonda sommissione." Arrigo Caterino Davila, *Dell' istoria delle guerre civili di Francia*, 6 vols. (Milan, 1807), vol. III, p. 187. See also the account in Sichel, *The Later Years of Catherine de' Medici*, esp. pp. 365–367.

38. Mendoza to Philip, Simancas, K. 1568, fol. 31. Cf. Davila, *Guerre civili*, III, 191–192.

39. L'Estoile, *Journal de Henri III*, III, 138; and Jean-Baptiste de La Fosse, *Journal d'un curé ligueur de Paris sous les trois derniers Valois* (Paris, 1866), p. 212.

40. Mendoza to Philip, Simancas, K. 1568, fol. 31.

41. Davila, *Guerre civili*, III, 201–202.

42. *Ibid.*, pp. 211–214.

43. *Ibid.*, p. 215. De Thou, who saw Guise that day reports that the duke and his men went about with "an air of gaiety and confidence." *Histoire universelle* (1734), X, 260.

44. Philip to Mendoza, S. Lorenzo, 2 June 1588, Simancas, K. 1448, fol. 189.

45. Mattingly, *The Armada*, p. 244; and cf. Parma to Philip, Bruges, 8 June 1588, Estado, 594, fol. 73, Manuscrits divers, reg. 1096, fol. 58, abstracted in Lefèvre, *Correspondance de Philippe II*, III, 315.

46. Quoted in Hübner, *Sixtus the Fifth*, II, 183–184.

47. Edouard Maugis, *Histoire du Parlement de Paris, de l'avènement des rois Valois à la mort d'Henri IV*, 2 vols. (Paris, 1913–14), II, 51–53.

48. Mattingly, *The Armada*, p. 244.

49. L'Estoile, *Journal de Henri III*, III, 141–142, 149.

50. La Fosse, *Journal d'un curé ligueur*, pp. 215–217.

51. See Alfred Maury, "La commune de Paris de 1588," *Revue des Deux Mondes*, 95:132–159 (1871).

52. *Registres des délibérations du Bureau de la ville de Paris* [hereafter cited *Bureau de la Ville*] (Paris, 1902), IX, 118; and "Acte de la Ligue," Bibliothèque Nationale, coll. Dupuy, vol. 87, fol. 247, in Loutchitzki, *Documents inédits*, XIV, 227–228.

53. Maury, "La commune de Paris," pp. 149–151.

54. L'Estoile, *Journal de Henri III*, III, 147–149; La Fosse, *Journal d'un curé ligueur*, p. 215.

55. *Bureau de la Ville*, IX, 118–122. Poëte, *Une vie de cité*, III, 231–232; and Frémy, *Les diplomates*, p. 199.

56. Mendoza to Parma, 21 May 1588, Simancas, K. 1568, fol. 43. Cf. P. Richard, *La Papauté et la Ligue française: Pierre d'Epinac, archevêque de Lyon* (Paris, 1901), pp. 296–301.

57. De Thou, *Histoire universelle* (1734), X, 268.

58. Registre de l'Hôtel de Ville, vol. XII, fols. 167, 169, 174, cited in Capefigue, *La réforme et la Ligue*, V, 21–27. Also "Marchans et eschevins de Paris à les messieurs, eschevins, etc., de Châlons," 30 May 1588, in Georges Hérelle, ed., *La réforme et la Ligue en Champagne: Documents*, 2 vols. (Paris, n.d.), I, 143–146; and Goulart, *Mémoires de la Ligue*, II, 337–341.

59. Henry III to Philip, Chartres, 20 May 1588, Simancas, K. 1568, fol. 41.

60. Baguenault de Puchesse, "La politique de Philippe II dans les affaires de France," *Revue des Questions Historiques*, 25:37–39 (1879).

61. Philip to Mendoza, S. Lorenzo, 17 July 1587, K. 1448, fol. 132.

62. "Je sçay qu'il [Mendoza] faict profession d'escrire par deçà en termes fort esloignez de ce qui pourroit servir à maintenir une bonne et vraye intelligence entre ces deux couronnes; et son naturel est de procurer tout le mal et la division qu'il peult ez Estatz des princes aupres desquelz il est, et de diminuer, s'il peut, leur reputation et grandeur, et troubler leurs affaires." Longlée to Henry III, Madrid, 6 February 1588, Bibliothèque Nationale, fonds français, 16110, fol. 220; and in Albert Mousset, ed., *Dépêches diplomatiques de M. de Longlée, résident de France en Espagne* (Paris, 1912), p. 346.

63. "Pour homme insolent, mal intentionne et tres pernicieux," *ibid.*, p. 351; and Bibliothèque Nationale, fonds français, 16110, fols. 222, 226.

64. Cavriana to Serguidi, Paris, 14 February 1588, Desjardins, *Négociations avec la Toscane*, IV, 757–760.

65. Mousset, *Dépêches de Longlée*, pp. 386–390, Simancas, K. 1568, fol. 71. Croze, *Les Guise*, II, 86.

66. Philip to Henry III, S. Lorenzo, 26 July 1588, K. 1568, fol. 79.

67. "El Embaxor Don Berdno de Mendoça procede muy conforme a la buena amistad y hermandad que entre sus Magdes ay, es lo que mas encargado le tiene en sus instructiones, y se le haria cosa bien nueva que de su parte se huviesse hecho mas de aquello a que obligasse la defensa y seguridad de los payses baxos y el bien de la causa Cathca a que siempre su Md. ha hecho y haze tanta profession de acuidir." Simancas, K. 1568, fol. 81 bis.

68. K. 1568, fol. 81.

69. Philip to Mendoza, S. Lorenzo, 31 July 1588, K. 1568, fol. 83.

70. "Requeste présentée au Roi par Ms. les cardinals, princes, seigneurs et les deputés de la Ville de Paris et autres villes Catholiques associes et unis pour la defense de la religion Catholique, Apostolique et Romaine," Goulart, *Mémoires de la Ligue*, II, 342–350.

71. Edouard Frémy, "La médiation de l'Abbé de Feuillants entre la Ligue et Henri III, 1588–1589," *Revue d'Histoire Diplomatique*, 6:228–243, 449–473 (1892).

72. Mouton, *Un demi-roi*, pp. 207–210.

73. L'Estoile, *Journal de Henri III*, III, 153–155.

74. Henri de l'Epinois, "La réconciliation de Henri III et du duc de Guise: d'après les documents des Archives du Vatican (mai-juillet 1588)," *Revue des Questions Historiques*, 39:52–94 (1886).

75. Catherine to Villeroy and to Henry III, 2 June 1588, Baguenault de Puchesse, *Lettres de Catherine de Médicis*, IX, 365–369; and "Les négociations de Catherine de Médicis à Paris après la Journée des Barricades," *Academie des Sciences Morales et Politiques*, N.S., 1:697–709 (1903).

76. Mendoza to Philip, 24 July 1588, Simancas, K. 1568, fol. 77; also see fols. 53, 61.

77. "Edit du roi, sur l'union de ses sujets Catholiques," in Goulart *Mémoires de la Ligue*, II, 368–373. Cf. Palma Cayet, *Chronologie novennaire*, pp. 58–59.

78. Articles of Peace, Simancas, K. 1568, fols. 60, 65; and Mendoza to Philip, fol. 61.

79. L'Estoile, *Journal de Henri III*, III, 175. Guise to Mendoza, Chartres, 6 August 1588, Simancas, K. 1567, fol. 95. Cf. H. C. Macdowell, *Henry of Guise and Other Portraits* (London, 1898), pp. 151–152.

CHAPTER VIII. Triumph of the League

1. "Si algunos baxales de mi armada aportaren con temporal a sus puertos, ordene que sean tratados conforme a la buena paz y hermandad que entre nosotros aya, quitando le por aqui la sospecha destas fuerças y grangeando le para lo que se pretende." Philip to Mendoza, S. Lorenzo, 24 April 1588, Simancas, K. 1448, fol. 175.

2. Mendoza to Philip, 5 April 1588, K. 1567, fol. 51; also K. 1568, fol. 33.

3. Mendoza to Philip, 30 May 1588, K. 1568, fol. 48. Cf. Forneron, *Histoire de Philippe II*, III, 290–315.

4. *Harangue au Roy très-chrestien, faite à Chartres par Monseigneur Don Bernardin de Mendoça, ambassadeur pour le Roy d'Espagne vers sa Majesté* (1588). This sixteen-page brochure was published, probably at Paris, shortly after the speech was delivered, although there is no place of publication indicated on the first edition. Two copies can be found in the Bibliothèque Nationale in Paris, LB34.472. A slightly different version (also 1588) was printed in Lyon. There is also one copy of this eight-page edition in the Bibliothèque Nationale. The British Museum has one copy of the Lyon brochure, C. 33. b.25, as well as some of Mendoza's other noteworthy addresses, including his pronouncement against the Dutch delegation in 1585. *Harenge de l'Ambassadeur d'Espaigne prononcee à sa Majesté tres-Chrestienne, lors de l'arrivee de Deputez des Estats de Flandres* [Ghent?], 1585. British Museum, T. 1716(4).

5. Philip to Mendoza, S. Lorenzo, 18 July 1588, Simancas, K. 1448, fol. 196.

6. Mendoza to Parma, 21 May 1588, K. 1568, fol. 43; and Guise to

Parma, fol. 42. Cf. with Parma's frequent solicitations to Philip for such a force. Van der Essen, *Alexandre Farnese*, V, 165, 174, 218–220.

7. Mendoza to Parma, 23 May, K. 1568, fol. 45.

8. K. 1567, fols. 85, 86, 93; and K. 1568, fols. 55, 63, 69, 74.

9. Mendoza to Philip, 8 August 1588, K. 1567, fol. 97. See J. S. Corbett, *Drake and the Tudor Navy* (London, 1898), II, 202–226, and especially Mattingly, *The Armada*, pp. 352–355.

10. Mendoza to Philip, 9 August, K. 1567, fol. 98; and Philip to Mendoza, 18 August, K. 1448, fol. 202.

11. Capelo to Mendoza, K. 1567, fol. 101, and anonymous, fol. 102.

12. Forneron, *Les ducs de Guise*, II, 369.

13. Philip to Mendoza, 18, August, K. 1448, fol. 202.

14. Noticias de Asan, K. 1567, fol. 104; and also fols. 109, 110, 120, K. 1568, fols. 92, 94. On the problem of Parma's rendezvous, see Mattingly, *The "Invincible" Armada and Elizabethan England* (Ithaca, 1963), pp. 19–20.

15. On September 24, he reported a ship from the Armada making port at Calais, and also tells of the *Santa Ana* (flagship of Recalde's squadron) at the bay of St. Vaast la Hougue. K. 1567, fol. 131. On November 2, Mendoza told of another at Le Havre, and the arrival of a ship at "Morvien" (Le Morbihan?) in Brittany, both from the Armada; K. 1568, fol. 123.

16. K. 1567, fol. 109B.

17. K. 1567, fol. 131. Cf. René de Bouillé, *Histoire des ducs de Guise* (Paris, 1850), vol. IV, for a different version of this episode.

18. "En la mar Norte auia encontrado a la Arm^{da} de V.Md. en numero de 115 a 120 velas muy grandes, la qual caminaua en orden y con buen tiempo"; Mendoza to Philip, K. 1568, fol. 112.

19. K. 1568, fol. 88. This decree was registered by the Parlement de Paris on August 6.

20. "Lettres patentes de Henri III données à Chartres le 6 août, 1588; Archives Nationales, X. 8639, fol. 207.

21. Mendoza to Philip, 9 August 1588, Simancas, K. 1567, fol. 100.

22. "Lettres patentes," 17 août, Archives Nationales, X. 8639, fol. 208.

23. Bibliothèque Nationale, fonds français, 15909, fol. 140.

24. Cavriana to Serguidi, Blois, 13 September 1588, Desjardins, *Négociations avec la Toscane*, IV, 822–823.

25. Mendoza to Philip, Simancas, K. 1568, fol. 113.

26. Villeroy, *Mémoires d'Estat*, in Michaud et Poujoulat, *Nouvelle collection des mémoires*, XI, 130.

27. Mendoza to Philip, 24 September 1588, Simancas, K. 1568, fol. 114. Sutherland accepts the view, from a letter in Croze, *Les Guises*, II, 374, dated 24 October, and also cited in Baguenault de Puchesse, "La politique de Philippe II," p. 41, that Mendoza believed "The ac-

tions of this prince all contradict each other to such an extent that these dismissals . . . do not appear to be the result of a plan drawn up in advance"; *The French Secretaries of State*, pp. 299–300.

28. Guise to Mendoza, Blois, 21 September, K. 1568, fol. 104. For the letters of convocation see François Isambert, *Recueil général des anciennes lois françaises*, 29 vols. (Paris, 1821–1833), XIV, 613–616.

29. Guise to Mendoza, 4 September, K. 1568, fol. 98.

30. *Ibid*. Cf. Forneron, *Les ducs de Guise*, II, 371–375.

31. Mendoza to Philip, 24 September, K. 1568, fol. 113. In October, Mendoza moved to the village of Saint-Dié to be nearer the proceedings at Blois.

32. Picot, *Histoire des États généraux*, III, 374–375. Also Ulph, "The Estates General and the Catholic League," pp. 182–184. These figures vary slightly for the second and third estates from those given by Russell Major, *The Deputies to the Estates General in Renaissance France* (Madison, 1960), pp. 164–165.

33. See Anquez, *Histoire des assemblées*, pp. 39–57; and H. M. Baird, *The Huguenots and Henry of Navarre*, II, 60–78.

34. Croze, *Les Guise*, II, 125 ff. Mendoza, as revealed in his notes to Henry, Guise, and Philip, expressed immediate surprise and concern over the invasion.

35. Guise to Mendoza, Blois, 9 October 1588, Simancas, K. 1567, fol. 150B.

36. Guise to Mendoza, 13 October, *ibid*. Cf. Felix Rocquain, *La France et Rome pendant les guerres de religion* (Paris, 1924), pp. 356–360.

37. "Séance des Etats de Blois," Charles Joseph Mayer, ed., *Des États généraux et autres assemblées nationales* (Paris, 1788–89), XV, 276–286.

38. La harangue faite par Henri III, Roi de France et de Pologne, à l'ouverture de l'assemblée des trois États-Généraux de son Royaume, en sa ville de Blois, le 16 d'Octobre, 1588," Mayer, *Des États généaux*, XV, 350–351. There are many accounts of Henry's speech, each varying somewhat in content and phraseology. Cf. Pierre Matthieu, *Histoire des derniers troubles de France* (Lyon, 1594), I, 119a–124b; and Goulart, *Mémoires de la Ligue*, II, 481–500.

39. "Rémerciement fait au Roi, par M. l'archevêque de Bourges, patriarche, primat d'Aquitaine, au nom des Etats de ce Royaume, sur la proposition faite par sa Majeste à l'ouverture de ses Etats . . . ," Mayer, *Des États généraux*, pp. 397–407. "Rémerciement fait au nom de la noblesse de France, par le Baron de Senecey," pp. 407–408. "Harangue de Monsieur le Prévôt des Marchands, président pour le Tiers-Etats," pp. 409–410.

40. "Declaration du Roi sur son Edit de L'Union de tous ses sujets Catholiques," *ibid.*, p. 412.

41. Guise to Mendoza, Blois, 24 October, Simancas, K. 1567, fol. 160.

42. See K. 1448, fols. 213-214, 221; K. 1567, fols, 147, 150, 174, 180, 186, 195; K. 1568, fol. 137.

43. Guise to Mendoza, K. 1567, fol. 172; and Mendoza to Philip, fols. 174, 186.

44. Mendoza to Philip, 2 November, K. 1567, fol. 165; 26 November, fol. 180.

45. The most complete account of the assassination is found in Cimber et Danjou, *Archives curieuses*, XII, 57-107: "Le martyre des deux frères, contenant au vray toutes les particularitès plus notables des massacres et assassinats commis de personnas de messieurs le cardinal et le duc de Guyse par Henry de Valoys." For Mendoza's succinct account see Simancas, K. 1567, fol. 196.

46. Mendoza to Philip, Saint-Dié, 26 November 1588, K. 1567, fol. 179; 9 December, K. 1568, fol. 135.

47. Davila, *Guerre civili*, III, 296-297.

48. Guise to Mendoza, Simancas, K. 1568, fol. 104; also Mendoza to Philip, K. 1567, fol. 190.

49. "Discours de ce qui est arrivé a Blois jusques a la mort du duc et du cardinal de Guyse," Cimber et Danjou, *Archives curieuses*, XII, 144-145. Cf. Valois, *Histoire de la Ligue; oeuvre d'un contemporaine*, I, 260. Mendoza reports that the king was going hunting.

50. "Information faicte par Michon et Courtin, conseillers au parlement, pour raison des massacres commis à Blois ès personnes des duc et cardinal de Guyse." An inquest made by the Parlement de Paris at the petition of Guise's widow, Cimber et Danjou, *Archives curieuses*, XII, 194.

51. Davila, *Guerre civili*, III, 300-302.

52. See Henry's note to the papal legate, quoted in L'Epinois, *La Ligue et les papes*, p. 265, from Tempesti, *Storia di Sisto Quinto*, II, 133. Also cf. Desjardins, *Négociations avec la Toscane*, IV, 842, 849.

53. Recorded by the king's personal physician, Miron, in his famous relation of the events of that day. "Relation de la mort de messieurs les duc et cardinal de Guise, par le sieur Miron," Cimber et Danjou, *Archives curieuses*, XII, 109-138. In his own brief account, Mendoza makes no mention of the paper referred to by Miron.

54. De Thou, *Histoire universelle*, VII, 353. Mendoza relates the murder of the cardinal in a passing sentence, but devotes several pages to the steps taken by the king to arrest the others. He then comments on the thoroughness of Henry's preparations, and concludes (though probably incorrectly) that he had been planning the move for a long time. Simancas, K. 1567, fol. 196, also cf. Croze, *Les Guises*, II, 385-388.

CHAPTER IX. Mendoza Leads the Paris League

1. Mendoza to Philip, Saint-Dié, 23 December 1588, Simancas, K. 1567, fol. 189.

2. Mendoza to Philip, K. 1567, fol. 190.

3. K. 1567, fol. 191. Parma too was stunned by the belief that the League had been destroyed. See Lefèvre, *Correspondance de Philip II*, III, 379.

4. Philip to Mendoza, Madrid, 14 January 1589, K. 1449, fol. 2.

5. Philip to Mendoza, K. 1449, fol. 3.

6. L'Estoile, *Journal de Henri III*, III, 233. Héritier, *Catherine de Médicis*, pp. 688–689.

7. Mendoza to Philip, Saint-Victor, 20 January 1589, K. 1570, fol. 18.

8. Forneron errs in his assertion that Mendoza remained at Saint-Dié after the assassinations: "Bernardin de Mendoça avait continué selon instructions à habiter Saint-Dié, près Blois, jusqu'au moment au il avait appris l'arrivet de Mayenne à Paris," and, "Il étaint encore à Saint-Dié le 1er février, 1589"; *Histoire de Philippe II*, IV, 4. Actually, Mendoza went from Saint-Dié to Blois on January 5 and apparently did not return again to Saint-Dié after that. On January 20 he retired to Saint-Victor, where he remained until March 5. On March 6 he was in Orléans, and sometime between that date and March 16 he returned to Paris.

9. "Le roi à noz chers et bien amez les mayre et eschevins de nostre ville de Chaallons," 24 December 1588, Hérelle, *La réforme et la Ligue*, I, pp. 155–157.

10. De Thou, *Histoire universelle*, VII, 368.

11. Picot, *Histoire des Etats généraux*, III, 426–431.

12. "Lettre du Cardinal Giovanni Francesco Morosini, Légat en France," in Desjardins, *Négociations avec la Toscane*, IV, 868–872.

13. See Félix Rocquain, *La France et Rome pendant les guerres de religion* (Paris, 1924), pp. 361–371.

14. Richard, *La papauté et la Ligue française*, pp. 341–347, and notes.

15. *Journal de François, bourgeois de Paris, 23 décembre 1588–30 avril 1589*, ed. Eugène Saulnier (Paris, 1913), pp. 13–14. L'Estoile, *Les belles figures et droilleries de la Ligue*, pp. 27–29. Poëte, *Une vie de cité*, III, 234.

16. See La Fosse, *Journal de un curé*, pp. 222–229.

17. Palma Cayet, *Chronologie novennaire*, p. 87. Saulnier, *Journal de François*, p. 37.

18. "Responsvm Facultatis Theologicae Parisiensis"; Simancas, K. 1579, fol. 8.

19. *Bureau de la Ville*, IX, 212–213. Also see Saulnier, *Journal de François*, pp. 21–23, 27; L'Estoile, *Journal de Henri III*, III, 203–204; Palma Cayet, *Chronologie novennaire*, p. 97; Mendoza to Philip, Blois, 5 January 1589, Simancas, K. 1570, fol. 3; and Poëte, *Une vie de cité*, III, 237–238.

20. Goulart, *Mémoires de la Ligue*, III, 511–523.

21. "Declaration et Resolvtion de par les Maievr, Prévost et Éschevins de la Ville et cité de Amyns"; Simancas, K. 1570, fol. 1.

22. See "Extraits des deliberations du conseil de la ville de Toulouse," in Loutchitzki, *Documents inédites*, XIV, 242–255, and "Extrait des registres du Parlement de Toulouse," *ibid.*, pp. 256–260. Also Cimber et Danjou, *Archives curieuses*, XII, 283; and Chalambert, *Histoire de la Ligue*, pp. 138–139.

23. See Jean Boucher's *De justa abdicatione Henrici tertii* (1589), and *La vie de l'hypocrite Henri de Valois*, in Labitte, *Les prédicateurs*, pp. 61 ff. Cf. Saulnier, *Journal de François*, pp. 19–20.

24. L'Estoile, *Journal de Henri III*, III, 249.

25. *Bureau de la Ville*, IX, 289, 295–296. La Fosse, *Journal d'un curé ligueur*, p. 223; Saulnier, *Journal de François*, pp. 58–60; and Forneron, *Histoire de Philippe II*, IV, 8–9, who also includes the cardinal of Lénoncourt and lists the lawyers and soldiers by name.

26. Mayenne to Philip, Paris, 22 March 1589, Simancas, K. 1570, fol. 97.

27. L'Estoile, *Les belles figures et droilleries de la Ligue*, pp. 64–65.

28. "Ordonnance des chefs de l'Union Catholique pour la diminution des impôts," Paris, 19 January 1589, Simancas, K. 1570, fol. 17.

29. Chalambert, *Histoire de la Ligue*, p. 141.

30. *Bureau de la Ville*, IX, 309–310. Pasquier, Lettre XXIV in *Oeuvres choisies d'Etienne Pasquier* (Paris, 1849), II, 327–328.

31. For an interesting letter justifying his action to Brisson, see Jean Bodin, *Lettre de Monsieur Bodin* (Paris, 1590); also Bibliothèque Nationale, Anc. fonds fr. 4897, f. 34, in Summerfield Baldwin, "Jean Bodin and the League," *Catholic Historical Review*, 23:174 (1937).

32. Mendoza to Philip, 13 February 1589, Simancas, K. 1570, fol. 63.

33. Palma Cayet, *Chronologie novennaire*, pp. 108–110.

34. "Declaration du Roy sur l'attentat, felonnie et rebellion, etc.," Simancas, K. 1570, fols. 52, 53; and Goulart, *Mémoires de la Ligue*, III, 211 ff.

35. "Declaration du Roy sur la treve accordée par Sa Majesté au Roy de Navarre, etc."; Goulart, *Mémoires de la Ligue*, III, 300–308. Cf. "Articles du traicté de la trefue negotiée par M. Du Plessis, de la part du Roy de Navarre, avec le Roy Henry III," Tours, 3 April 1589; Du Plessis-Mornay, *Mémoires et correspondance*, IV, 351–355.

36. Mendoza to Henry III, Simancas, K. 1570, fol. 120.

37. L'Estoile, *Journal de Henri III*, III, 276–278. Mariéjol, *La ré-*

forme et la Ligue, p. 297. Some accounts give the date as April 13, but this is undoubtedly an error. Vassière reminds us that this meeting took place in the park of the Château where Jeanne d'Albret, Navarre's mother, spent her melancholy childhood; *Henri IV* (Paris, 1928), p. 321. See Navarre's report of the reconciliation with the Comtesse de Guiche, dated May 17; *ibid.*, pp. 322–323.

38. Philip to Mendoza, 15 January 1589, Simancas, K. 1449, fol. 2.

39. Henry III to Philip, Tours, March, K. 1569, fol. 2; Henry III to Mendoza, 10 April, K. 1570, fol. 108.

40. Philip to Mendoza, Madrid, 17 March 1589, K. 1449, fol. 10.

41. Mendoza returned to Paris via Orléans, where he was received with hearty acclaim and given many friendly assurances of support in the Spanish-League cause. Mendoza to Idiáquez, Orléans, 6 March 1589, K. 1570, fol. 91. Also see Philip to Mendoza, K. 1449, fol. 10.

42. Cavriana thought Guise had elements of greatness: "Aveva il duca tutte le condizioni de grande: bellezza, grandezza, forza, dolcezza, ardiere, prudenza, pazienza, dissimulazione, segretezza; ci mancava la fede, per la quale sarebbe stato il maggiore del mondo, e si sarebbe mantenuto poco meno che re." Cavriana to Serguidi, Blois, 31 December 1588, Desjardins, *Négociations avec la Toscane*, IV, 847.

43. For a revealing contemporary Politique evaluation of Mayenne, see De Thou, *Histoire universelle* (1734), X, 476–477.

44. Mendoza to Philip, 11 April, Simancas, K. 1570, fols. 112, 113.

45. Mendoza to Philip, 21 April, K. 1570, fols. 122, 125, 131. Croze, *Les Guises*, II, 166–171.

46. Mendoza to Philip, 1 April 1589, K. 1569, fol. 9.

47. Philip to Jacobo [Mayenne], S. Lorenzo, 6 May 1589, K. 1449, fol. 22.

48. Philip to Moreo, May 1589, K. 1449, fol. 20.

49. Philip to Mendoza, 5 May, K. 1449, fol. 18.

50. "El Rey como el duque de Umena y los de la Liga, con quienes vos procedeys como conviene y les aconsejays lo que importa assi lo hazed adelante, procurando siempre que la cause Cat^{ca} prevalezca." Philip to Mendoza, 11 May, K. 1449, fol. 24.

51. Henry III to Philip, Tours, 29 April 1589, K. 1569, fol. 29.

52. "Lettre de créance du sieur de Fresne Forget, mai 1589," K. 1568, fol. 80 (misfiled at Simancas among documents for the year 1588).

53. Philip to Henry III, S. Lorenzo, 18 June 1589, K. 1569, fol. 59.

54. See Henry to Mendoza, Camp de Beaugency, 16 June, K. 1569, fol. 51; and Mendoza to Henry, 12 June, fol. 48; and 22 June, fol. 65.

55. Mendoza to Philip, 21 June, K. 1569, fol. 61.

56. Mendoza's doctors called his malady "flatus" or a "ventosidad caliente." Mendoza to Idiáquez, 16 July 1587, K. 1448, fol. 130.

57. "Yo he estado dias fatigadissimo de los ojos por el humor que

me havia cargado a ellos y con tanto dolor por ser caliente que me hara terrible dolor aun el mobellos." Mendoza to Idiáquez, 1 June 1585, K. 1563, fol. 75.

58. "Por haver se me acabado de quajar una cataracta en el ojo izquierdo, que me ha ympedidio totalmente la vista de el, se han resuelto los medicos y ocolistas deste lugar que me disponga a la aguja." 24 June 1586, K. 1564, fol. 94.

59. Mendoza to Idiáquez, 20 November 1586, K. 1564, fol. 227.

60. Philip to Mendoza, S. Lorenzo, K. 1449, fols. 33, 41.

61. Philip to Mendoza, K. 1449, fols. 34–38, 40.

62. L'Estoile, *Journal de Henri III*, III, 286–289.

63. Mendoza to Philip, 18 May 1589, Simancas, K. 1570, fol. 149.

64. ". . . procuri vostra Maestà di vincere, che al sicuro le consure saranno rivocate, ma se saremo vinti, morremo cretici e condannati," Davila, *Guerre civili*, III, 415.

65. Mendoza to Philip, 27 July 1589, Simancas, K. 1569, fol. 82.

66. Mendoza to Philip, 2 August, K. 1569, fol. 86. Cf. "Discours aux François, avec l'histoire véritable de la mort de Henry de Valois, advenure à Sainct-Cloud-lès-Paris le 1er aoust 1589," in Cimber et Danjou, *Archives curieuses*, XII, 361–371. Also Forneron, *Histoire de Philippe II*, IV, 1–6, and Mariéjol, *La réforme et la Ligue*, pp. 298–301.

CHAPTER X. The Struggle for a Throne

1. Clément apparently consulted the learned men of his Order and sought absolution from his confessor before carrying out the deed. The reply he received, according to De Thou, was that if it were done without vengeance and for the good of the church and the state, and with the love of God, it could be done without sin. In fact, it would be counted as a meritorious act. *Histoire universelle* (1734), X, 667–669. De Thou also makes quite a point of the fact that Mayenne had more than a hundred Politiques arrested on the eve of the assassination; *ibid.*, p. 670. There is no doubt that Mayenne knew of the plot and that the more fanatical preachers had been advocating tyrannicide from the pulpit. See Cimber et Danjou, *Archives curieuses*, XII, 358; also *Satyre Ménippée*, II, 436–511.

2. Mendoza to Philip, 8 August 1589, Simancas, K. 1569, fol. 93.

3. See Navarre's letter to the nobility of the Republic of Berne, 18 August 1589, K. 1569, fol. 97.

4. "Extract d'un discours d'estat de M. de Sancy," *Mémoires de Nevers*, II, 590–594.

5. Vassière, *Henri IV*, p. 333. The exact number of troops thus acquired by Navarre is impossible to determine, but estimates and conflicting contemporary reports range between 12,000 and 20,000.

6. "Declaration du roy Henry IV, St. Cloud, 4 August 1589," in Henry IV, *Lettres missives*, VII, 357-359; and "Declaration du roy Henry IV," in Simancas, K. 1569, fol. 90.

7. Actually, there was a considerable amount of discontent and protest on the part of the Huguenots, who felt the declaration was a great betrayal. See *Mémoires du duc d'Angoulesme*, in Michaud et Poujoulat, *Nouvelle collection des mémoires*, XI, 542.

8. Mendoza to Philip, 2 August 1589, Simancas, K. 1569, fol. 86.

9. Mendoza to Philip, 8 August, K. 1569, fol. 93; also fols. 87, 94. De Thou quotes a letter of submission sent by Mayenne to Philip on August 21, which was subsequently intercepted at Bordeaux. *Histoire universelle* (1734), XI, 667-668.

10. Philip to Mendoza, Madrid, 7 September 1589, K. 1449, fol. 50. Philip rushed a letter to Parma on the same day indicating his approval of Charles X, and instructing Parma to send 300,000 escudos to Mayenne. Lèfevre, *Correspondance de Philippe II*, III, 437.

11. Philip to Mendoza and Moreo, K. 1449, fol. 51.

12. Mariéjol declares that the army of the two kings was reduced by almost one-half after the assassination of Henry III; *La réforme et la Ligue*, pp. 305-306.

13. See John B. Black, *Elizabeth and Henry IV: Being a Short Study in Anglo-French Relations, 1589-1603* (Oxford, 1914), pp. 13-15; and Croze, *Les Guise*, II, 199-201.

14. Philip to Mendoza, S. Lorenzo, 7 September 1589, Simancas, K. 1449, fol. 53.

15. Mendoza to Philip, 30 October 1589, K. 1569, fol. 145.

16. Philip to Tassis, El Pardo, 6 November 1589, K. 1449, fol. 71.

17. Philip to Mendoza, K. 1449, fol. 50; and Philip to Cardinal Cajetan, El Pardo, 6 November, fol. 72.

18. Petitot, *Introduction aux mémoires*, 1st ser., XX, 233.

19. Villeroy to Bellièvre, 29 April 1589, Bibliothèque Nationale, fonds français, 15909, fol. 252. See the valuable article by Joseph Nouaillac, "La fin de la Ligue: Villeroy négociateur des Politiques. Essai d'histoire nes négociations de 1589 à 1594," *Revue Henry IV*, 1:37-58, 69-81 (1905); and 1:197-217 (1906).

20. Villeroy to Mendoza, Amiens, 27 October 1589, Simancas, K. 1569, fol. 142.

21. Prior to Henry III's death, Mayenne made an urgent request of Philip for money, which had not yet arrived by the middle of August. The money was to be delivered to him from Flanders by Juan Iñiguez. On August 27, Mendoza reported that "Jacobo [Mayenne] is chafing at the bit over the absence of news from Flanders or from Juan Iñiguez" ["Jacobo esta tan colgado de los cabellos . . ."]. Mendoza to Philip, 27 August, K. 1569, fol. 91.

22. See the excellent article by Michel de Bouard, "Sixte-Quint,

Henry IV, et la Ligue: la légation du cardinal Caetani en France (1589–1590)," *Revue des Questions Historiques,* 20:59–140 (1932). Henri de l'Epinois' older "La légation du cardinal Caetani en France," *ibid.,* 30:460–525 (1881), is also very useful, as is Henri Drouot's "La mission du légat Caetano et sa traversée de la Bourgogne (Nov. 1589–Jan. 1590)," *Revue d'Histoire Moderne,* 3:371–388 (1928), on his journey and arrival.

23. Philip to Mendoza, Tassis, and Moreo, 6 November 1589, Simancas, K. 1449, fol. 70.

24. "Siendo el hereje tan obstinado y confirmado que mamo la herejia con la leche." Article 7. The passage originally read, "Que aviendo heredado la herejia en el vientre se crio con ella" (having inherited heresy in the womb, he was nourished on it), but this phrase was struck out and the other inserted.

25. "Tras esto como yo tiro al suave reparo desse Reyno mas que a interesses propios, facilmente me absternia de las pretensiones que me tocan con saber que son muy bien fundadas." Article 18.

26. "Finalmente procurareys que todo se encamine como mas convenga para el servicio de Nro Señor y el bien de la causa Cathca que es lo que sobre todo os encomiendo, y de que se seguira la quietud y sossiego desse reyno." Article 26.

27. "Articles accordés, jurés et signes entre le roy de France et de Navarre et les prelates, etc." L'Estoile, *Les belles figures et drolleries de la Ligue,* pp. 152–157.

28. Croze, *Les Guise,* II, 196.

29. Points of Alliance between the duke de Maine and Spain, Simancas, K. 1570, fol. 193.

30. Mendoza to Philip, 21 February 1590, K. 1571, fol. 27.

31. Saulnier, *Le rôle politique,* pp. 238–242.

32. "Lettres patentes du roi Charles X ordonant de frapper monnaie à son effigie," Paris, 15 December 1589, Archives Nationales, musée piece 745.

33. Mendoza to Philip, 22 December 1589, Simancas, K. 1569, fol. 173.

34. "Arrest de la cour de Parlement, par lequel est enioint de recognoistre le Roy Charles X pour vray et legitime Roy de France, et deffendu aucun traicté de paix avec Henry de Bourbon." Cimber et Danjou, *Archives curieuses,* XIII, 223–226.

35. L'Estoile, *Journal de Henry IV,* V, 266–268.

36. Moreo to Mendoza, Aumalle (Camp of Mayenne), 12 October 1589, Simancas, K. 1569, fol. 137.

37. Mendoza to Moreo, K. 1569, fol. 141.

38. Moreo was only ten years younger than Mendoza, but the difference in their health made it entirely probable that Moreo would have many more years ahead of him than Mendoza. As fate would

have it, however, Moreo was killed in August of the following year by one of Navarre's patrols (D. Pedro de Moreo [brother of Juan] to Idiáquez, near Lagni, 12 September 1590, K. 1573, fol. 103), while Mendoza lived on, in spite of the unprecedented hardships of the 1590 siege, for another fifteen years.

39. "Pero atiendase a la emienda, y dexados todos otros respectos, os bolved a conformar enteramente." Philip to Mendoza, 7 January 1590, K. 1449, fol. 89; and Philip to Moreo, fol. 92.

40. Philip to Tassis, 8 January 1590, K. 1449, fol. 93.

41. Mendoza to Idiáquez, 10 December 1589, K. 1569, fol. 169. Mendoza's letter of 1 October 1590, concerning Moreo's death, discloses a touching and sincere appreciation of his rival, and expresses deep sorrow over his untimely death; Mendoza to Idiáquez, K. 1571, fol. 138.

42. See Moreo to Philip, 13 March 1590, K. 1574, fol. 36. Also Armstrong, *French Wars of Religion*, p. 73.

43. Mayenne to Mendoza, Soissons, 3 April 1590, K. 1571, fol. 70.

44. "Calunias de los Politicos contra don Bernardino de Mendoza," in Antonio de Herrera, *Historia de los sucessos de Francia, desde el año de 1585 que començò la Liga Catolica* (Madrid, 1598), bk. III, p. 141. (This is the official history written by Philip's "Cronista mayor de las Indias.")

45. Mayenne to Philip, Soissons, 22 March 1590, Simancas, K. 1573, fol. 73 bis.

46. The fullest contemporary account of the Battle of Ivry is the "Discours véritable de la victoire ont enue par le Roy en la bataille donne pres le village d'Yri le quatorziesm jour de Mars," Goulart, *Mémoires de la Ligue*, IV, 254–271. Vassière considers it the most popular of Navarre's victories because it symbolized his military genius and his personal valor; *Henry IV*, p. 356. Also see *Cecil Papers*, pt. IV, pp. 20–23.

47. *C.S.P., For.*, XX, 61, 154. Angoulême reported that the English brought with them "200,000 livres, toute monnoye d'argent et du pays; 70 milliers de poudre à canon, 3,000 boulets de canons, à sçavoir, 500 pour grosses pièces, et le reste pour couleuvrines bastardes et moyennes; de bleds, biscuits, vins et bières, avec des draps, jusques à des souliers" Angoulême, *Mémoires*, p. 81.

48. See Pedro Cornejo's "Bref discours et véritable des choses plus notables arrivées au siége mémorable de la renommée ville de Paris, et défence d'icelle par Monseigneur le Duc de Nemours, contra le Roy de Navarre" in Cimber et Danjou, *Archives curieuses*, XIII, 227–270. Also "Bref traité des misères de la ville de Paris," *ibid.*, pp. 271–285; and "Autre discours sur le siége de Paris," *ibid.*, pp. 286–290. Cf. Goulart, *Mémoires de la Ligue*, IV, 272–316.

49. Mendoza to Philip, 23 April 1590, Simancas, K. 1571, fol. 84.

50. Mendoza to Philip, 22 May 1590, K. 1571, fol. 112.

51. *Satyre Ménippée*, I, 430–432; II, 362. Petitot, *Introduction aux mémoires*, 1st ser., XX, 241.

52. *Satyre Ménippée*, I, 38, 109, is one source of this story. Pedro Cornejo and Pierre de l'Estoile also testify to its veracity. See Cornejo, *Compendio y breve relación de la Liga y confederación Francesa* (Brussels, 1591), p. 45; and L'Estoile, *Journal de Henri IV*, IV, 26. Also Goulart, *Mémoires de la Ligue*, IV, 276–303.

53. Cabrera de Cordova, *Felipe II*, III, 397.

54. Mendoza to Philip, 22 May 1590, Simancas, K. 1571, fol. 112; and 24 June, fol. 115. Mendoza and Cardinal Cajetan were also able to get the cardinal's brother out of Paris and send him for help. He reached Parma a few days later and informed the duke of their plight. Cabrera de Cordoba, *Felipe II*, III, 419.

55. Van der Essen, *Alexandre Farnese*, V, 277–289.

56. *Ibid.*, pp. 283–299. Also see Parma to Philip, 1 June 1590, in Lefèvre, *Correspondance de Philippe II*, III, 497–498; and Suárez Inclán, "Liberación de Paris en 1590," *Neustro Tiempo*, 1:100–108 (1900).

57. "Arrest de la Cour de Parlement sur le pouvoir de Monseigneur le duc de Mayenne, Lt. gen. de l'Estat royal et couronne de France," L'Estoile, *Belles figures et drolleries de la Ligue*, pp. 245–246.

58. Consultation on the right of the Infanta to the crown of France, Simancas, K. 1499, fols. 83, 84.

59. "Discours du Sorbonne," K. 1579, fol. 35.

60. "Declaration del duque de Mena sobre llamar los Estados generales," in Herrera, *Historia de los sucessos de Francia*, bk. IV, pp. 217–225. Simancas, K. 1450, fol. 5.

61. Simancas, K. 1579, fol. 74.

62. Philip to Mercoeur, S. Lorenzo, 10 August 1590, K. 1449, fol. 150; and "Instructions to Juan del Aguila, commander of the tercio in Brittany," fol. 152. Diego de Maldonado had previously been sent to Brittany as Philip's special envoy to the duke of Mercoeur, where he was also of great help in relaying Mendoza's diplomatic pouches. Instructions to Maldonado, 12 September 1589, K. 1449, fol. 59; also fol. 74.

63. Instructions to Fontaine, K. 1449, fol. 136; Philip to Ledron, 15 October 1590, fol. 168; and Joyeuse to Philip, Narbonne, K. 1574, fol. 99.

CHAPTER XI. Collapse of the League

1. Instructions to Ibarra, El Pardo, 18 November 1590, Simancas, K. 1449, fol. 172.

2. Philip to Mendoza, 18 November, K. 1449, fol. 177.

3. Mendoza to Philip, 31 December 1590, K. 1571, fol. 162.

4. "Que antes pediria paso al enemigo que quedar en la ciudad que en tan peligrosos terminos se hallaba sin remedio." Quoted by Cabrera de Cordoba, *Felipe II*, III, 459.

5. Mendoza to Philip, Guise, 16 January 1591, Simancas, K. 1578, fol. 2; Mendoza to Idiáquez, 21 and 27 January 1591, fols. 8, 12; and Mendoza to Philip, fol. 6.

6. Mendoza to Philip, Mons, 19 February 1591, K. 1578, fol. 19.

7. Philip to Mendoza, Madrid, 15 March 1591, K. 1450, fol. 30.

8. "Me ponia en camino, gozando de la licencia." Mendoza to Philip, Mons, 25 July 1591, K. 1578, fol. 55.

9. Mendoza to Idiáquez, K. 1578, fols. 70, 79; Mendoza to Philip, fol. 69.

10. There is frequent mention of Mendoza's negotiations and correspondence in relation to France down to 1598. See Simancas, K. 1592, fol. 104; K. 1450, fols. 185, 188; Palma Cayet, *Chronologie novennaire*, p. 528; Cabrera de Cordoba, *Felipe II*, IV, 98; and Forneron, *Histoire de Philippe II*, IV, 216.

11. *Commentaires memorables de don Bernardin de Mendoçe, chevallier ambassadeur en France pour le Roy Catholique, des guerres de Flandres et Pays-bas depuis l'an 1567 jusques à l'an mil cinq cens soixante et six-sept* (Paris, 1581). This first edition bears a dedication "A la noblesse Catholique de France," dated 15 October 1590, from the convent of the Célestins de Paris. See Morel-Fatio, *Études*, p. 470.

12. See J. L. Saunders, *Justus Lipsius: the Philosophy of Renaissance Stoicism* (New York, 1955).

13. Reference is made by Francisco de Aldana, a close friend and military companion of Mendoza's, to one of his poems entitled "Mi Guadalajara," Morel-Fatio, *Études*, p. 487. See Simancas, K. 1569, fol. 148 for an ode which he wrote in 1589 to Don Juan de Idiáquez. He patterned it, he explains, after Horace's "O Navis." Cf. Morel-Fatio, *Études*, pp. 486–488.

14. Some of these were published in 1593 by Diego Alfonso Velázquez de Velasco in his *Odas a imitación de los Siete Salmos Penitenciales del Real Profeta David* (Antwerp, 1593).

15. "Tengo sus obras poéticas que son dignas de ser más conocidas." Francisco Torres y Pérez, in Catalina García, *Biblioteca de escritores de la provincia de Guadalajara*, pp. 331–338.

16. Philip to Ibarra, S. Lorenzo, 30 June 1591, Simancas, K. 1450, fol. 46; Ibarra to Philip, 5 February 1592, K. 1581, fol. 2; and Council of the Sixteen to Ibarra, 7 April 1592, fol. 45.

17. K. 1579, fol. 73.

18. Pasquier to Sainte-Marthe, treasurer general of France, Lettre XXXI, *Oeuvres choisies d'Etienne Pasquier*, II, 349–356. François Leger, *La fin de la Ligue, 1589–1593* (Paris, 1944), pp. 15–16.

19. "Discours sur la mort du monsieur le président Brisson," in

Cimber et Danjou, *Archives curieuses*, XIII, 319–331. De Thou, *Histoire universelle* (1734), XI, 438–443. Paul Gambier, *Au temps des Guerres de Religion: Le Président Barnabé Brisson ligueur (1531–1591)* (Paris, 1957), pp. 97–112.

20. *C.S.P., For.*, XXV, 66. See R. B. Wernham, "Queen Elizabeth and the Siege of Rouen, 1591," *Transactions of the Royal Historical Society*, 4th ser., 15:163–179 (1932).

21. Wilkinson, *History of the League*, pp. 119–120; also Baird, *The Huguenots and Henry of Navarre*, II, 283–293, and notes.

22. Van der Essen, *Alexandre Farnese*, V, 340–355, 383.

23. "Declaration de Enrique de Borbon contra la convocation del duque Mena en Paris," 29 January 1593, in Herrera, *Historia de los sucessos de Francia*, pp. 232–239. Ulph, "The Estates General and the Catholic League," pp. 249–251; and Major, *The Deputies to the Estates General*, pp. 25, 32. Indispensible for any study of this assembly is Auguste Bernard, ed., *Procès-verbaux des États généraux de 1593* (Paris, 1842).

24. Simancas, K. 1450, fol. 240; K. 1584, fol. 14; K. 1585, fols. 9, 10, and esp. 48–72.

25. Bernard, *Procès-verbaux*, pp. 111–115. Mariéjol, *La réforme et la Ligue*, pp. 369–371. De Thou, *Histoire universelle* (1734), XI, 756–760.

26. Bibliothèque Nationale, fonds français, 3997, fol. 15; and Simancas, K. 1585, fol. 48. Guillaume Rose, bishop of Senlis and ardent League pamphleteer, was among those who rejected Feria's proposal; see Ulph, "The Estates General and the Catholic League," p. 280; and Boullée, *Histoire complète des États-généraux*, II, 96–97.

27. De Thou, *Histoire universelle* (1734), XI, 781–784. *Satyre Ménippée* (1711 ed.), III, 353–357. Boullée, *Histoire complète des États-généraux*, II, 108–111.

28. *Mémoires de Sully*, vol. XVI of Michaud et Poujoulat, *Nouvelle collection des mémoires*, p. 109. Cf. François de la Noue, "François de la Noue et la conversion du roi: Lettre de Monsieur de la Noue (Bradefer) sur le changement de religion," Henri Hauser, *Revue Historique*, 36:311–323 (1888).

29. See L'Epinois, *La Ligue et les papes*, pp. 581–634.

30. "Pereat societas judaica cum tota gente iberica." Maurice Wilkinson, "A Provincial Assembly during the League," *Transactions of the Royal Historical Society*, 3rd ser., 9:76 (1915). L'Estoile, *Journal de Henri IV*, V, 296; X, 180–187. Mathorez, "Les Espagnols," pp. 103–108. Félix Rocquain, "Les Espagnols en France sous Henri IV: Le roi et la nation," *Séances et Travaux de l'Académie des Sciences Morales et Politiques*, N.s., 86:135–155 (1916).

31. See Leger, *La fin de la Ligue*, pp. 29–50; also Arthur Tilley, *The Literature of the French Renaissance* (New York, 1959), II, 233–

242; and Lenient, *La satire en France*, pp. 414–456. For a look at another interesting and brief anti-League pamphlet of the same period, see Alain Dufour, "Le Catéchisme du doctor Pantelon et de Zani, son Disciple (1594)," in *Aspects de la propagande religieuse*, pp. 361–372. M. Dufour has also published a new edition of the moderate Leaguer book by René de Lucinge, *Dialogue du François et du Savoysien* (1593) (Paris and Geneva, 1961).

32. Black, *Elizabeth and Henry IV*, p. 69.

33. Merriman, *Philip the Prudent*, p. 644. Cf. Mariéjol, *La réforme et la Ligue*, pp. 386–389.

34. On the war with Spain see particularly Rocquain, "Les Espagnols en France . . . ," *Séances et Travaux*, pp. 145–155; and Luis Fernández de Retana, *España en tiempo de Felipe II* (Madrid, 1958), tomo XIX, vol. II of Ramón Menéndez Pidal's monumental *Historia de España*, pp. 567–592. On the final phase of the League resistance in Champagne see the documents in Hérelle, *La réforme et la Ligue en Champagne*, I, 368–394, and II, 518–604, and in Burgundy the excellent study by Henri Drouot, *Mayenne et la Bourgogne: Étude sur la Ligue, 1587–1596*, 2 vols. (Paris, 1937), II, 342–466.

35. Louis Calendini, "Notes sur le traité de Vervins," *Revue Henri IV*, 1:86–88 (1905), and *Mémoire historique concernant la négociation de la paix traitée à Vervins l'an 1598*, 2 vols. (Paris, 1667). The text of the treaty is in Dumont, *Corps universelle diplomatique*, I, 561–564.

36. See in particular, Benoist, *Histoire de l'Edit de Nantes*, I, appendix pp. 62–85, which contains the text of the edict; and Anquez, *Histoire des assemblées*, pp. 79–168, 456–502. Also "Troisième centennaire de l'Edit de Nantes," *Bulletin de la Sociéte Historique du Protestantisme Française*, 47:169–392 (1898); Lecler, *Histoire de la tolérance*, II, 120–130; and Mariéjol, *La réforme et la Ligue*, pp. 415–423; and the brief but perceptive discussion by Emile G. Léonard in *Histoire générale du protestantisme*, vol. II, *L'établissement (1564–1700)* (Paris, 1961), pp. 141–149.

37. Michel de Montaigne, *The Autobiography of Michel de Montaigne*, ed. Marvin Lowenthal (New York, 1956), p. 230, from *Essais de Montaigne*, bk. III, chap. X.

INDEX

✦ ✦ ✦